THE LIBRARY OF HOLOCAUST TESTIMONIES

With a Yellow Star
and a
Red Cross

The Library of Holocaust Testimonies

Editors: Antony Polonsky, Martin Gilbert CBE, Aubrey Newman,
Raphael F. Scharf, Ben Helfgott MBE

Under the auspices of the Yad Vashem Committee of the Board of
Deputies of British Jews and the Centre for Holocaust Studies,
University of Leicester

My Lost World by Sara Rosen
From Dachau to Dunkirk by Fred Pelican
Breathe Deeply, My Son by Henry Wermuth
My Private War by Jacob Gerstenfeld-Maltiel
A Cat Called Adolf by Trude Levi
An End to Childhood by Miriam Akavia
A Child Alone by Martha Blend
The Children Accuse by Maria Hochberg-Marianska and Noe Gruss
I Light a Candle by Gena Turgel
My Heart in a Suitcase by Anne L. Fox
Memoirs from Occupied Warsaw, 1942-1945
by Helena Szereszewska
Have You Seen My Little Sister?
by Janina Fischler-Martinho
Surviving the Nazis, Exile and Siberia by Edith Sekules
Out of the Ghetto by Jack Klajman with Ed Klajman
From Thessaloniki to Auschwitz and Back
by Erika Myriam Kounio Amariglio
Translated by Theresa Sundt
I Was No. 20832 at Auschwitz by Eva Tichauer
Translated by Colette Lévy and Nicki Rensten
My Child is Back! by Ursula Pawel
Wartime Experiences in Lithuania by Rivka Lozansky Bogomolnaya
Translated by Miriam Beckerman
Who Are You, Mr Grymek? by Natan Gross
Translated by William Brand
A Life Sentence of Memories by Issy Hahn, Foreword by Theo Richmond
An Englishman in Auschwitz by Leon Greenman
For Love of Life by Leah Iglinsky-Goodman
No Place to Run: The Story of David Gilbert by Tim Shortridge and
Michael D. Frounfelter
A Little House on Mount Carmel by Alexandre Blumstein
From Germany to England Via the Kindertransports by Peter Prager
By a Twist of History: The Three Lives of a Polish Jew by Mietek Sieradzki
The Jews of Poznań by Zbigniew Pakula
Lessons in Fear by Henryk Vogler
To Live is to Forgive ... But Not Forget by Maja Abramowitch

With a Yellow Star and a Red Cross

A Doctor in the Łódź Ghetto

ARNOLD MOSTOWICZ

Translated from the Polish by
HENIA and NOCHEM REINHARTZ

Foreword by
ANTONY POLONSKY

VALLENTINE MITCHELL
LONDON • PORTLAND, OR

First published in 2005 in Great Britain by
VALLENTINE MITCHELL
Suite 314, Premier House
Edgware, Middlesex HA8 7BJ

and in the United States of America by
VALLENTINE MITCHELL
c/o ISBS, 920 NE 58th Avenue, Suite 300
Portland, Oregon 97213-3786

Website: www.vmbooks.com

First published in Polish as *Żólta świazda i czerwony krzyż*
Copyright © Arnold Mostowicz, Warszawa 1988

Translation copyright © 2003 Henia and Nochem Reinhartz
Library of Congress Txu 1-093-302

Maps on pp. xxii and xxiii reprinted from Lucjan Dobroszycki, *The Chronicle of the Łódź Ghetto, 1941–1944* (1984) with the permission of Yale University Press

Copyright © 2005 Vallentine Mitchell & Co. Ltd

Printed in Great Britain by Antony Rowe Ltd, Chippenham, Wiltshire

*This translation is dedicated
to the memory of the
Łódź ghetto Jews who perished
in the Holocaust*

Contents

Plates

Photographs from Y. Tabaksblat, *Khurbn-Lodzh* (The Destruction of Łódź), Buenos Aires, 1946; A. Wolf Jasni, *Di Geschikhte fun Yidn in Łodzh in di Yorn fun der Daytsher Yidn-Oysrotung* (The History of Jews in Łódź in the Years of the German Extermination of the Jews), Tel Aviv, 1960.

The Library of Holocaust Testimonies

It is greatly to the credit of Frank Cass that this series of survivors' testimonies is being published in Britain. The need
for such a series has been long apparent in a country where
many survivors made their homes.

Since the end of the war in 1945 the terrible events of the
Nazi destruction of European Jewry have cast a pall over our
time. Six million Jews were murdered within a short period;
the few survivors have had to carry in their memories whatever remains of the knowledge of Jewish life in more than a
dozen countries, in several thousand towns, in tens of thousands of villages, and in innumerable families. The precious
gift of recollection has been the sole memorial for millions of
people whose lives were suddenly and brutally cut off.

For many years, individual survivors have published
their testimonies. But many more have been reluctant to do
so, often because they could not believe that they would
find a publisher for their efforts.

In my own work over the past two decades I have been
approached by many survivors who had set down their
memories in writing, but who did not know how to have
them published. I also realized, as I read many dozens of
such accounts, how important each account was, in its own
way, in recounting aspects of the story that had not been
told before, and adding to our understanding of the wide
range of human suffering, struggle and aspiration.

With so many people and so many places involved,
including many hundreds of camps, it was inevitable that
the historians and students of the Holocaust should find it
difficult at times to grasp the scale and range of events. The
publication of memiors is therefore an indispensable part of
the extension of knowledge, and of public awareness of the

crimes that were committed against a whole people.

Sir Martin Gilbert
Merton College, Oxford

Foreword

Not to forget …You have eyes – look carefully.
You have ears – listen attentively. Remember
everything because there may come a day
when you will not be certain whether this has
been the truth or perhaps a nightmare.

Arnold Mostowicz

The late Arnold Mostowicz was well known in Poland as a public intellectual, having been a journalist, an editor of various publications, and an author. His autobiography, which appeared in Warsaw in 1988 under the title *Żołta gwiazda i czerwony krzyż?* and was translated into German in 1992, and now appearing here in English as *With a Yellow Star and a Red Cross*, tells the story of his experiences in the Łódź ghetto. Although Mostowicz's later career was literary in nature, his intial training was as a medical doctor. It is from this unique perspective, as one charged with the health of the ghetto and with the relative freedom of movement that provided, that Mostowicz writes of his ghetto experiences.

Mostowicz was born in 1914 into a large and diverse Jewish family in Łódź. His father, who was born in Krosniewice, near Kutno, earned his living in the textile industry, but also pursued his literary and theatrical interests and wrote for the local Yiddish press. He was an important member of the literary-musical society *Hazomir*, and Mostowicz has described his father's activities in this organisation in a documentary film made in 1996 about its American reincarnation, the Boston-based Zamir chorale. He fled to Warsaw at the beginning of the war and was a successful actor in the Yiddish theatre in the ghetto. He was deported to his death in Treblinka in 1942.

Unable because of the anti-Jewish restrictions to obtain entry to a medical school in Poland, Mostowicz enrolled as a medical student in Rouen (his family could not afford to send him to the more expensive Paris). He returned to Poland, having just qualified as a doctor, shortly before the outbreak of the war, fleeing in September 1939 from his native Łódź to Warsaw, where he worked in a hospital during the German seige of the Polish capital. He returned to Łódź after the German defeat where he became a doctor in the 'Sanitary Service' of the ghetto. After the liquidation of the Łódź ghetto, he was deported to Auschwitz and later to a labour camp at Jelenia Góra, where he worked in an artificial fibre factory and nearly died from typhoid, Warmbrunn, Doernau and Erlenbusch, where he lived out the war.

After the war he remained in Poland. He had already become active in the communist movement while a student in France and after the war he joined the Polish Workers' Party, working as a journalist, first in Silesia, where he was editor of *Trybuna Dolnoślaska* and later in Kraków, where he was on the editorial board of *Gazeta Krakowska*. He observed later:

> I do not regret my support for communism. Stalinism caused suffering, but I accepted it because I was certain that it would be replaced by something better. And in 1956 things did change.

Already in 1955 as the thaw developed, he had been appointed chief editor of the humorous magazine *Szpilki*, where he assembled a lively and creative team of writers. He lost this position in 1969 as a result of the 'anti-Zionist' purge that began in 1968. He worked first in the monthly *Ty i Ja*, where many of those who lost their jobs as a result of the purge found employment. When this was closed down, he earned his living by writing scientific and medical articles. He refused to leave Poland, partly because he did not want to leave behind the grave of his 15-year-old son, who had died in 1964, and partly because, as he explained in an interview in April 2001, 'If I had emigrated, I would have done what they wanted me to.'[1] He became increasingly active in the reviving Jewish life in Poland and was one of the founders in 1991 of the Jewish Combatants Association.

In addition to this work, he published a number of books. They include *Biologia uczy myśleć* (Biology teaches you to think, Warsaw 1988); *Łódź, moja zakazana miłość* (Łódź, my forbidden love, Łódź, 1999); *Karambole na czerwonym suknie* (Ricochets on a Red Skirt, Warsaw, 2001) and *Lekarska ballada* (Medical Ballad, Łódź, 2003). He was also the narrator and script-writer of the film *Fotoamator* (Camera Buff), made in 2001 by Dariusz Jabloński, which contrasted the beautiful colour slides taken during the war by the Austrian chief accountant administering the Łódź ghetto with the death and degradation that characterised ghetto life. He died in 2002.

Shortly before his death, in April 2001, he concluded his interview with Joanna Podgórska with the following words:

> What am I today? More a Jew or more a Pole? I don't know. I feel myself a patriot and, as George Bernard Shaw used to say, a true patriot is one who is dissatisfied with his homeland.

This double perspective of a Jew and a Pole is one of the important aspects that make this autobiography so striking. It took Mostowicz over forty years before he was able to return to his traumatic past. He generally describes his experiences in the third person – as if his connection with the person who lived through these nightmarish occurrences is too painful to acknowledge directly. He gives not a chronological account of what he went through, but a series of vignettes that illustrate the essence of the tragic years of Jewish martyrdom and also frequently refer to Jewish life in interwar Poland and to the history of his own family. These finely wrought and often deceptively artless accounts give a remarkable picture of what it was like to live through what he calls the 'time of indifference' (p. 111), when the world observed uncaringly the mass murder of the Jews. Each chapter is devoted to a different aspect of the nightmarish world of the Nazis and infused with Mostowicz's subtle commentaries on human nature.

In the first, he describes the brutality that accompanied the establishment of the ghetto. Although diarists, photographers and later memoir writers and film makers have tried to describe the horror and confusion of Jews given a few minutes' notice that they must gather their belongings and leave their homes for ever, Mostowicz is able to relate this tragic experience as one responsible for treating those unable to keep up and recording those who were killed by this brutal evacuation. He describes his neighbors' actions during the 'resettlement' noting the actions of one Polish woman who assisted Jews in the only way she knew how, through kneeling down in the courtyard and praying over the body of a fallen Jew (p. 6).

In the second chapter, describing a visit to the Roma (Gypsy) camp, Mostowicz writes from the unique experience of one of the few Jews allowed inside the Roma section of the ghetto. Very little primary source documentation of that area survived the war. All the Roma interred in the Łódź ghetto were killed by the Nazis, leaving no witnesses. A few Jewish sources offer fragmentary evidence of the Roma experience and only a few pages remain among the German records to bear witness to the tragedy of the Roma in the Łódź ghetto. Illegal photographs were taken of this portion of the camp but were destroyed during the 1948 War of Independence in Israel when the kibbutz in which they were housed was bombed. Mostowicz thus stands alone as a first-hand witness of the last days of a people who were killed at the hands of the Nazis.

Mostowicz does not limit himself to describing what he saw inside the Roma camp but also offers an analysis of Roma–Jewish relations, or at least Jewish perspectives of the Roma, during the war. As he points out:

> No refined psychological insight is required to surmise that situating the Gypsy camp in a few buildings detached from the ghetto was a factor that in a peculiar way boosted the morale of the Jewish population. First, by some unusual logic, this fact had reassured the Jews that at least for the time being that the Germans did not intend to liquidate the ghetto. The second reason was more easily

understood. The news reached the ghetto about the conditions in which the Gypsies lived (news that did not even describe the horrible truth) improved the morale of the Jews enclosed in the ghetto because it meant that it was not they who were at the bottom. At the bottom of degradation, misery, hunger. There was no compassion in the ghetto for the Gypsies as most likely there was not compassion among the Gypsies for the Jews ... Both groups were considered by the surrounding Christian-Catholic society at least as aliens, if not enemies. And experience teaches that in such cases solidarity is out of the question. What arises is something akin to competition for a gesture of kindness, for the alms of a kind word. (p. 24)

It was not only the hidden world of the Roma which Mostowicz was able to see as a medical physician which his fellow ghetto dwellers could not enter. He was also able to see the world of the Western Jews and comment on the changes that occurred among the new arrivals as hunger set in. As a native of Łódź, his perspective and commentary on the situation is very different from, for example, that of Oskar Rosenfeld, a writer who had arrived in a transport from Prague and wrote on the transformation as a western Jew himself.[2] Mostowicz also had entry into a variety of people's private homes – people from all walks of pre-war and ghetto life. Even before the Second World War, the majority of the Łódź Jewish community had been poor, consisting mostly of artisans and textile workers. There had, in addition, been a significant minority of industrialists, intellectuals, and professionals. The pre-war Jewish community was diverse not only in its economic stratifications but also in its religious observance. Although the great majority were religious, there were a variety of traditions including various hasidic sects. Mostowicz's descriptions and discussions of individuals reflect this diverse pre-war community.

One place where this becomes personal is in Mostowicz's description of his extended family, which encompassed a variety of economic and religious backgrounds. One tragic episode depicts how religious feeling played a role in furthering the anguish of one of his cousins, a deeply religious Jew who, because of malnutrition and illness, could not fulfil what he regarded as his religious obligation to have intercourse with his wife.

One of the most memorable pieces describes the end of the way in which the three leaders of the Łódź Jewish underworld enforced a crude but effective justice in the period between the two world wars. In this piece, Mostowicz condemns Jews who willingly collaborated with the Gestapo. He is more reflective in his evaluation of others who found themselves forced into the dirty work of the Nazis. For example, he gives his own assessment of Mordechai Chaim Rumkowski in a chapter entitled, tellingly, 'There Once Was a King ...' In it he argues that the usual attempt to contrast the moral heroism of Adam Czerniaków, who committed suicide rather than comply with the Germans demand that he assist in the deportation of the Jews of Warsaw, and the constant attempts of Rumkowski to placate the Germans is misplaced. Given the total abandonment and isolation of the Jews, their leaders could count only on a miracle to save them. Had the Soviets broken through the German lines in 1944, or had the plot against Hitler's life succeeded, that miracle would have occurred. Rumkowski might still have been condemned for his many acts of cravenness, but he would have saved perhaps 60,000 Jews. Even without this miracle, one has to remember that 'from the Łódź ghetto after all there remained alive more than 10,000 Jews whom death in the camps had not had time to swallow. Almost no one survived from the Warsaw ghetto, except those few who found shelter on the "Aryan" side' (p. 126).

One of the most moving pieces gives a rare glimpse into the struggles of a Jew who, as part of the ghetto administration, is charged with sifting through the ghetto inmates to choose those who will be permitted to live and those who will die. Mostowicz describes a conversation with a Czech Jewish philosopher who refuses his offer to class him as physically capable of work so that he can avoid deportation to certain death. The philosopher adopts his stance because he wants to be able to choose the moment of his own death and because he does not wish that someone else should die in his place. The account concludes:

> He heard the man open the door and still say something at the threshold. It reached him like a voice from another world, another space.
>
> 'Let us say you survive the ghetto ... That would be a miracle ... And the decisions you made today and perhaps not only today are praised ... Perhaps even one of those whom you saved at the expense of others survives ... He will worship you ... You will hear compliments ... And those who were deported to die instead of the others will not voice any reproach, any reproach, any reproach ...'
>
> He raised his head. There was no one in the cell. 'Not good,' he thought. 'I am hallucinating.' (p. 107)

Another moving piece describes the tragic fate of his friend Jerzy, a fellow medical student in France, who was betrayed to the Gestapo by his Maronite wife, who had become a strong antisemite and Vichy supporter, and died in Auschwitz.

The last chapters describe his experiences, first in Auschwitz and then in the labour camps of Jelenia Góra, Warmbrunn, Doernau, and Erlenbusch. As the war approached its end, the Nazi world began to exhibit some strange contradictions. A number of SS men ask individual prisoners if it was true that Jews are being murdered *en masse* in Auschwitz. Acts of humanity, like the organisation of a football match between the SS and their prisoners, alternate with mindless brutality and killing. A previously 'humane' guard loses his temper and viciously beats up the author, a sign that the Soviet offensive is succeeding. The prisoners also sometimes behave bizarrely. A German Jewish doctor, as a group of prisoners are being marched to the camp in Hirschberg, asks to change places with Mostowicz in the column. He is frightened that someone who knew him from the days when he came skiing in this area will recognise him in his shameful concentration camp garb.

In one of the last chapters, he describes how, in the 'memorable year 1981', which saw the flourishing of the Solidarity movement in Poland, he was invited to a scientific conference in Cieplice, where as a camp prisoner he had nearly died of typhoid as the war came to its end. He comments:

> The evacuation of the Cieplice camp was a story altogether different. When he started out at that time on an unknown road, he left behind a stage of suffering that, while occupying little space in his biography, had carved in him deep traces. He was not always aware of the existence of those traces, or rather scars. He thought that the current of life would erase those traces as the sea erases footprints in the sand on the beach. But this was an illusion. He was returning to the Cieplice of his memories and what was worse, he was returning to it in nightmares. He had never returned to a place to confront his memories and dreams with reality. A least, with what remained of the reality of that other time. Perhaps it was laziness. Perhaps its was a superstition that he could not understand. In a certain period, it was fear. The fear of delving too much in his own past, because that meant that he was getting old. For the same reason, he did not like to look at photographs that recalled the old days...
>
> Standing here now, in front of the five buildings that at one time made up the Cieplice camp, he felt a kind of regret that the had treated his past that way. And not only his past at the camps. He had treated it as if it belonged to someone else. And this was, after all, a deception. One cannot create an artificial separation between the different periods of one's own life as he had done – between the period of his life that ended with the liberation. You are what you are: the tears of your mother, the laughter of your friend, the stone that was thrown at you because of your ethnic origin, the song with which you bid farewell to the train with volunteers that

went to the Spanish front, the yellow star that you wore attached to your chest, the dead person's bread that saved you from death ... (p. 214)

The book ends with what is ironically described as a *Finale Giocoso*. When the prisoners at Erlenbusch are liberated, a young Soviet officer makes a characteristically optimistic speech describing 'the suffering and determination of the Soviet people ... [and] the casualties it incurred for the final victory' (p. 243). He is then brought to the place where the prisoners, who have been deprived of food for 36 hours, are dying in filthy and degrading conditions. Mostowicz comments characteristically:

> For a few moments, the young officer looked dumbfounded at the view before him. He had not had time to extinguish the smile on his lips when he turned pale, staggered and was at the last moment supported by the prisoners who stood near him. When he was literally pulled out of the hall, he vomited. Luckily, he did not soil his uniform or the medals that bore witness to his courage.
>
> From the nearby church the bells were ringing for Angelus. The sound was spreading joyfully far and wide and announced the arrival of the era of peace. In Europe the guns fell silent. Bells were ringing everywhere in praise of the victory. There was rejoicing in London, Moscow, Paris and Warsaw. Hosanna! Never ag ...

Antony Polonsky
Brandeis University
Waltham, MA

NOTES

1 Interview with Joanna Podgórska, *Polityka*, 5 April 2001.
2 For a first-hand perspective on the early days of the western Jews' experience, see Oskar Rosenfeld, *In the Beginning was the Ghetto: Notebooks from Łódź*, trans. Brigitti M. Goldstein (Evanston: Northwestern University Press, 2002). For more information on the relationship between the Eastern and Western Jews in the Łódź Ghetto, see Avraham Barkai, 'Between East and West: Jews from Germany in the Łódź Ghetto,' *Yad Vashem Studies* (Jerusalem: Yad Vashem, 1984).

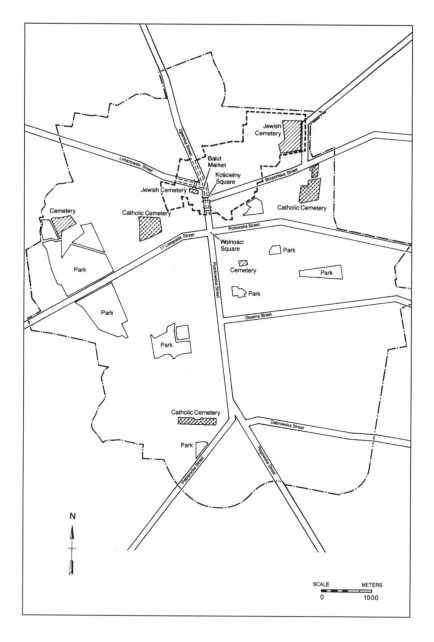

Map 1
The city of Łódź as of 1939 and the area designated for the ghetto

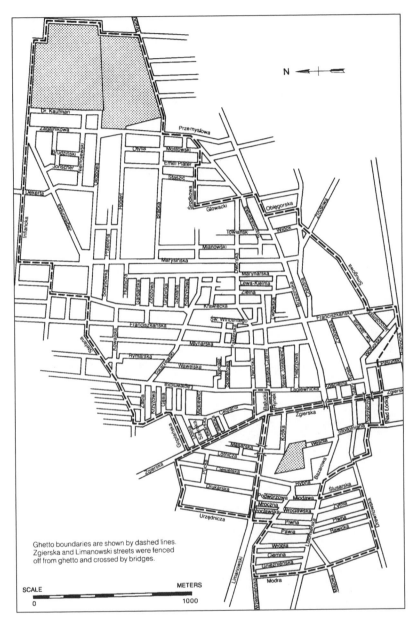

N

Dr. Kaufman
Zagainikowa
Brudzinski
Jonscher
Dekerra
Inflancka
Przemysłowa
Okrina
Mostowski
Emili Plater
Staszic
Glowacki
Obiegorska
Towlansk
Widok
Mianowski
Marysińska
Marynarska
Lewa-Kielma
Zielna
Krawiecka
Sw. Wincentego
Franciszkańska
Mlynarska
Kowalska
Rybnarska
Wawelska
Lagiewnicka
Zgierska
Bałucki Rynek
Zgierska
Mazelska
Łotnicza
Ciesielska
Drukarska
Podworzowa Miodawa
Mroczna Wroclawska
Wroclawska
Urzędnicza
Piwna
Pawia
Wróbla
Ciemna
Modra

Ghetto boundaries are shown by dashed lines.
Zgierska and Limanowski streets were fenced
off from ghetto and crossed by bridges.

SCALE   METERS

0   1000

Map 2
Street map of the ghetto of Łódź

Translators' Introduction

Arnold Mostowicz, the author of *Żółta gwiazda i czerwony krzyż* (Państwowy Instytut Wydawniczy, Warsaw, 1988), of which this book is the English translation, was a Polish Jew, a native of Łódź. To outsiders, Łódź was an ugly, grey industrial city. It was a young city without traditions, pedigree or roots in the distant past and therefore had little architectural or historical interest. But the citizens of Łódź loved their city, and Łódź – particularly the Jewish Łódź – is very prominent in Mostowicz's work.

Łódź was and remains the second largest city of Poland after Warsaw. As a settlement, it already existed in the fourteenth century. But it began to develop only in the nineteenth century. In 1820, the authorities of the Polish Kingdom, at that time part of the Russian Empire, chose Łódź to become a centre of the textile and clothing industry. Master weavers from Silesia, Bohemia and Saxony were induced to settle in Łódź and start enterprises there. Łódź developed at lightning speed and in a short time began to attract people from all parts of the country, for whom it was 'the Promised Land'. Among them were a large number of Jews.

In 1825, a decree limited Jewish access to a number of occupations and forced most Jews to reside in a Jewish district. The congestion and poverty in that district was great. Still, Jews from surrounding smaller towns flocked to Łódź After the decree was rescinded in 1862, Jews were able to settle in other parts of Łódź and to participate more fully in the growth of the city. By the middle of the nineteenth century, Jews were among the three most important ethnic groups in Łódź, constituting 17 per cent of the population. The other two groups were Germans (44 per cent) and native Poles (35 per cent).

While Germans had been the pioneers of the Łódź textile

industry, Jews also contributed to its development. Initially they were engaged only in the commercial side of the industry by supplying its raw materials and marketing its final product. Later in the century, they also engaged in the production of textiles as entrepreneurs and workers. The majority, however, worked as entrepreneurs and workers in what were considered traditional Jewish trades – tailoring, shoemaking, and furniture-making – and in commerce and services. As its industry developed, the population of the Łódź increased and its composition changed. On the eve of the Second World War, the Łódź population of 672,000, while mostly Polish, included 231,000 Jews and 86,000 Germans.

Łódź was 'the Polish Manchester', and as such played a very important role in Poland's economy. It had an active political life and strong labour movements, and became a cultural centre with a vibrant artistic milieu. It was the first city in Poland to introduce and implement a general obligatory education system. In 1928, it established a university; museums and art galleries followed. Famous artists, writers and musicians, well known in Poland, originated from Łódź, and some became internationally known, for instance Artur Rubinstein and Artur Szyk. While the majority of Jews were religious and traditional, a large number were secular, creating modern Jewish cultural institutions, and also contributing to the mainstream Polish culture.

On 1 September 1939, the army of Nazi Germany invaded Poland. On 7 September Łódź was occupied, and on 7 November it was incorporated into the Third Reich and renamed Litzmannstadt (after the German general Karl Litzmann, who fell in the conquest of Łódź during the First World War). From the very beginning of the German occupation, Jews were subjected to many restrictions and to persecution. Religious practices were prohibited and synagogues were burned. Many Jews were expelled from their dwellings and had their bank accounts frozen; they were subjected to physical abuse, robbery, beatings, round-ups for forced labour and ransom demands. The occupying authorities were assisted in their actions against the Jews by gangs of local Nazi Germans. A decree of 16 November 1939 forced the Jews to wear a yellow armband on the right arm. This was later replaced by a yellow badge in the form of a Star of David with the inscription JUDE (Jew), to be worn on the front and back of the outer garment.

On 8 February 1940, the Nazis established a ghetto for the Jews. Some 160,000 Jews from all parts of the city were forced to resettle in an area of 4.3 square kilometres in the slum area of Łódź, Bałuty. The ghetto was surrounded by a barbed-wire fence, which was guarded by German police. In May 1940, the ghetto was sealed and became completely isolated from the outside world. While the various branches of the Gestapo were in charge of security in the ghetto and the enforcement of the German decrees regarding its inmates, Hans Biebow, a Nazi businessman from Bremen, was in charge of the ghetto's food supply and economic affairs. The Germans appointed a Council of Elders (*Judenrat*), with Mordecai Chaim Rumkowski, as the Eldest of the Jews, charged with implementing Nazi policies in the ghetto. As 'King of the Ghetto', Rumkowski organized a Jewish police and created a variety of services, including a ghetto currency and postage stamps.

The Germans insisted that the ghetto pay for its own food. Initially, the food was paid for with the valuables that Rumkowski had extracted from ghetto inmates with the help of the German authorities. When this source began to run out, he came up with a plan to transform the ghetto into a labour camp that worked for the Germans. He was helped in this plan by Biebow, who saw in the ghetto a skilled labour force that could be both a source of profit for himself and of benefit for Germany. The Germans delivered raw materials and the Jews made the final products. They were paid for their work with food distributed by ration cards. For the majority of the ghetto population, the food rations were at starvation level. The food was delivered to the ghetto in bulk, confiscated by Rumkowki's officials and then distributed by them. Control over the ghetto food supply thus strengthened Rumkowski's hold on the ghetto.

In 1941, the 'final solution of the Jewish problem' – that is, the direct genocide of the Jews – began to be implemented. Besides being a labour camp, the ghetto then became a holding facility for Jews destined for extermination. Some 25,000 Jews from the Old Reich (Germany, Austria, Czechoslovakia) were brought to the Łódź ghetto. Since they were mostly of the upper middle class, few of them could adapt to the ghetto conditions and find work in the ghetto industries, and most remained unemployed. Soon the unemployed began to be deported to the extermination camp at Chełmno, some 35 miles from Łódź. For a time, there was a Gypsy camp attached to the ghetto; its inmates were also deported and exterminated. One of the most tragic days in the life of the ghetto was 4 September 1942, when Rumkowski demanded that parents offer their children for deportation. When the people refused, the Gestapo helped the Jewish ghetto police enforce this demand. When the extermination camp at Auschwitz came into being, the Nazis increased their demands for people for deportation – the elderly, the sick, the unemployed, children, and those who were out of favour with the authorities. Periodically the Nazi requests halted because the German army needed the products produced by the ghetto population of 75,000.

Throughout the existence of the ghetto, in spite of hunger, disease, deportations, and the constant fight for physical survival, the ghetto inmates also attempted to survive spiritually and intellectually. The devout tried to continue their religious practices; the pre-war political parties organized meetings and lectures; the ghetto orchestra played occasional concerts; many groups ran clandestine schools and libraries. Secret radio receivers kept the ghetto inmates informed about the progress of the war.

As the Soviet army advanced in Poland, the order came to liquidate the ghetto. On 29 August 1944, the last transport of ghetto Jews left for Auschwitz. The number of Łódź ghetto inmates who survived the war is estimated at between seven and twelve thousand.

Arnold Mostowicz was a physician in the Łódź ghetto. After the liquidation of the ghetto, he found himself in Auschwitz and in a number of concentration camps of the Gross-Rosen camp system. The present book was described by its Polish publisher as a literary take on the author's experiences in the Łódź ghetto and the Nazi concentration camps. As a physician in the ghetto, and intermittently in the camps, he was a witness to and participant in situations that have received very little attention. For example, the book contains a unique account of a worker demonstration in 1940, and a description of the Gypsy camp that the Nazis created on the edge of the Łódź ghetto. He gives a unique analysis of how the antagonism between the Łódź Jews and the German and Czech Jews deported to the ghetto played itself out in everyday life. Through flashbacks, he also depicts slices of pre-war Jewish life in Poland and in Łódź.

But the memoir is more than an account of events and situations. Mostowicz also deals with the moral dilemmas of life in the ghetto and the camps. In situations where the fate of other people depended on his admittedly very limited power to make decisions, he questions the morality of his own actions and describes the inner tensions and ambivalences associated with those actions. Through the unusual strategy of writing the memoir in the form of a third-person account, he becomes also an observer of his own actions and thoughts. He invites the reader to bear witness to his actions and leaves them to judge them for themselves. Throughout he attempts to find a psychological explanation for the actions of the ghetto and camp inmates and imaginatively to understand how people made choices in order to survive within the ghetto and the forced-labour system created by the Nazis.

The memoir was written some forty years after the events it deals with. This was probably how long it took for the author's psychological wounds from his war experiences to heal. From this retrospective point of view, he challenged many of the accepted judgments about people and events, for instance, the blanket condemnation of Rumkowski by many survivors and historians. Looking back, he could also see that the planned genocide of an entire people was a crime of which not only the Nazi machine but also the world's indifference was culpable. As he says, 'the book is a record of matters and events that our wonderful twentieth century swallowed without choking.'

The Polish original of this book had been on our shelves for more than thirteen years. It was rescued from there by Irene Kohn, of the Ontario Institute for Studies in Education, who is researching little-known literary material on the Łódź ghetto. Our children, Adele and Abe, read and commented on parts of it, and our grandson Mordechai Walfish read it in its entirety. Our thanks to them all. We also want to thank Jadwiga and Ryszard Mostowicz in Warsaw for granting permission to translate the book.

1 The Overture

Not to forget. With tens of millions of people on this continent he had entered the state of war. If he could, he would have gladly inserted a filmstrip into his memory to register events, images and facts that came to form the everyday reality of the last months. For the time being, every day brought new experiences and every night stretched the bitter taste of anxiety into infinity. Only yesterday – yesterday? No, several months ago – in the besieged Warsaw, he had learned the language of the total war that the Germans had launched against Poland. It had been his war as it had been the war of 35 million Poles. He took part in it on the street, at home, in improvised little hospitals, and finally in one hospital. The defeat of Poland was his defeat. However, he had no time to reflect on it. Before he could evaluate his losses, the Germans had launched a new war, one against the Jews. Again against him. He was drawn into the whirlwind of war twice over: a few months earlier, as an anonymous Pole, the bombs that Warsaw had been expiring under had been murdering him; today, as an anonymous Jew, he had a part in a spectacle the première of which had taken place a long time ago, and which the future conquerors decided to repeat on the occasion of the new war.

You have eyes – look carefully. You have ears – listen attentively. Remember everything because there may come a day when you yourself will not be certain whether this has been the truth or perhaps a nightmare. The truth for whom? For someone who will wait at the finish line and to whom you will bequeath it as a priceless treasure you guarded during your entire run for life? Or perhaps the finish line will be haunted by the emptiness of death, and only the wind will disperse dust and ashes into the four corners of the world. Ashes and dust, as it now disperses the content of the fiber

1

suitcase entangled under the feet. On the suitcase are the remains of white canvas, like an obituary notice, with letters written in ink: Gold ... or perhaps Geld.

He could not believe that the truth about those times and the events in which he had been a participant would be lost to memory, even if it was becoming ever more difficult for him to realize he had participated in them. To forget is good for the fate of an individual.

History repeats itself. What was happening now had already happened many times before. He had studied this conscientiously in school, but had never surmised that he would come to experience those lessons himself. His forefathers had been expelled from Israel and Judea, expelled from Spain, Flanders and Champagne, from German and Italian cities, from Kishinev[1] and Anatevka.[2] The pursuers were changing but not the quarry. What had not changed were the despair and bewilderment in the black eyes that glanced for the last time in the direction of the burning Jerusalem, the palaces of Cordoba, the narrow houses of Speyer or Worms, the wooden huts of Ukrainian villages. Today those eyes turned in the direction of the black, gloomy, dilapidated apartment blocks of Łódź where the exiles have left the possessions of a lifetime and a fraction of their homeland.

He found himself in the rear, behind the last dawdlers of a column of people surrounded by gendarmes. Near the sidewalk, where it was less crowded, a tall, gray-haired man walked as though benumbed. What was strange about him was that with both hands he pressed to his chest a pot containing a beautiful fuchsia. His wife trotted near him with little steps and supported his arms as if she had wanted to help her husband bring this holy relic to its destination. The woman wore two coats and her husband's hat. It was not difficult to guess what had happened earlier. Running and screaming as usual, the Germans had entered the couple's home, threatening to shoot them, and ordered them to get out in ten minutes. Ten minutes. Just enough time to master their fright, comb their hair, have a glance at the walls, the furniture, the curtains, the wedding picture above the bed, the pots, all the things that had formed the domestic part of their life. And at the last moment they grabbed what was the closest at hand and what

2

they had nurtured lovingly over the years. The doors were sealed. Germans from Estonia would be arriving soon. The Jewish furniture, pots, linen and shirts would bring the caring German fatherland closer to their hearts.

He walked slowly behind the others. In this performance, which the Germans observed with the satisfaction of a director looking at a play for which many repeat performances were planned, he himself had a somewhat privileged part. He was not among the exiles. He was a first-aid doctor. His presence was intended to indicate the Germans' serious care about the proper course of this spectacle ... He walked at the rear of the crowd, so could not see the face of a man who dragged two heavy suitcases. The man was probably crying. Or perhaps was having a coughing fit? After a while he realized that the man was both crying and coughing. Worst of all, he was falling behind increasingly. It was obvious that he was making an extraordinary effort to catch up with the column. If he had left behind at least one of the suitcases, he would certainly have made it. A German in a green uniform approached him. For a moment it seemed that he kindly wanted to help the overburdened man. But it turned out he wanted to wrest the suitcases from the man's hands. The man defended himself desperately. Now he could see his face. It was enclosed in a long, gray beard. His ear-locks slipped out from under a simple cap. Yes, that Jew had certainly been in similar situations in the past. Perhaps he had been dealing with the soldiers of Isabella and Ferdinand[3] who, in the name of the holy cross, cleansed Spain of the Jews. At this moment he struggled with a gendarme who in the name of the broken cross – the swastika – was cleansing Łódź of the Jews. The German finally succeeded in wresting a suitcase from the hand attached to it. He kicked it aside. The man did not give up and ran after the remnants of his possessions. The German seemed to have been waiting just for that. Swiftly he took the sub-machinegun off his arm. – No! – Before the German pulled the trigger a scream was heard. After it, a series of shots ... Apparently someone else had screamed – the scream had not come from the man with the side-locks, who now lay quietly near his possessions and did not interfere with the resettlement any more. The German bent over him to make sure he had done his job properly.

3

Now he must play the part assigned to him. Together with a male nurse, he ran up to the man to ascertain that he was indeed dead. He did it with a movement similar to the one that the German had made. There was no more life in the man than in the suitcase spread out near him. He instructed the nurse to check the dead man's documents. The Germans made certain that their victims had a name, a surname, and an address. Then the victim would become an item on the list that the director of the first-aid service would send the next day to the authorities, and the authorities would add those names to the list of people killed for offering opposition.

After a while he wrote down a fifth name in his notebook. This was just the beginning. Then he heard another series of shots.

Not long ago, on a different occasion, he had heard similar shots. The Germans were celebrating New Year's Eve. The conqueror bathed in joy. Everyone hid behind closed windows and barred doors. From the street one could hear shooting and strong, joyous singing. Now there was shooting but no singing. Well-brought-up Germans know that it is not proper to sing when one seriously performs one's duties.

A month before that New Year's Eve he had been posted to work at the first-aid service. More precisely, at the Jewish first-aid service. And even more precisely, at the first-aid service subordinated to the Eldest of the Jews.[4] The doctors in that service had the right to help only Jews. To help an Aryan would be punishable by jail and a fine. It was an old laryngologist who informed them at the first organization meeting of the Germans' decision to create a Jewish first-aid service. Unexpectedly he finished off with the Latin quotation: '*Quidquid id est timeo Danaos et dona ferentes.*'[5] With this he exhibited not only his knowledge of Virgil but also his far-sightedness. He, the old Jewish physician and Laokoon, knew both: that only the naïve and the blind can count on the favour of the gods, and that to oppose them is not in the power of a human ... On top of the first-aid service for the Jews, there was one more gift – a Jewish ghetto in Bałuty.[6]

Well, now was not the time to reminisce about events from months or even weeks ago. Now he must play well the role

4

assigned to him in the spectacle. And he must make certain that the German lords did not show their displeasure.

The column kept growing in size, he thought, seeing how the gendarmes dragged new groups of people with yellow stars from the doorways of the houses. After all, this action was begun because the Germans had become nervous, and rightly so. They had announced the creation of the ghetto and had made known its boundaries, but only a few Jews believed that this was not just a threat or a joke. Only those who believed it got in touch with Poles who lived in Bałuty and bought out the better dwellings for good money. The choice was not great. The better dwellings, those with sanitary facilities, were only three or four hundred out of a total of forty thousand. The rest of the Łódź Jews waited several weeks. Waited for what? Perhaps for the rumours of unknown origin and spread by unknown people to turn to reality. Rumours that the war was at an end, that Hitler was dead, that the French offensive, that Russian tanks, that Rumania, that ... Wishful thinking. Who in the Jewish district had ever heard of Sikorski before?[7] At most the few people who read newspapers. Now every child knew of him.

What street is it? In the darkness all streets look alike, particularly in Łódź. Zachodnia (Western) Street, it seems. In the West something should start any day now ...

Suddenly the nurse called him from the other side of the street making gestures that got lost in the darkness. He ran in the indicated direction and he heard a scream: 'Ambulance! Someone is lying in the doorway!' And when he was in the doorway, he saw that someone was also lying in the courtyard. Using his elbows, he squeezed through the crowd that now was stretching the whole width of the street. In the doorway a woman had simply fainted. He instructed the nurse to give her the appropriate injection. He himself kneeled near the person needing medical help in the courtyard. On the cobblestones in the courtyard lay an elderly man with a jacket thrown on top of his pyjamas. A kind person had put a pillow under his head. But actually the head did not need a pillow any more. It was half-smashed because an SS man had tried out the butt of his rifle on it.

Not to forget! Not to forget – he constantly repeated to

5

himself. On the ground floor a woman stood in a window and cried. She had not been touched – she was Polish. But to look out of the window was already an act of courage. From the house another woman came out, also Polish. She knelt near the dying man and prayed. The courtyard was drowned in darkness.

He sent the nurse for a stretcher, and after a while they carried the dying man in the direction of the *droshky*, the horse-driven carriage. Skilfully they placed the stretcher with the dying man on the *droshky* and secured it. He ordered the driver to drive to the hospital. Should he hurry? No, he should not. He reached for his notebook and registered one more name, which the reliable nurse had found out. It was true the man was still alive, but … Tomorrow when he calls the hospital he'll make sure. Tomorrow? Will there be a tomorrow? A moment of rest. At least until the *droshky* comes back.

When he began to work at the first-aid service, he received a certificate from the German authorities giving him the right to violate the curfew without punishment. This was very convenient. But he did not abuse that right. Very soon he realized that the evening and the Jewish loneliness on an Aryan street created a very risky situation. He was once returning home late in the evening and as usual the passers-by looked at him as at a strolling monkey. But this time they were more determined. To provoke Aryan passers-by with a yellow armband should not go unpunished. Because at that time there were still armbands. The yellow stars were introduced later … Later? Come on – remember your history lessons:

'You, there, in the last row! Yes, I have you in mind. Stop playing sea battle with your neighbour and tell me what you know of the Lateran Council.'[8] – 'The Lateran Council?' … 'The Lateran Council.' 'The Council decided that all Jews must wear a special patch on their clothing to distinguish them from Christians.' 'The year?' – 'Of the Council?' 'Yes, in which year had the Council met?' 'In 1215, professor'… 'Indeed, in 1215.'

Now the year is 1940. Exactly 725 years ago. The Germans knew how to honour such an anniversary …

Not far from the Zielony Rynek (Green Market) he heard something familiar: 'Where are you rushing to, you little Yid?' Two students (or perhaps young doctors) had asked him exactly the same question in the middle of September in the courtyard of a Warsaw hospital, where he had worked after he had escaped on foot from Łódź. At that time there were no yellow arm-bands but his features were as telling an indication of a shameful origin as an arm-band. This time the question was asked indeed in native Polish but as it turned out it came from the mouth of a newly baked *Volksdeutsch*.[9] In any case, two men had taken him energetically by the arm and led him to the nearest police station. There a non-commissioned officer examined his certificate and regretfully let him go, adding only: 'You, Jew, are a lucky swine.' This time it indeed ended by respecting an official document. But this would not always be the case ... The other time, at the hospital, the incident also had a happy ending. Two doctors with whom he had been working explained something to the two students, and the first, the one who had accosted him, approached him with an outstretched hand: 'Pardon me, colleague, we did not know that ...'

'Doctor, the *droshky* has returned,' the nurse interrupted his thoughts. He did not even notice that he had been sitting on a pile of bricks. Something must have happened because everything had come to a halt.

Indeed, the column stood as if rooted to the roadway. Together with the nurse, he began to squeeze himself through the silent, dense crowd. Even children did not cry. Some people rested sitting on their suitcases. Others were afraid to show the Germans such insubordination. Withered faces, sunken eyes, hunched backs – the eternal wanderers were waiting for a sign to continue on. It turned out that the resettlement of the Jews from a number of streets had not proceeded as smoothly as the Germans had hoped for. This involved the Jews from Zachodnia, Wólczańska, Zawadzka, and Cegielniana Streets. The first street to cause problems had been Piotrkowska Street, which on becoming Adolf Hitler Strasse should have been the first to be declared *Judenfrei*.[10]

Together with the nurse he reached the head of the column. Some thug was standing there. He wore a yellow star but also an arm-band. Obviously the Germans had invested him with the power to direct the mass of exiles. He acted as though delighted with his new power. From time to time he turned either to the first row of the column or, with proper

7

respect, to the group of SS officers and non-commissioned officers who stood nearby. Like a prophet transmitting God's word, he sermonized loudly with a raised hand to the wanderers. The thug's red face swelled up from the effort. He did not seem to be someone who would realize that he too was an actor in a play performed many times during the centuries, but who knows? Perhaps he saw in the uniformed SS men the soldiers that had accompanied the Jews expelled from Jerusalem on their way to Babylon.

To forget nothing? Indeed!

The column was moving slowly along the gray houses of Zachodnia Street. He walked more slowly than the crowd to let the people pass. Before he set out on this assignment he had received the order always to keep at the rear of the column. From time to time some German shouts reached his ears, but he continuously heard the rustle of the snow that was trampled ever deeper between the cobblestones of the pavement.

Finally he and the nurse found themselves at the rear of the column and had before them, wrapped in the darkness of the night, the view of an empty street as if the street had taken leave of the departing crowd of exiles. But no, it only seemed that way. Dark figures came out of the doorways of the barely noticeable houses. They quickly loaded in bags, baskets or suitcases, whatever the Jews on their march to the ghetto had left behind. Hyenas smelling carcasses, and the number of carcasses was growing. Some of the Germans made a game. With one skilful kick they would knock out a suitcase from the hands of the scavengers who stood in front of the houses. Those behind them were happy to collect the bountiful harvest. It seems that the occupation is not so bad after all!

The nurse points at them and mumbles something under his breath. He wants to answer that if the situation had been reversed, and those who are humiliated today would have been in the place of those who remained untouched, more than one of them would have behaved the same way. He did not however have the time to do so because he noticed an elderly woman in a yellow, flannel dressing-gown lying near the wall of one of the houses. The old woman was dead. They put her on the stretcher. At the questioning glance of the nurse, he mumbled: 'You see for yourself, she died of natural causes.'

8

Again they put the stretcher on the *droshky*. Before they had secured the stretcher, and before he had given the driver the appropriate order, the column moved on. Now they had to hurry to catch up with it. There was constantly new information about killings in the courtyards, the apartments, on the stairs of houses in the streets intersecting Zachodnia Street. Together with the nurse he was now rushing to and fro. It was not of course to help anyone; in any case, there was no need for help. The purpose was to have everything written down correctly so that the data in the report would agree with the number of corpses, if it would occur to anyone to count them the next day.

The column, stretching the whole width of the street, resembled a rapidly flowing river running through a dark canyon. At a certain spot, closed off by a double row of gendarmes, the river suddenly ended.

Not to lose anything …

All of a sudden, books began to mark the traces of the march in the snow and mud. Thick, thin, big, small. The number of books kept increasing, and the shoes of the men and women trample on them ever more deeply into the soggy roadway. The nurse, surprised, picked up one book – the Hebrew characters and the specific arrangement of the pages indicated that this was most likely a commentary on the Talmud or the Bible … After a while they were not surprised any more. Several men were pulling a handcart with books, probably the entire property of some synagogue or *cheder*[11] … Two men in green uniforms did not like it and began systematically to throw books into the snow until at the end they turned the whole handcart upside down. The view of the scattered content of the handcart greatly amused the Germans. And the nurse managed a black joke: 'Want a bet, doctor, that the scavengers in the back won't touch those books?'

Suddenly it looked as if the stream of exiles from the side streets had stopped. The expulsion from the apartments was halted. The Germans probably wanted to go to sleep. In any event, they had achieved their purpose … The next day as the news of the expulsion spread, the Jews would start moving to Bałuty of their own accord. Of course, they would be able to take more things with them, and there would be less loot for those who would come to occupy their homes, but it would be a temporary reprieve.

'Doctor! Come here! She fainted,' someone yelled from the crowd. He ran after the nurse. Surprisingly, the Germans allowed them to pull out from the crowd a young, pale woman without opposition. She was choking. Asthma? Yes, asthma. He looked questioningly at a gendarme. 'We have to take her to the hospital …' A wave of the hand indicated: 'Do with her whatever you want.' A good man. The nurse took the woman to the *droshky*. The asthma attack was over. A happy ending. 'I am pregnant.' The woman had divulged this information before the *droshky* began to move. With this proud information she wanted to cover up the weakness resulting from her asthma. This would be one of the first ghetto babies, he thought.

And again at the head of the column that by now had already reached the Bałuty Market, the thug with the red face lifted both his hands: *'Schneller, kinderlech! Schneller!'*[12] In Yiddish? In German? How low you have fallen, Jeremiah!

How many hours had passed since the beginning of this action? Three? Four? From Zachodnia Street to the Bałuty Market the distance was no more than three kilometres. He reviewed his list. He could probably start summing up. He stopped. Best not to invite an evil eye. Full of pride, touching his navy cap with earflaps with two fingers in a military salute, the thug reported something. The German did not hide his satisfaction. He even treated the thug to a cigarette. He said something and disappeared into one of the buildings … The column is waiting. The nurse circulated in the crowd with some drops and treated everyone with them as with good brandy on a holiday.

The waiting is prolonged. What are they going to do with us? Will they immediately find lodgings here for us? And perhaps they will let us go back home? The last question indicated that the Jews quickly saw through the psyche of the executioners, who were capable of gigantic actions for the sole purpose of torturing them. But the optimistic sense of the question did not measure up to the reality of the situation. Returning to the closed and sealed homes was out of the question.

Gradually the discipline of the crowd became relaxed. The worst was that the gendarmes were losing their patience – they were dreaming of a warm bed after a job well done. And who could predict what an impatient gendarme is capable of? In spite of this, the column in its entire length lost it compactness and began to fall apart. Men relieve themselves near the walls of the houses; women indeed as well. Conversations get louder. Even children understand that the time to cry has arrived.

He was so tired that suddenly this spectacle, like a frame cut out from a film about medieval times, did not strike him any more ... He was cold and was shivering ... 'Doctor,' this was the nurse, 'what happened?' A change of shift.

Only now had he remembered that at four o'clock another first-aid team was to replace them. Indeed. A well-rested and lively twosome – a doctor and a male nurse – took over the *droshky* and the medicine chest. He still had the time to hand over the list of those killed to the other doctor. 'Perhaps you won't have to add to it,' he said with a barely noticeable smile. However the other doctor did not look at him but looked somewhere to the side, behind his head. He turned around and still managed to notice how the officer who a while ago had treated the thug to a cigarette, now punched him in the face and kicked him after he fell to the ground. This had not impressed him. He nodded goodbye to his colleague and still had time to thank the nurse ...

As if in a trance, he went home through the empty streets of Bałuty to his new abode in a room above a former pharmacy. Six beds, sofas and couches stood along the walls of the room. The couch under the window was at the moment the only place on earth he could call his own ... In order not to wake anyone, he had not turned on the light, but could not help making a noise. After a while a little lamp near someone's bed came on. Several pairs of eyes stared at him.

'Well, why did they call you out? What was it?' That was Bronek.

'Resettlement. Over 10,000. Anyway, who the hell knows, perhaps more. From downtown to Bałuty.'

Silence.

'So what?'

'Twenty-three killed.'

'Impossible.' This was Marysia, Bronek's wife. 'They sleep together.'

11

'The Nazis, they are what they are.'

'But they are murderers. And sadists,' said Heniek, a young engineer who was covered with his blanket up to his ears.

He lay down, sharing his fatigue with the couch. He was already falling asleep when suddenly another question reached his ears:

'Were they killing children, too?' The question came from a nightmarish dwarf who together with his young wife was lying on a large bed standing near the couch. His wife had been one of the most beautiful and sought-after young women of Łódź. She married this super-rich dwarf. But the war broke out before she could profit from her investment. In the dim light of the little lamp, he saw the nightgown open on her breast.

'Not a single child was killed,' he reassured them.

'So, you see,' the dwarf said.

'You see yourself,' said Marysia.

He was falling asleep. For a while he could still hear a promising rustle from the bed nearby. Whatever the situation, the dwarf did not forget his conjugal rights. Since the Germans had not killed even one child ... Indeed, why hadn't they? In Kishinev, the Cossacks did kill children ... In Spain, the Dominicans forced them to be baptized. And what about here?

Everything has its time – as the book of Ecclesiastes says.

Notes

1. In Kishinev, in Bessarabia which at that time was part of the Russian empire, a pogrom took place in April, 1903.
2. A mythical village in which lived and from which was expelled Sholem Aleichem's hero, Tevye the Dairyman.
3. Reference to the rulers of Spain in 1492 at the time Jews were expelled.
4. Mordecai Rumkowski.
5. Be it what it may, I fear the Danaans, though their hands proffer gifts. (*Aeneid*, 2:48).
6. A slum area inhabited mostly by Jews, where the ghetto was located.
7. The prime minister of the Polish government in exile in London.
8. An ecumenical council held in the Lateran Palace in Rome, the residence of the pope until the removal of the papal court to Avignon.
9. An ethnic German living outside Germany.
10. Free of Jews.
11. Religious school.
12. Faster, children, faster.

2 A Report on the Gypsies

Dear Sir!

In your letter, you asked me for a detailed account of the events that I had mentioned briefly in our conversation. In connection with this conversation you also asked me, if possible, to write in more detail about myself. Such a request is understandable: you hope to utilize the information that I would pass on to you, but since that information cannot be verified, you need to know more about the informant. The particulars about me could thus become an essential point of reference.

It is true that in our conversation I had little occasion to talk about myself. I realized at once that you were primarily interested in the matters that had been the subject of your investigations for a long time, both historical and literary. Now I shall attempt to write about myself in greater detail. I trust you will forgive me if my remarks have the character more of a report or account than a letter. I feel it would be easier for me to write if I did not have to think at all times that I was writing to a particular person – that is to you. This impersonal approach will perhaps enable me to avoid the constraints I would feel knowing that the words I put on paper are read (and remembered) by a recipient whom I know.

But let us begin.

When I attempt to organize my ghetto memories, I always look for a point in time, a point that would enable me to introduce some order in those memories and establish the actual sequence of events. For instance, it is easier for me to say that an event had occurred right before the liquidation of the ghetto or after the great *Sperre*[1] than to specify the year or month when it occurred. Though, on the other hand, I doubt if the sequence of events has any significance today, after so many years? At most, perhaps, certain facts can be rendered more credible, but is even that necessary? The ghetto years were all alike: one did not bid farewell to the year that passed, and one expected of the incoming year more than it could bring. But, for instance, the September *Sperre* during which mothers were forced to give their children to the Germans for deportation, that is for death; when hospital patients were gathered by the Nazis like homeless dogs by a dog-catcher; when sons carefully put their helpless mothers on wagons that took them straight to the trucks that were actually primitive gas chambers – that *Sperre* divided the ghetto time into two rhythms, as in a dreary sonata composed by Satan. The events about which I am about to relate occurred before the *Sperre* but after the resettlement of the German, Austrian and Czech Jews to the ghetto: for them this had been but a short intermezzo in their ordeal.

At the time, I was working at the hospital for infectious diseases. The hospital was of course in the ghetto, on Drewnowska Street. This is certainly not essential to the events to be described, but I would like to explain (since I decided also to write about myself) how I had come to be at that particular hospital. Right after the ghetto was closed off – this is a very important time reference – I had already had some brief experience with the first-aid service and volunteered to work at the hospital's internal diseases ward. Obviously, my practical knowledge was not broad enough for me to claim the right to work independently. I had finished my studies shortly before the war broke out, and in my dreams of the future I saw myself in a laboratory rather than at a sick-bed. If, however, in spite of some inner resistance, or perhaps dislike, I began to practice medicine, it was simply because my medical studies were some foundation on which I could build my immediate future. Right after the Jewish authorities (or rather the Eldest of the Jews – to employ the Nazi terminology) created a Health Department, I presented myself for work at the first-aid service.

First-aid service! When I think today of the audacity I showed by undertaking such work without any experience in that field, I can explain it only by the courage of youth. And also by the times that formed the background to this decision. The world was breaking down. There were ever more signs

14

that a long, heavy night was in the offing and that it would be a long time until dawn. It must be added that few doctors were eager for first-aid work. That was work for young people such as myself, who believed in themselves. I also counted on the help of older doctors but, as I soon realized, that hope was not justified. This is not the place to go into this, but immediately after the occupation of Poland, it was difficult for many older doctors to free themselves of customs and habits formed in normal times. How many of them had not grasped that before crossing the ghetto gates it was necessary at least to refresh those habits! Indeed, as a result of this situation the need arose at the very beginning to bring a group of doctors to the Łódź ghetto from the Warsaw ghetto. Their arrival was supposed to break the monopoly of their Łódź colleagues in many special-ities, a monopoly which they used to blackmail the Ghetto authorities... But here, I have digressed into matters that have little bearing on the main subject of this report.

In any case, by my first night out with the first-aid ambulance, it became clear to me how much I needed help. Without help, this first independent move would already have had a dismal ending. Luckily, help came from an old, experienced male nurse. It was a cold December night, before the ghetto was set up. The first-aid ambulance was called out to a case of 'loss of consciousness,' as noted by the reception-ist who took the call. I stood before an elderly unconscious patient. I paid no attention to *who* he was, although this proved to be not entirely without significance. I rather tried to determine what was wrong with him because for a loss of consciousness there could be at least fifty reasons. When after the first attempts at a diagnosis I looked helplessly at the patient, the old nurse who accompanied me drew nearer to me and so that no one could hear him quietly whispered: 'He is smoking a pipe, doctor ...'

And indeed, while breathing, the patient's mouth formed a grimace reminiscent of the exhaling of smoke by someone who smoked a pipe. Even a young doctor, if he remembered something about pathology, would know that 'smoking a pipe' is a phenomenon that accompanies a brain haemor-rhage. Nurse Gutentag – this seems to have been his name – must have had a lot of experience prompting at school.

15

Nobody heard his remark. Gutentag had worked in the first-aid service for forty-five years, and probably three generations of first-aid doctors started out with him. Later, in the ghetto, he died of hunger ...

After that things went more briskly. The letting of blood (yes, yes), the appropriate injection – now I was on familiar grounds. In any event, due to his age, the patient's prognosis was poor.

Fate had ordained that my first patient was someone whom I had indeed seen for the first time in my life but about whom I knew almost everything. His name was Zachariasz Warszawski and he had been for many years, before the war, the owner of a wholesale store of textiles. And it was there, at the beginning of this century, that my father became an errand boy and had begun his working life. My father, a man with literary abilities (he had been writing steadily for the Yiddish press) and a considerable thespian talent (in the Warsaw Ghetto he was an actor) could tell stories for hours about Zachariasz Warszawski: his manner of speaking, his way of life, his habits and life experiences, his attitude to his employees and clients. And by chance it so happened that when, at end of the former world I had become independent and started my medical work, the first person for whom I filled out a death certificate (the day after my night visit) was someone with whom my father, after coming from far-away Krośniewic, had started his independent life forty years before.

But I have become side-tracked from the essence of my report, because I still have to explain how I came to specialize in infectious diseases. As I have already mentioned, in the beginning I was a volunteer in the internal medicine ward. It should be noted that this was an unusual ward. The older male patients there had been foisted on the hospital to get rid of them at home. The female patients, on the other hand, were all young and handsome women. If the first fact could have been all too easily explained by the ghetto conditions, the second was the result of the erotic exploits of the head of the ward, Dr M., who was otherwise a charming and cultured person. His weakness was women. In his ward, he did not allow female patients older than thirty. His rounds always created a sensation. Nurses from all over the hospital rushed to witness them. He had several tricks he used in his exami-

16

nations, depending on the situation or on the external attributes of the female patient. For instance, he would examine
the stomach of a female patient only under the blanket, as if
not to expose her to others and cause her embarrassment. He
also liked to have a female patient lie on her stomach and
explore beneath her belly-button. Aural examinations were
always conducted in such a manner that one hand of Dr M.
rested on the patient's breast. The nurses who observed his
manipulations laughed their heads off, and the doctors who
assisted him looked at his tricks with both jealousy and
understanding. And the patients? In general, they did not
object; the most they did was blush.

Now, the same Dr M., who liked me and who had often
been nice to me, offered me the job – for which I would be
paid! – of an assistant at the hospital for infectious diseases. (Dr
M., who later again played an important role in my life,
perished in strange circumstances. After the liquidation of the
ghetto, the Germans left him together with a group of 800
Jews, to 'clean up' abandoned homes and workshops. One day
he went out of town with a group of workers and never came
back. The whole group was liquidated in Chełmno.[2]) In any
case, I was fed up with seeing old patients die without treatment and women pawed instead of being treated. I agreed to
be transferred to the infectious ward, even if it was risky, and
on top of it, I had to learn everything from the scratch.

Luckily, I found Karwacki's manual which was basic for
that branch of medicine, at the hospital library. I crammed the
content of Karwacki's manual into my, head and since I
already had a lot of hospital experience I slowly began to feel
more confident. The confidence resulted from the fact that
more often than in the internal ward I saw patients recover-
ing. This was of course connected with the abnormal conditions in the ghetto, but it still enriched my medical practice
with a pinch of optimism. The typical temperature chart of a
typhoid fever patient, in spite of the ghetto fence, and in spite
of hunger and hopelessness, imbued one with faith in the
immutable order of the universe. Actually, in the hospital for
infectious diseases there were no hopeless cases. That is,
except for tubercular meningitis. Patients who were terminally
ill with this disease were transferred to another hospital – here

17

there were only cases of tubercular meningitis whose character still had to be diagnosed. The diagnosis depended on the appearance of the fluid obtained from the spinal tap: clear or cloudy. Clear fluid indicated a death sentence: tubercular meningitis of a type for which at that time (not only in the ghetto) there was no cure. Anyway, such cases were frequent and, luckily, the patients themselves were not aware that the verdict depended on the appearance of the first drop of fluid that fell into the test-tube.

Of course, these details have no special relevance to the main topic of this report, though it is worth noting that I was to some extent a specialist in these matters (perhaps this is an exaggeration) and this eventually made me almost the main witness, or more precisely the only witness alive, of the subject about which I am about to writet.

A few words about my superiors because that too is quite important in this case. The chief physician of the hospital had been Dr Sz., a decent numbskull. On the other hand, Dr W., the head of the ward and my immediate superior, was a good doctor who was not so young and who with some justification reckoned he should have been the head of the hospital. Luckily, that ambition of his had not affected the hospital's operation.

That year autumn was fair, harsh and cool. The sky was always cloudless, as if it had tried to bring with its immaculate blue some hope, or even joy, to the bleak course of affairs in the ghetto behind the fences. But there was no season or weather that could counteract the bitterness, troubles, calamities or defeats that the Germans handed out to each ghetto resident. Even the few trees that grew in the ghetto had become adapted to the conditions of the ghetto: they did not grow leaves until the end of spring and lost them by August. Behind the hospital for infectious diseases there was a dirty-brown piece of land on which the odd person tried to grow a miserable crop, but the soil did not favour the pariahs. Besides, the road to the hospital went through this land. The hospital was so awkwardly situated that right near its front entrance was the barbed-wire fence that indicated the ghetto boundary. An armed German gendarme was always standing there. That gendarme could always be seized by the desire to practice shooting at a Jew; the first-aid service reports had a lot to say on this topic. Ghetto residents would also approach an SS man to ask for a liberating bullet, though this was relatively rare considering the conditions of ghetto life behind the barbed-wire fence.

By the end of November, the field behind the hospital was drowning in mud. No breakneck attempts to avoid the dirty flood were successful, and the mud had to be laboriously scraped off one's shoes and trousers. I was busy with this everyday task in the doctors' room before going on my rounds, when one of the nurses ran into the office without knocking. She was not just 'one of the nurses.' She was the best-looking nurse in the hospital who in spite of the ghetto conditions did not try to make up for lost opportunities. She was very frugal in bestowing her favours. Panting, she told me immediately to report at full speed to the superiors. She was obviously scared and the urgency of the matter was obvious.

In the ghetto, there were enough reasons for panic day and night. At the hospital for infectious diseases, even more so. Without making my shoes and trousers decent, and putting on my white coat on the run, I ran up to the second floor office of the hospital director. As the door was half-open, I entered without knocking and stopped flabbergasted. On the couch on the right side lay Dr Sz., the hospital director. On the couch on the left side lay the chief of my ward, Dr W. A puzzled nurse stood nearby, and a hospital doctor was giving the hospital director an injection. In addition, there was a terrible stench in the room. When my colleague finished the injection, Dr Sz., upon noticing me, lifted himself onto his elbow, glanced at me pitifully and said emphatically:

'Colleague, report immediately to the Kripo.'[3]

Stunned by this command, I did not react. The other actors in this scene were also silent. With a gesture, Sz. invited me to come nearer and added:

'They are waiting for you there.'

'How come they are waiting for me? Why for me? What might they want from me?'

'Not exactly you.'

'Then for whom?'

'They phoned and demanded that a doctor from the hospital for infectious diseases come to them right away.'

19

'So why do I have to go?'

'Because, you see, I fainted. The heart … It's too much at my age …'

He lifted himself higher on his elbow.

'And he,' he pointed to the other couch, 'can't you smell it? He shat himself.'

Now a few more words about the Kripo because there is need to explain why a summons to report to that institution would cause such panic. Kripo, or Kriminalpolizei (Criminal Police) established itself at Kościelny Square (Church Square) in the parish house. As its name indicated, one of the duties of that institution was to take care of ordinary crimes. But in the ghetto, this institution had been charged with a special duty. The Jewish police handled crimes and regularly reported to Kościelny Square. The Kripo's essential activity in the ghetto, on the other hand, was to complete the constant and systematic plunder of Jewish property. The task was to squeeze out from every Jew anything that could be of value to the Great Reich, before he was swallowed up by the gas chamber, if he had not already died of hunger. Some Jews had dared, in spite of orders to the contrary, to hide or give away for hiding such things as diamond rings, stocks of yarn, fur collars, or German marks. The Kripo's duty was to confiscate such things. But before they could do that, they had to find out whether anything had been hidden and where. For this there was one method, in principle an infallible one. A person suspected of the crime of having hidden something of value was arrested and then beaten and tortured until he admitted, that means he told, what he had hidden and where, if indeed he had hidden anything. If however he already did not have anything, if he had not hidden anything, if he had not given away a golden wedding band to hide, a fur or a roll of woollens, then there was no way he would leave the Kripo alive. Informers from both sides of the fence kept the Germans supplied with knowledge about such treasures … In any event, to be called to Kościelny Square meant giving oneself up to extremely skilled sadists. Even though the Nazi power was constantly weighing heavily over the ghetto, the Kripo was the most visible and omnipresent tool of that power.

I had therefore no reason to be surprised at the reaction of the two doctors to the telephonic summons from Kościelny Square, although I might have been surprised by the eagerness with which they sent me there. After all, nobody knew what was the matter. Since I was sent I hoped that, if investigated, my young age would guarantee (to a certain degree) my ability to endure the known Kripo methods. This was obvious, and therefore I had been even more disgusted by Dr Sz.'s attempt to convince me that choosing me as a representative of the hospital for infectious diseases to Kościelny Square was evidence of unprecedented trust. In any case, my opinion did not count. I was obliged to submit to that decision, and I did. This fact brings us rapidly closer to the most important part of this report.

From Drewnowska Street to Kościelny Square was not far. One had to cross the muddy field to get to Lutomierska Street and then to go over the wooden bridge above Zgierska Street. Going over that bridge required great effort: for some physical, for others psychological. For people who were elderly, sickly, or weak, the steep stairs to the bridge presented great difficulty, particularly during winter-time. But standing on the bridge and looking southward, one had a view of part of Zgierska, Nowomiejska and Piotrkowska Streets, which cut through the city in a straight line. In this view some had tried again to find elements of big-city life, traces of life in the rest of the universe. Others rediscovered with longing the normality of the past in the distant contours of downtown – a normality often gray, empty and amorphous in which they were seldom happy – not anticipating that happiness could have different faces. Then one had to descend. On the right side was the church of the Holy Virgin Mary whose patron saint the Germans had resettled from Zachodnia Street like an ordinary Jewess.

Fifteen minutes after I had been called to the office of the hospital director, I found myself in front of the Kripo headquarters. Today I cannot remember what filled me more: fear or curiosity. In any case, they were waiting for me there. In front of the old parish house stood the *droshky* with two horses well-known to the ghetto residents, and in it sat two splendid representatives of the SS. One of them was a magnificent Siberian wolfhound with a fluffy, soft coat and brown

21

eyes like amber. Its hanging-out tongue expressed a joy for life. The other was an SS Oberscharführer whose name, as I later learned, was Jansen. Eugen Jansen was the most handsome man I had ever seen. The Oberscharführer (an SS rank corresponding to sergeant or top-sergeant in the army) was perfect in every respect. He wore the military cap perfectly, he rolled his eyes perfectly, his boots were shined to perfection, the SS uniform fitted him perfectly, and he had perfect Aryan features … Besides which, his manners were also perfect; at least in the beginning. With a well-studied motion he invited me into the *droshky*, ordered me to sit beside him, and to the wolfhound that had until now occupied this place of honour he indicated the pulled-out seat opposite. The horses behaved as if they had been waiting for my arrival. The *droshky* started violently through the ghetto streets and turned into Brzezińska Street. That street connected Łódź with Brzeziny – hence its name – a little town of perhaps the greatest Jewish poverty in Poland. There, for miserable pennies, entire families had been sewing ready-made garments on which the Łódź wholesalers made fortunes. Brzezińska Street was disappearing under the wheels of the *droshky*, and Jansen informed me that we were going to the Gypsy camp.

And now another indispensable explanation. Two or three months earlier, the Germans had evicted the Jews from a few three-storey tenement houses located right near the ghetto boundary at the corner of Brzezińska and Głowacki Streets. The space occupied by those buildings and the little square between them was fenced off with barbed wire – on one side that area bordered on the city, and on the other, on the ghetto. A barbed-wire barricade separated it from the ghetto. A few days after such preparation, trucks had arrived from which several thousand Gypsies were driven out. Thus, near the big Jewish ghetto, a little Gypsy ghetto bordering on it was set up. At the beginning, the camp had been a sensation for the ghetto, but after a while nobody showed much interest in it. The Kripo was ruling and supervising the Gypsy camp. Occasionally news of atrocities leaked out from that camp.

And it was precisely there that I was going with Oberscharführer Jansen. The presence of a doctor knowledgeable about infectious diseases was indispensable because some sickness had begun to spread among the Gypsies. The Oberscharführer expected me to diagnose the sickness and advise how to prevent its spread.

As I already mentioned, the Germans had put up a double row of barbed wire between the Gypsy camp and the ghetto. (What were they afraid of?) German sentries guarded the wire fence between the camp and the city as well as the wire fence between the camp and the ghetto. In addition, from the ghetto side, the Jewish police guarded the gate linking the two camps. Indeed, through that very gate we were let to pass respectfully and, together with the Oberscharführer, I found myself at the site of the Gypsy camp. (Three years later, when, after incarceration in the camps at Auschwitz and Jelenia Góra, I had been transferred to the camp at Cieplice, I recalled that visit to the Gypsy camp, because I found myself at that time in a quarantine area created inside the camp, a quarantine area that was separated from the other part of the camp by a barbed-wire barricade. Here there was an almost identical situation.)

The Kripo carriage stopped at the little square between the buildings that formed the camp. To maintain order in the camp the Germans had set up a police of sorts. Its tall representatives had been given wooden clubs as arms. This proved that the Third Reich held our Jewish police in greater esteem since they had at their disposal authentic rubber truncheons. Some of the Gypsy inmates selected to maintain order stood to attention before Jansen, others began to disperse the thickening mob that crowded the little square. As the Oberscharführer discussed something with the chief of the order service, who gesticulated like an actor in an Italian film, I moved near to the wall of the closest building and peeked inside. I stole a glance into the hall on the main floor and through the hall into two rooms whose doors were open. This was an unusual sight. What I saw in the two rooms was horrifying even to me, who had been used to the terribly crowded lodgings in the ghetto and in the camps for the arrivals from Germany and Austria. Still today, when I write this report, I cannot think of what it could be compared to. At that time it brought to memory a documentary film about a hospital in

23

India that I had seen before the war. As in the film, the rooms I saw from the corner of my eye did not have any plank beds, let alone real beds. The floor, scattered with straw and covered with rags, served as the place to sleep – for one hundred residents of that ant-hill. It was shocking.

While it is true that my report would not gain from it, I must digress to make some general observations.

No refined psychological insight is required to surmise that situating the Gypsy camp in a few buildings detached from the ghetto was a factor that in a peculiar way boosted the morale of the Jewish population. And that was for two reasons. First, by some unusual logic, this fact had reassured the Jews that at least for the time being the Germans did not intend to liquidate the ghetto. The second reason was more easily understood. The news that reached the ghetto about the conditions in which the Gypsies lived (news that did not even describe the horrible truth) improved the morale of the Jews enclosed in the ghetto because it meant it was not they who were at the bottom. At the bottom of degradation, misery, hunger. There was no compassion in the ghetto for the Gypsies as most likely there was no compassion among the Gypsies for the Jews. The executioner allowed the victims to observe each other, but it must be remembered that there was never any feeling of sympathy or common fate between the Jews and the Gypsies. Both groups were considered by the surrounding Christian–Catholic society at least as aliens, if not enemies. And experience teaches that in such cases solidarity is out of the question. What arises is something akin to competition for a gesture of kindness, for the alms of a kind word.

The conditions in which the Jews lived in the ghetto were awful. But what could be said of the Gypsy camp? In those three or four buildings, there could have been no more than 120 to 150 small rooms. And those rooms had to accommodate several thousand people. There those people lived, ate, were sick … The majority of the Gypsies probably did not move from their sleeping places. I noticed that those lying on the rags did not react at all to such an unusual event as Jansen's coming – at most, his wolfhound caused some confusion and fear. Luckily, he did not attack people, unlike other representatives of his race that had been trained by the Nazis. Just the opposite, in fact. He wanted to be caressed, and wallowed in the bedding scattered on the floor: it was obvious that this gave him special pleasure.

All this registered very clearly in my memory even if my survey lasted but a few minutes. Because very soon Jansen called me to order, making me understand that I was not to distance myself from him even for one step. Besides, he had become so upset with my insubordination that he lost his good manners on the spot and hit the chief of the order service with whom until then he had been quietly talking with his riding-whip. Perhaps he wanted to show me that I would not be treated with greater consideration.

Together we entered a little one-storey house at the right of the main gate. It appeared that in it two rooms were occupied by a little hospital, or, as it was called at that time, a *revier.* Jansen stopped at the threshold of one room, letting me go inside. Along the longer walls in each little room eight plank beds were lined up stacked two high. All were filled up, some of them with two sick persons. It is interesting that I cannot recall if there were any women among the sick. Looking back, I ask myself whether there were any women at all in that camp. I recall exactly many details I noticed at the time, but this aspect so important for the present report, I do not recall. While it is true that this does not change the essence of this report, by analogy I would still think that in that camp there were entire families, although I do not remember seeing any children either. The analogy refers to a part of the Gypsy camp in Birkenau where, until the liquidation of the Łódź Ghetto, entire Gypsy families lived and were murdered from day to day in the gas chambers. The concern there at that time was to make room for the Łódź Jews. Yes. There again the Germans had shuffled the fates of those two peoples.

I went over to a sick man on the lower plank bed at the left side. He was unconscious and had a high fever. It was enough to lift his shirt from his chest to make a quick diagnosis. There was no doubt that this was spotted typhus. While it was true that there was no need to examine the other sick people, still, firstly, I wanted to have a clear conscience, and secondly, I wanted to check the extent of the louse infestation there. I should have done this in the living-quarters, but after what I noticed among the sick, I did not need additional confirmation. The matter was clear as day, or rather threatening as the harbinger of an element that human powers were not in a position to subdue.

All this took no more than twenty minutes.

The conversation with Jansen was brief.

'So, what is it?'

'Typhus.'

'Is it life-threatening?'

'Very.'

'Is it curable?' (In German: "*Ist das heilbar?*")

Now I did not know what to say. The answer was not simple: To cure in the conditions there? Nevertheless, I answered:

'Yes, indeed. Medical supplies, medicines are required.'

'Is it very contagious?'

I thought he knew everything on this subject. The Germans were afraid of typhus most of all. There was no reason however to beat about the bush.

'Yes, it is very contagious. The sickness is spread by lice.'

'This I know.'

If he knows, he must also know the old epidemiological rule asserting that no barbed wire will stop a louse. And behind the barbed wire was first of all the ghetto with its dense population and terrible sanitary conditions (only one per cent of dwellings possessed so-called sanitary facilities), and then there was the city, the Aryan city. This thought I kept to myself. Yet I noticed that something had occurred to the Kripo Oberscharführer. He even smiled to himself.

We were again on the little square.

'I am going to show you something,' he said suddenly, 'I'll show you that this can be cured at once.'

He called the chief of the order service and gave him some order. After a short while two sick people were led down by some of his subordinates. That means that they were not so much led down as carried down and put on the ground. Jansen came over to them, observed them for a moment, then rapidly pulled his pistol from the holster and shot them in the back of the head. Only one of the men shot still twitched for a moment. The other one was motionless right away. All this before the eyes of the crowd of Gypsies who were kept in place by the order service. For a moment silence reigned in the little square. It lasted unnaturally long as if each onlooker of the scene had wanted to convince himself that he was not dreaming. And suddenly the silence was broken by a horrific scream. A scream from several hundred throats, a scream full of rage, and perhaps despair or sorrow. The crowd surged forward. This appeared so threatening that perhaps Jansen was also terrified. Not hiding the pistol, he jumped in the *droshky*. Next he pulled in the wolfhound and ordered me quickly to my place. The driver whipped the horses that went through the gate in a gallop, and we drove out again into the ghetto streets.

All this took not more than three, perhaps four, minutes. The earth did not stop spinning around the sun, women did not stop bearing children, the heavens remained mute and no saint helped the murdered souls find the road to eternal happiness. When the *droshky* turned into Brzezińska Street I had at my right the little square between the buildings of the Gypsy camp. I saw dark, gloomy faces retreating to the rear, some hands raised to heaven, and heard the weakening echo of a scream. What had actually happened? Nothing had happened. Two people sick with typhus were denied the chance to win the fight for life.

Jansen was silent the whole way back. After his cold performance, he now had the expression of a mischievous boy who had smashed a jar of marmalade. For a moment he raised his head as if he intended to say something – who knows to whom, to himself? To the dog? But he gave up this intention. The wolfhound did not take his eyes off his master. I was careful to sit as close as possible to the edge so as not to come in contact with the dog's fluffy coat. Before I descended the cab at the corner of Łagiewnicka Street, I turned to Jansen with a remark whose form in German I had carefully prepared in my mind:

'This dog of yours, Herr Oberscharführer, should in general not be admitted in the camp area. He can easily carry over lice in his coat.'

Jansen glanced at me as if he had seen me for the first time in his life. When I finished, he waved his hand and briefly said: '*Quatch!*' That meant I was talking nonsense.

When I found myself on the street, I breathed deeply. After the events of the last several minutes, the dilapidated, ruined houses of the ghetto seemed to me refreshing and quite charming, something familiar and cozy. All around people lived, froze and starved unaware of the threats hanging over the ghetto that I had witnessed just fifteen minutes before. I went straight to the Health Department. Its chief at the time was the same Dr M. who had sent me to the hospital for infectious diseases. He already knew about my visit to the Gypsies, but did not know the reason for it. So I reported everything to him, not leaving out any details. He immediately understood what the typhus epidemic in the Gypsy camp meant for the ghetto.

What happened later is public knowledge. Too many documents remain on the topic of further developments for me to need to elaborate on them. I shall only mention in brief that the German authorities issued the order that Jewish doctors take over the care of the Gypsy camp. This of course increased the probability that the epidemic would spread to the ghetto area. The Health Department then had the dilemma of choosing who to send on this dangerous assignment. One could not count on finding doctors who would on their own come forward to work in so dangerous a sector without being forced to do so. Neither could one count on anti-typhus vaccination. That was not for Jews.

After long deliberation, the problem was solved more or less democratically. The doctors themselves resolved that they would decide by drawing lots who would go to work at the Gypsy camp. The work period would be ten days. Two doctors would work together. After ten days, two other doctors would take their place. Only doctors without families would be subject to the draw. Since I had been married for a year, I was not threatened with being sent to the Gypsy camp.

And so it began. With perfect regularity, the pairs of doctors were changed every ten days. Their main task was quickly to separate the sick from the healthy. (In the prevailing conditions, thorough delousing was unthinkable.) And every 15 days a new pair of doctors fell ill with typhus. No precautions helped. About one of the doctors, Dr A., rumours circulated that, wanting to protect himself from contact with carriers of lice, he examined patients handling the stethoscope with a stick while standing on a table. But he too became ill. This went on for two months, perhaps somewhat longer. I cannot say exactly how many of the more than ten doctors survived. If I remember correctly – five. Luckily, in the ghetto itself the number of typhus cases had increased only slightly. It seems that the bacteria did not like the taste of the anaemic blood of the ghetto Jews incarcerated behind barbed wire – for them death by other methods had been planned. But among the Gypsies the bacteria could rage freely. Seldom were there anywhere or at any time conditions more favourable for a typhus epidemic to embrace such a large number of people. At the beginning some kind of statistics were kept at the Gypsy camp. Later that was given up. Even death certificates stopped being issued. The dead were buried nameless at the Jewish cemetery which was after all close by. Mother earth did not differentiate between those buried according to all the forms of the Jewish religious ritual and the Gypsies buried without tears and prayers.

This went on, as I have said, for about two months. Until one night trucks arrived in front of the Gypsy camp on which everyone, the healthy and the sick, was loaded and carted away. The Germans had not even made a secret of the fate that the camp residents met. In any case, from whom should they have kept it a secret? From the other sub-humans for whom a similar future was in store? All the Gypsies were murdered ... Some were shot, and some were gassed in trucks whose exhaust pipes were mounted to the inside. This method had already been tried earlier on Jews deported from the ghetto. The buildings that had formed the camp were returned to the ghetto, which meant they were behind a single row of barbed wire. They were thoroughly treated with insecticides and several dozen Jewish families were settled in their refreshed interiors before they too were gassed in Chełmno or Auschwitz. As it later became known, the decision to exterminate the Gypsy camp was apparently influenced by the increased number of typhus cases in Łódź itself. The Aryan Łódź, of course. How true this is, it is difficult to know.

This is everything I know about that matter. I surmise that I am the only person who had been in such close contact with this case, and this solely because of the weak heart of Dr Sz. and the weak sphincter of Dr W. But, but ... After all, this story had its happy end, if this notion can be used in relation to any stage of the events described above. Exactly fifteen days after his last visit to the Gypsy camp (that means the visit in which I had participated) Oberscharführer Eugen Jansen himself became ill with typhus. How a treacherous louse got to his body was not known. Perhaps from the fur of his beautiful wolfhound, perhaps some other way. In any case, the dog was immediately shot, which did not change the fact that after ten days of illness the condition of the sick man was such that the authorities had no choice but appeal to the most competent powers of this and the other world. German doctors were of no help; Jewish doctors from the ghetto were summoned – among them both my superiors. On top of it, the Kripo chief summoned all the ghetto rabbis (it seems there were four) and suggested to them that they started to pray intensively to the Jewish God for the return to health of the Oberscharführer because his death could bring terrible calamities on the ghetto. The rabbis then had to choose: if they were anxious for the fate of the ghetto, they could pray for the quick return to health of Eugen Jansen; but if they desired to reduce the number of enemies of Israel in the world, and also to reduce the deficit in the account of wrong-doings, they could pray for his fast demise.

It is not known what the rabbis had decided and for what they finally prayed. Neither is it known whether the Jewish Yahweh paid any attention to their prayers. The fact remained that two days later Jansen died and the ghetto survived him by two years and six months.

Notes

1. Closure. The Jews were not permitted to leave their houses and the Germans rounded up people for deportation. See later.
2. An extermination camp not far from Łódź.
3. Criminal Police (*Kriminalpolizei*).

3 The Confrontation

Groaning with its worn-out shock absorbers, the first-aid service's *droshky* was slowly and sleepily rolling over the cobblestone pavement of the Łódź ghetto. The *droshky* should have been retired a long time ago. But it still provided a priceless service. It gave the sick not so much help as hope, and this too was important, in the same way as the distilled water in the vial that acted at times as effectively as morphine and other pain killers. The only winner was the horse which, if not for the creation of the ghetto, would have ended up in the stomachs of the citizens of the Third Reich.

The male nurse settled down in the little front seat which, though not comfortable, was according to some old tradition designated exclusively for him. On his knees he held the famous medicine chest that he spasmodically clutched with both hands when passing over a bigger pothole so it would not slip out. A cold, gloomy November night descended on the ghetto. For the thousands of people shut in behind the walls of the ghetto houses, the night was no more gloomy and hostile than a November day, and a November day no more so than any day of any other month. During nights such as these, nights whose chill penetrated to his bone marrow and he was on duty and rode this rattling first-aid service *droshky*, he remembered a Yiddish theatre joke his father used to tell. So, two Jewish actors are dragging themselves in a *droshky* over the empty streets of a small town somewhere in Galicia[1] or in Congress Poland.[2] It is a cold, rainy night, and they huddle together to keep warm. One of them, pointing with a broad gesture to the houses they are passing, says: 'Look how lucky we are. Those people around us, locked in their houses, must be in their beds by now sleeping, we however have the opportunity to ride and ride!'

The horse's shoes as they hit the cobblestones emitted a

characteristic sound that sank in the heavy darkness as in a thick layer of cotton. A schoolfriend had once taught him to imitate that sound. When he tried at home to show off the skill he had learned at school, he was severely reprimanded by his mother who reckoned that a well brought-up boy does not use his mouth and tongue for such games. This remained with him. He was considered well brought-up. In the ghetto such a virtue was worth exactly as much as an old, leaky pot.

'Doctor,' the nurse's sharp voice swept out the nap that was embracing him. 'It is here.'

He stretched himself and opened his eyes. The cold wind wrapped him in an icy compress. In the darkness of the street, he barely noticed the contours of a lone one-storey house that stood on guard not far from the ghetto boundary. There were outlines of some figures clustered in front of the house. One of them headed in the direction of the *droshky*.

'It is here,' the figure echoed the words of the nurse.

He cautiously descended the *droshky*, careful of the slippery, inclined step.

He wanted to get quickly to some shelter to warm up.

'Is anyone of the family there?' said the nurse asking the first exploratory question.

No one answered. Apparently, there was no family. The man who was the one who came up to the *droshky* now walked beside him. Together they entered the dark little hallway where two more people stood. In the hallway doors led to the right and to the left as well as to the stairs which led to the first floor.

'Where is it?' he asked.

'Here,' said the man who accompanied him, and indicated the door on the right side.

He approached it and knocked.

'No need to knock,' said the man gloomily. 'Nobody will open anyway.'

He pushed the door. It was not locked. He quickly entered the premises behind it and retreated immediately, in a panic. In the few years of work in first-aid in the ghetto, he became used to the worst odours, but the dense stench composed of various odious smells that filled the room literally knocked him over. It was a mixture of decay, decomposing human remains, dirt and excrement.

32

The nurse had also entered the room but could not endure the stench either. In the hallway he asked again:

'Is anyone of the family here?'

'The whole family is there,' came someone's sensible answer in the darkness.

'Could you manage to go into the room and open the window?' he turned to the nurse. 'There is no other way.'

To prepare himself for that task, the nurse put away the medicine chest and covered his mouth and nose with a woollen scarf. He entered the room again and turned on the flashlight.

'Turn it off, goddamn it,' yelled the man. 'We are two feet from the barbed-wire fence. Do you want them to start shooting at us like they shoot at ducks?'

The nurse quickly turned off the flashlight and, breathing in deeply, ran through the dark room. After a while one could hear him fighting the window.

'Doctor,' this was the man.

'What is it?'

'Since you are already here ... That means ... Perhaps ... There, upstairs, my wife...'

'What is the matter with her?'

'She gave birth ... Now she is home and there is something wrong ...'

'So call a doctor from the infirmary.'

'But since you are already here ...'

'So what if I am here?" He called out enraged. ' am from first aid, do you understand? From first aid. We come only to emergencies. And your wife's case is not an emergency.'

'Yet, but ... It is only one floor up,' said the man as if begging for alms. "I shall pay ... With bread ...'

He waved his hand. He was accustomed to such proposals. Apparently, some doctors were not refusing.

The nurse left the room. He was breathing rapidly, with difficulty.

'Perhaps you could try now, doctor? But there is nothing for us to do there anyway. Perhaps someone would have a candle? Without a candle you won't see a thing.'

Someone brought the lit stump of a candle. The nurse was holding the candle in one hand and was covering it from the side of the window with his other hand. They went into the room together. The stench was no less but perhaps somewhat diluted by the air that came in from the open window. He felt that in a moment he was going to vomit … but he controlled himself. He could not make a spectacle of himself in front of the people in the hallway and the nurse. He looked around. The only furniture in the room was two plank-beds, a table, and near the table a little wooden stool. There was no stove or range. Nor was there a sink. Near one of the beds stood a rusty bucket with frozen urine. A few dirty plates and two pots lay scattered on the table. The walls as well as the floor were covered with a thick layer of dirt. Stepping carefully so as not to slip, he approached a plank-bed, the one closer to the window. It was not even a pallet, only a jumble of remnants of bedding and rags which at one time were probably some outer garments. Even in the dim light of the candle one could see on the plank-bed and near it remnants of dried out faeces. Across it lay the body of a tiny, perhaps eight-year-old, boy. He bent over him. At the last moment, the nurse caught him by the hand:

'What are you doing? Don't you see what is going on here?'

Only now had he realized that the child's face, his body as well as everything on the bed, was covered with a thick layer of nimble lice. On the skin, they looked like mobile speckles. They crept into everything – the eyes, the nostrils, and the mouth of the boy. The child was indeed dead but the layer of crawling lice gave the illusion that the boy's face was still alive.

This sight called forth in him the feeling of a superior duty. He pulled up the sleeves of his coat and jacket and touched the cheeks of the child.

'He has been dead for a good many hours. They called when nothing could have been done, goddamn it.'

He approached the plank-bed on the left. It looked exactly like the first one. The only difference was that there were two bodies on it. Likewise dirty, emaciated and wasted. Likewise covered with lice. A woman and a child – it looked like a girl. The woman had embraced the girl with her arm as if to protect her from danger. He bent over her. A superficial glance was enough to conclude that she was dead. The child, however, was showing some signs of life. It was breathing its last. With a piece of gauze, he shook off a layer of lice from her face.

'She should be taken immediately to the hospital,' he said in a voice he himself did not recognize.

The nurse looked at him in disbelief.

'With what, doctor? How? How will you pull her out? All our things will be covered with lice ... perhaps tomorrow ... the sanitary squad ...'

The nurse of course was right. But leaving the child until the morning meant convicting her to an inevitable death. Perhaps she was already convicted in any case? He glanced at the plank-bed again because it seemed to him that the little girl had let out a groan.

'Go out in the hallway and find out who was the one who asked me to see his wife. Tell him I'll examine her if he'll give me – no, lend me – some kind of a sheet. Could be a used one.' He came to think, this was always less costly than a bread ration, anyway.

The nurse was not convinced.

'How will we pull the child out from the plank bed? And besides who knows if it is not spotted typhus?'

'They will confirm that at the hospital. It does not seem to me as if this is exactly typhus ... Go already and speak to the man from upstairs.'

The nurse shrugged his shoulders and left. When he remained by himself in the room he again approached the plank-bed on which lay the woman's mortal remains. Holding the candle low, he carefully looked at the dead woman. Her face seemed familiar, though all the emaciated, wasted and black-from-dirt and hunger faces resembled each other ... But he was certain that he had seen this face somewhere else. Before he mustered the effort to open in his mind the circumstances that would help him place the features of the woman, the nurse was already back.

'He said he'll bring the sheet soon. But how will we manage?' He was worried again. 'Oh, they already climbed up on you!' The nurse shook off a brownish louse from his sleeve.

'We'll try. First we'll have to put the plank-bed in the middle of the room.'

With difficulty, they succeeded in pushing away the bed from the wall so that there would be access to it from both sides. In the meantime, the man from upstairs brought the sheet. He told the nurse and the other man to hold the sheet stretched out right near the plank-bed, and he himself, using the wooden stool, lifted the body of the child to the edge of the bed and then onto the sheet. This was performed quite efficiently, although at one moment the little girl almost rolled down onto the floor. Together with the nurse they now rapidly rolled up the sheet and put it on the stretcher. They placed the stretcher lengthwise on the *droshky*.

'You go with the child to the hospital, and I'll wait upstairs.'

Before the *droshky* departed, he remembered something else.

'I have not given you a referral for the child. You will have to justify yourself to the doctor on duty anyway. Tell him I'll give him the appropriate piece of paper tomorrow, and in general blame everything on me.'

The nurse's name was Lerer. He knew he could rely on him. He was witty, smart, but not with the ghetto smartness that many in the fenced-in by barbed-wire Jewish quarter had rapidly developed. It was smartness that resulted from the experience of having to deal with institutions that sheltered themselves behind barricades of pieces of paper, certificates and documents. The nursing school he had graduated from instilled in him the notion that everything should be in the service of the sick. In the ghetto conditions, when all the liberated bad demons hidden on the bottom of the human soul ruled people's behaviour, such a nurse was a treasure.

He went in again to the hallway and with the light of the candle checked thoroughly the sleeves of his coat, jacket and shirt. He found two more lice, which did not look threatening. Besides, he was convinced that it had not been spotted typhus. In this room, the fight against death was a long and stubborn one –that was obvious. In the case of spotted typhus, the illness rapidly disables a person.

'So, now take me upstairs,' he said to the man who had watched him in silence. 'But better check whether the vermin have attached themselves to you.'

'I have checked as much as I could. They probably have not jumped on me. Anyhow, there is more light in my place, so we'll check everything again.'

Along winding stairs, they went up to the first floor. The man took him to premises located on the side opposite to the place downstairs occupied by the dead woman. The room where they found themselves was thoroughly blacked-out, therefore two kerosene lamps could safely burn. For the first moment, their brightness blinded him. They checked their sleeves and collars again. It appeared that they had conducted the whole operation quite safely. He now looked more favourably at the man to whom he became quite unexpectedly connected by the transfer of the dying child to the hospital. He was a short, neatly-dressed man. He was no older than his forties, although the conditions of life in the ghetto had rapidly carved the furrows of old age on human faces. The room where they found themselves was crowded beyond imagination. Some three beds or sofas. On all of them, the bedding was remarkably bright with freshness. From under the bedding on two beds, five or six pairs of frightened black eyes looked at him. The room even had running water, which already was an unusual luxury. Right near the door stood a table and near it a third bed which was occupied by a middle-aged woman, neither pretty nor ugly but obviously exhausted and, like the children, looking at him in fear.

'Are you the sick lady?' he asked mechanically opening his briefcase with the stethoscope.

She did not reply. He repeated the question.

'Have you given birth?'

'It is her, her,' the man hurried with an explanation. 'Since she returned from the hospital she is somehow strange ...'

He did not manage to finish his explanations before suddenly the woman had thrown off her eiderdown with one violent motion, turned around, lifted her shirt and spreading with both hands her thin buttocks, piercingly screamed in Yiddish:

'Now you see? I am shitting with children! I am continually shitting with children!"

This was so unexpected that for a long while he kept staring at the buttocks, the anus, at the rusty hairiness of the parts of shame of the woman who was turned with her back

37

to him. It seemed to him as if indeed the head of a child coming into the world would soon appear ...

The man rapidly ran up to the sick woman and scuffling with her, endeavoured to force her to pull down her shirt. He talked to her with so much warmth and tenderness that indeed the woman calmed down.

'You see,' he said, 'since her return from the hospital she is like that all the time.'

'Where is the baby?' he asked just to say something.

'It was stillborn.'

'How many children do you have?'

The man smiled a smile in which was combined sadness and pride.

'Four, doctor.'

'Your wife, mister ...' he looked inquiringly at the man.

'Goldsztajn.'

'Your wife, Mister Goldsztajn, suffers from a kind of psychosis. It came from this unlucky childbirth. In such a case, the prognosis is usually favourable. ('To hell,' he thought, 'why am I using such terminology? I am losing it.')

'Does it mean, she will get out of it?'

'She should get out of it. I shall give you a referral to a neurologist, he will certainly come tomorrow.'

'But now? Perhaps some injection?'

Of course, such a request was bound to come. All those who called a first-aid doctor had the unique belief in the magic power of injections. Even very pious Jews had considerably less trust in the help of heaven than in the help of the content of a glass vial; although, between God and the truth, in both cases the bases of trust were identical. Luckily, in this case the situation was not bad. In the little first-aid kit, there still were several scopolamine injections. From the old stock.

'She'll get an injection.'

Before he went away, the nurse had left the medicine chest with him. He pulled out a syringe from its holder, filled it with the liquid from the vial and, stretching the skin on the arm of the sick woman, injected her with the appropriate dose of the medicine.

Again he looked around the room. At the side, near the little iron stove, stood a chair. He sat down heavily on it and closed his eyes. For a moment he thought he would fall asleep – because in the room such a silence prevailed as if everyone around had decided to respect his fatigue. But sleep was out of the question. He kept returning constantly to the image from downstairs, to that woman whom he was certain he had at one time encountered. Suddenly the circumstances of where and when dawned on him. He painstakingly pulled out from the bottom of his memory, as though from a deep well, the particular details of that event.

Early in the spring of that year the ghetto had been struck by the news that the Nazis intended to resettle tens of thousands of German Jews there. As had most rumours that contained bad news for the ghetto, this one also proved true. The unbearably crowded ghetto had to absorb thousands of new deportees. Shortly the first transports arrived, and after them more. From Berlin, Hamburg, Cologne, Munich, and also Vienna and Prague. The deportees were lodged in various places: schools, factories and barracks were all turned into temporary camps. From there, the deportees were later supposed to be placed in some miraculously found dwellings.

At that time, he was managing a large medical infirmary. One day he received an order from the Health Department to go immediately to one of those camps that was in the district of his medical infirmary. He was to set up a first-aid station there to provide the deportees with constant medical help. The camp was located in a large and gloomy five-storey building that until the outbreak of the war, and perhaps until the formation of the ghetto, was the seat of the Order of Mariavites.[3] He went there with some curiosity. The German Jews formed a completely unique society in Europe, both with regard to the role they had played in the economic and cultural life of Germany until the Nazis came to power, and with regard to the completely unique mentality they developed over the last hundred years. This mentality had many elements, but above all, it was the conviction of their own separateness and exceptionality. His father, like the majority of Polish Jews, did not like the German Jews and told him a little about them. He learned a lot more about them during his studies in France, at the time when Hitler came to power. Many German Jews succeeded in finding refuge on French soil, a refuge they saw as temporary, thinking that the whole Hitler adventure was bound to pass soon. For a time, he was involved with a girl whose father had been a typical representative of that specific society. He ranked highly in the German social democratic movement and had even been the owner of a newspaper that derived its name and pedigree from a newspaper established in his day by Marx. So, on the basis of his own observations, and on the basis of the girl's stories that were at times simply amazing, he formed for himself an opinion of the German Jews which he thought to be objective. At that time, not many years before the German occupation of Poland, he had been in touch with them in a situation produced by the shock of Hitler's coming to power, but in spite of it within the framework of a civilization with which they both identified, the Western civilization. Now fate had decreed that the remnants of that society found themselves behind the barbed wires of the Łódź ghetto. Face to face with those from whom they had always set themselves apart, with whom they never wanted to have anything in common. Face to face with the gloomy, hopeless reality of the ghetto. Here they had to live and, as they were assured, to work.

The building of the former Order of Mariavites was filled with deportees. In the large halls as well as in the smaller rooms, hundreds of beds made of rough planks had been stacked two-beds high. The beds stood so close to each other that one could only pass between them going sideways. All the nooks, places under the beds, between the beds and on the top of them were taken up by suitcases, bags, packages, bundles, bedding, drying laundry, pots, cans of conserves, plates, clothing. A wonder there was still room for people. Since, however, they had to find room somewhere, they most willingly lay on the beds and guarded the remnants of the possessions that the authorities had let them bring along.

He immediately understood that those people had not fully realized where and in what conditions they had found themselves. The mood here resembled that of a picnic, an outing, a trip to the unknown. For the time being, the local people were not allowed in, and the deportees were not in a hurry to make contacts with the outside. But in spite of this, social life blossomed. They visited each other in the various rooms, they became acquainted with each other, joked around – really! – they even arranged receptions for guests coming from another floor or hall. The suitcases served as tables and the beds as chairs. The deportees had not yet experienced hunger. They complained somewhat of the sanitary conditions but were rather more curious than scared or horrified.

During the first inspection of the camp at Franciszkańska Street he limited himself to a superficial evaluation of the sanitary conditions and to a check to see whether or not there were any infectious diseases among the deportees. He also organized a first-aid station which was all the more easy because among the deportees was quite a sizeable group of doctors. By a miracle, he managed to find a little room that the deportees themselves undertook to bring to an appropriate condition. A doctor was always to be there on duty. And after a few days, he also sent over there a small medicine chest.

He returned to Franciszkańska Street a week later. Officially, his purpose was to survey the operation of the first- aid station, unofficially to see what changed there. He was driven by an unhealthy curiosity of which he was ashamed but which he could not resist. He experienced a similar feeling when he was little. In their home, a mouse had been caught in a trap and it was decided to drown it in a bucket of water. At that time he had to see how *that* looked. Now he had to see how *this* looked. What? This he could not yet fully make clear to himself. There were reports of a few cases of poisoning among the deportees, and even one case of acute appendicitis, but those were one could say luxury sicknesses, sicknesses of normal times.

Ostensibly, nothing had changed there. The crowding remained the same, the beds were still encumbered with things, but something had happened that after all was bound to happen. Something that would perhaps have had an historical dimension and been noted in chronicles or records; something about which in normal circumstances people would talk for years either in tragic or anecdotal terms, had in the conditions of German captivity, in the starving ghetto, acquired the form of a caricature. Something that in other circumstances would have deserved the pen of a Shakespeare now demanded the lines of a Daumier.

The deportees, camp had been transformed into a fair, a market-place, where each bed was a stall and everything was traded. When the modest provisions that the deportees had brought with them were about to end, and they understood that the ghetto food rations were not sufficient to keep them alive, the time for barter and exchange had arrived. All the more so because the transition from a relatively normal nutrition to the ghetto starvation had happened suddenly. The newcomers bought up any amount of bread, potatoes, and turnips – all that could always be obtained illegally and usually at exorbitant prices. As demand increased, the food prices began to rise so furiously that the deportees had to sell off their possessions in a hurry. There was a demand for those possessions, if not among all the ghetto residents, certainly among a large part of them. But since the deportees were in the situation that they were forced to sell in order to buy, their bargaining position was weakened ... Besides, the locals were richer, richer in the experience of life behind the barbed-wire fence, while the newcomers did not have enough imagination at once to fully realize their defeat. As a result, then, the deportees had to deal with the mercy and hostility of those who had the unusual luck of having been put behind the barbed wires earlier. This was a commercial victory of the locals over the newcomers. But this commercial victory took on at the same time the character of a triumph of one brand of Jewishness over another. And on top of it, of the one that had been the despised one over the proud and boastful one. So, it had been a peculiar triumph and a peculiar revenge.

Literature occasionally attempted to deal with the theme of the contact between those two worlds. Life in copying literature supported it at times with examples, but no philosopher, politician or historian had sufficient imagination to predict the form the clash would take when the rules would be dictated by the Nazi madness and the conditions of life in the ghetto. Such a scenario no one could predict.

What linked those two worlds? Formally – religion, but it too was differently perceived in regard to philosophy and ritual. Historically – common roots in the distant past and for many centuries the same fate. Race? This was already a pseudo-scientific argument. What divided them? Two centuries of European development. Two centuries of emancipation which had only barely touched the life of the Jews in the east of Europe, but had fundamentally transformed the life of the Jews in the west, in the first place the life of the German Jews.

The East European Jews, in their majority Orthodox-Hasidic, had cut themselves off from any external influences. They remained faithful to the mysticism and religious philosophy of the Baalshemtov.[4] A minority succumbed to the ideas of Medem[5] and Borochov,[6] which while modern still had set Jews apart from the society surrounding them. The German Jews, on the other hand, had ever so rapidly, though it proved only superficially, integrated themselves with the German nation and, consistently following the views of Moses Mendelssohn,[7] had stubbornly assimilated themselves.

All this he had learned at school and all those matters had been passionately discussed at home. When during his studies he lived in France, after Hitler had come to power and the first Jewish emigrants from Germany appeared in France, those problems became more acute and the discussions more passionate. Although the views discussed and the ferocity with which they were expressed did not appeal to him, he knew that the majority of Polish Jews considered any form of assimilation to be an apostasy. He also had the opportunity to learn that the German Jews not only viewed the adherence to the Hasidic mysticism or the setting themselves apart from the surrounding society as obscurantism and backwardness, but also showed a plainly racial dislike of every Jew of East European descent. Even in emigration, even in conditions of exile. Not even once had he gained the honour of being invited to his girlfriend's parents' home. Indeed! He knew that even his family name was anathema in her home.

And here came the clash of those two worlds. Not in the form of a discussion or exchange of ideas, but in the form of furious bargaining, in the form of an exchange of goods on the plank-beds of the camp of deportees in the Łódź ghetto. The exchange of sweaters for turnips, of shoes for onions, of pots and bed linen for bread had allowed those despised Polish Jews to pay back. For the humiliation that the Germans had inflicted on them, they took revenge on the newcomers, and by some twisted reasoning made them responsible for their own fate. They got even not only for the pride of the others, for their showing off their Zweigs, Einsteins, Reinhardts, but also for their own miserable existence, for their stagnation in the little towns shrunk on the edge of history, for the pogroms, for the ghetto benches at the universities.[8] Those who came here had not yet realized the full extent of their defeat. Those who received them did not want to realize that the defeat was mutual. Thus the exploitation of the newcomers t acquired lofty reasons and, if this was not sufficient, the newcomers were burdened with the guilt of having caused reduced food rations, even greater crowding and increased suffering.

'Would you like some tea, doctor?'

'What? Perhaps. Please,' the man's question pulled him out of the half-sleep half-reminiscence state. He was cold and was shivering. The proposal to have tea was at the least an exaggeration. Ghetto tea had been a solution of burned sugar and did not at all resemble real tea. Still, it did not matter to him. He wanted only to warm up a little.

It was spring when the Germans Jews were deported, and the newcomers were thoughtlessly getting rid of their warm clothing. The locals, having had the experience of two winters in the ghetto, were buying up that clothing. The halls and the rooms of the building on Franciszkańska Street resounded with the noisy hubbub of market bargaining. He stopped near one of the beds and listened in on the concluding stages of a transaction. Its outcome was that a beautiful blue sweater became the property of a buyer for the sum of a few dozen ghetto marks, a sum for which it was even difficult to buy a kilogram loaf of bread. The buyer spoke in Yiddish, the seller in German. They understood each other perfectly and covered up their mutual dislike perfectly. For a moment, he intended to intervene in the bargaining and inform the newcomer that one could no more survive the ghetto without a sweater than without bread … He gave up this intention. In any case, he did not at that time wait through to the end of the transaction. He decided to run away as fast as possible from this disgusting market-place. When he was about to leave the hall, he was suddenly pushed by a little boy and almost knocked over. The boy was running and loudly calling: 'Liese! Liese!'

'Be careful, child,' he said. 'This is not a place for games. Haven't your parents told you?'

'I am sorry, sir. Liese is my little sister. My mother asked me to find her.' Saying this, the boy pointed to one of the plank-beds near the door.

He looked in that direction and saw a woman of thirty, perhaps thirty-five sitting on a bed with her feet bent underneath ...

'What was the name of the family downstairs?' he asked the man who was pouring him a glass of hot liquid.

'Reiser, doctor. They came from Hamburg.'

'Have only the three lived here?'

'In the beginning there lived with them also some ... When they deported all the German Jews who did not work from the ghetto, he too was taken away.'

Yes. Almost all the deportees had been taken away. That means, all those who until then had not succumbed to hunger. The Nazis thought that the newcomers from Germany and Czechoslovakia should be the first to go. Besides, the ghetto authorities had been of the same opinion.

He went over to the woman on the bed fascinated by her unusual beauty. When he came closer, she gave him a look in which girlish naïveté and unspecified promise melted into a dull indifference. She shook off a lock of fair hair from her forehead, and having realized that the man who came over to her had a while ago been pushed by her son, said:

'I am very sorry, but it is difficult here to keep the children near oneself.'

'Nothing happened. Can I be of any help?'

'Help?' she appeared surprised. 'How could you help me?'

From the plank-bed above her, as if from a canopy, a man bent over and said:

'The woman's husband, Dr Reiser, was arrested by the Gestapo. He was sent to a camp.'

'Was your husband a doctor?'

Too late did he notice that he had used the past tense. She did not reply. However, the one above replied. Probably he too realized that the past tense was the more appropriate one:

'No. He was a lawyer.'

For a long while everyone was silent. The woman was

45

apparently not inclined to talk. When he intended to take his leave, the man on the bed above addressed him. He was a relatively young man with a pale, almost white face.

'Are there any neurologists here?'

'There are. Of course there are. Why do you ask?'

'I am ill. You must have heard about such an illness. *Sclerosis multiplex*. Multiple sclerosis.' First he gave the Latin name and later repeated it in German. 'I have difficulty walking. Even more difficulty working. They told me in Hamburg that if I have the proper medical certificate, I shall be excused from work and get a pension and a double food ration.'

'They told you that in Hamburg?' he tried not to make the question sound ironic but had not quite succeeded. 'I shall send you a neurologist.'

He cast another glance at the woman who was explaining something to the children and not paying him the least attention, and went on his way.

'Mister Goldsztajn, the one who lived downstairs, did he have difficulty walking? That means, were his legs sick?'

'Yes, yes. He hardly ever went out.'

After two or three weeks, the deportees from the west were allocated lodgings. It was however difficult to use this term in relation to the places they received. Even if the ghetto authorities had the best intentions – and in that case they certainly had not – it was impossible to allocate rooms or apartments that would permit a normal life to all those who were resettled to the ghetto. Even before the arrival of the German Jews, the housing conditions had been horrible. Besides, the people who represented the ghetto authorities thought along the same lines as the majority of the local population. For them the deportees were not only intruders from the outside. They were Jews who had been punished for having rejected their Jewishness. Everything resulted from that punishment.

Later on, the newcomers from the West began to die out *en masse* … From TB, from dysentery, from typhus and most often simply from hunger. Then, on every occasion when the Germans demanded a number of Jews for deportation, the newcomers were close at hand.

It was an open secret that in most cases the deportees were

sent to their deaths. It was also an open secret that the Germans intended the same fate for all the Jews. The ghetto people constantly deluded themselves with the hope that the Germans would not have sufficient time. They tried to convince each other that it would not be worth liquidating the ghetto, given the revenue the ghetto generated for them. They therefore also accepted, with thinly-hidden relief, the news that for the time being only the strangers, who in addition had not been working, were being removed from the ghetto. This created the hope that if there were fewer mouths to feed the ghetto would last longer. Such a calculation, actually an inhuman one, would have been justified if the relation of the Germans to the Jews incarcerated in the ghetto were based only on profit considerations, that means on the calculation that the slave labour could produce maximum gain at minimum cost. The brief experience of the first ghetto years was sufficient to conclude that the insanity of the racist ideology had overshadowed economic reasons. But perhaps they played some role: it is not impossible that not utilizing the gas chambers and crematoria ovens made their amortization difficult …

He woke up. The room was quiet. The sick woman was asleep. So were the children. He looked at his watch. The male nurse had been away for more than an hour. He reached for the medicine chest and pulled out a notebook which detailed calls to sick people. There were still nine addresses. All of them with the note: heart attack. The callers knew that only this way would they secure the fast arrival of the first-aid doctor. As a rule those heart attacks usually turned out to be weakness from hunger and exhaustion. Besides, the rapid arrival of the first-aid doctor was an illusion in any case. Since there were no telephones, the caller had to go on foot to the office of the first-aid service, and a doctor with help could arrive in the best case only after a few hours. A great improvement in the work of the first-aid service turned out to be the second *droshky*. Since the two parts of the ghetto were separated by a fence but linked by bridges, each *droshky* served one part.

At last, he heard steps on the stairs. The door opened and the nurse stepped in bringing with him the chill of the night.

'All done, doctor. For the two from downstairs death certificates will have to be filled out.'

47

He forgot about that.

'I shall fill them out soon. Have they admitted the little girl?'

'Better not to ask. At first when they saw the package they were stupefied, and later when they looked inside they went delirious.'

'Did the doctor on duty examine her?'

'From a distance. They put the child in a bath-tub and washed off the lice with streams of water. The doctor said she won't survive anyway.'

'Give me the forms. Those downstairs must have had some documents or papers.'

They were found. They were in a drawer of the table. The woman's name was Maria Louise Reiser, she was thirty-six years old. The name of the boy was Ludwig. The little girl had two names – Sara Elizabeth. This proved that she was born when the German Jews were already compelled to give their children at least one Jewish name … Mechanically he filled out the death certificate and for the little girl a referral to the hospital.

'The death certificates will have to be taken tomorrow to the Administration Department.'

'Who will do it, doctor?' the man became anxious.

'Someone must do it. Because otherwise no one will take away the dead bodies from here!' the nurse became irritated.

He understood that since his wife was emotionally sick, the man could not go to work and in general could not leave the house.

'All right, you can stay tomorrow the whole day with your wife. First-aid will let the Administration Department know. They will send a hearse. I think a psychiatrist will also come … Goodbye. Thanks for the sheet. We'll try to send it back …'

The next day after his shift he did not go home to sleep as usual but went straight to the hospital. Partly out of curiosity, partly in order to ward off a storm on the spot. He knew that what he had done was unacceptable.

In the reception office, he asked about the little Reiser girl whom the ambulance had brought to the hospital at night. They could not tell him anything specific. He went up to the first floor to the doctor on duty. As soon as the doctor on duty saw him, he handed him a copy of the report he intended to send to the Health Department without saying a word.

'The hospital is defending itself from lice infestation, and somehow we are succeeding. And you, as if this did not matter, are sending over a child with enough lice for three hospitals.'

'Have you examined the child?'

'I have examined her today.'

'Is she alive?'

'She is alive and, what is surprising is that she is going to live. She'll get over it.'

'If we had to wait until the morning for the sanitary squad, and for the sanitary squad to refer her to the hospital after delousing, what do you think, would she still be alive?'

'You know very well that this is not an argument. In the ghetto, one cannot practise philanthropy, and that at the expense of a whole hospital …'

'Send out the report if you wish. I know that had you been in my place you would have done the same.'

There were two doctors on duty. The one with whom he talked had the reputation of an extremely decent person. Not waiting for a reply, he left. When he was closing the door, he noticed from the corner of an eye that the other was reading with concern his report again.

He went to the ward. The child was still unconscious. On the white pillow, her little face stood out with its dark grayness. In the corners of her mouth and in the furrows near her nostrils were black stripes that obviously were not yet possible to wash off. The little girl had fair hair like her mother, which was visible even after it had been shaved off.

The first week he visited her almost every day. At the end of the second week, she could already walk a little, although her legs, thin like matches, bent under her. She now waited for him and snuggled up to him like a little puppy. The nurses had told her that her mother and little brother were not alive. She accepted the news with the seriousness of an adult. And it seemed that she too had become used to death in the few months of life in the ghetto. After a month in the hospital, she had almost become the happy little girl of the temporary camp on Franciszkańska Street whom her brother was trying to find. The nurses and doctors adored her. Unfortunately, she could not remain at the hospital any longer. It was necessary to transfer her to the orphanage where he could visit her considerably less often.

But half a year later, together with the other children of the orphanage, she was loaded during the great September *Sperre* on to a wagon, and from the wagon on to a truck that the Germans converted into a hermetically sealed chamber. Like almost all the ghetto children, including the Goldsztajn children, in that truck she had been gassed.

He later wondered whether those who opened that truck had paid attention to her most beautiful hair. He regretted that then, during his shift on duty, he broke the regulations. If she had died on her pallet, waiting for the sanitary squad, she would not have had to look death in the eyes. And in addition, it was said that dying from exhaust fumes takes more than ten minutes. *Zyklon* apparently worked considerably faster.

Notes

1. At the end of the eighteenth century, Poland was partitioned by its neighbours – Russia, Prussia and Austria. Galicia was part of Austrian Poland.
2. The 'autonomous' Kingdom of Poland, within the Russian empire, established after the Congress of Vienna in 1815. It had the Russian czar as its monarch.
3. The Order of Mariavites was founded in Poland by a Third Order Franciscan, Sister Maria Felicja Kozlowska. It was declared schismatic and suppressed by an encyclical letter of Pope Pius X in 1906. However the Polish government recognized it. The order did not die out but expanded to France, Germany, England, Lithuania and the Americas.
4. The founder of the Chassidic religious-mystical movement at the end of the eighteenth century.
5. A leader of the secular socialist labour party 'Bund'.
6. A leader of the secular Poale-Zion-Left (left wing of the labour–Zionist party).
7. Jewish philosopher in eighteenth century Germany who initiated the Jewish Enlightenment.
8. In the 1930s, most Polish universities restricted the numbers of Jewish students, and those who were admitted were required to attend lectures in segregated areas of the classroom. Thus, the Jewish students were ghettoized.

4 Crossing the River Styx[1]

In the ghetto, this apartment was considered luxurious. It had its own toilet and even a bathroom, although not everyone had access to it. The apartment had four rooms. Two of them were occupied by the four-member family of a man who was a sort of minister of finance in the ghetto. Before the war, he had been a decent, quite intelligent bank cashier. Entangled in the affairs of the Łódź ghetto Jews, he suddenly found himself in a position that exceeded his knowledge and abilities but not his ambitions. His family was privileged. Not only did it occupy the greater part of the apartment, but it also had the monopoly of use of the bathroom. The larger of the two remaining rooms was occupied by four people. Had they been the heroes of a nineteenth-century novel, each of them would have deserved a separate chapter. The occupants of that room were the two Rozenblatt brothers, the wife of one of them and her mother. The Rozenblatt brothers were the third-generation descendants of a completely Polonized family of textile-industry barons. The younger of the brothers, an eccentric and an ascetic, was *a priori* condemned to ruin in the ghetto conditions. The older one – brilliant and smart – held a relatively important position with the chairman.[2] The two brothers could not stand each other, which was not surprising since one was the antithesis of the other. The wife of the older Rozenblatt lived as if she had found herself behind the barbed-wire fence only temporarily and of her own will. She had nothing in common with Jewishness and in the ghetto she felt completely alienated. Her life until then had had a strange pattern. Her present husband was her fifth in a row, and if it had not been for the war, he would have probably not been the last. Her mother, the seventy-five-year-old widow of Dr A., had once been one of the most beautiful women in Łódź. It was said that her life had been a string of romantic successes. Here, in the ghetto, she hardly ever left her bed and was waited on by her daughter. From morning until evening, she studied French because she was certain that that language would be useful to her after the end of the war.

And finally, he and his wife occupied the fourth and smallest room. He was the least important of the residents of that apartment, and yet he held the office of medical officer. Someone always had urgent business with him. Most of the doorbell rings, in the morning and in the evening, were connected to his duties. The doorbell rings at those times of the day caused anxiety, which was understandable. In the second year of the ghetto's existence, all the duties of a medical officer had actually become meaningless, except for one: the filling out of death certificates. Previously the medical officer had been filling them out only if an infirmary doctor had not been taking care of the deceased or if a first-aid doctor had not been called to the dying person. The greater the number of people in the ghetto who died from hunger or exhaustion, the greater the number of such 'stray' deaths became. The Germans scrupulously made certain that no one was buried without a death certificate. The German bureaucracy had strengthened the crossing of the River Styx with detailed regulations, and the obligatory toll for crossing the river was replaced with a gray card filled out by the doctor. After all, Litzmannstadt[3] was in the Third Reich, and in the Reich everything had to be treated in the accurate German manner, even Jewish deaths. It was only somewhere in the *Generalgouvernement*[4] that one could croak anonymously from hunger, cold, or from a German truncheon or bullet, and be equally anonymously buried ...

When he began to act as a medical officer, he considered it his duty to verify each reported death. In the beginning this still was possible – later it was neither possible nor sensible. It became necessary to believe the family that the deceased had not died a violent death, had not been murdered, or was not being buried alive ... The risk appeared when there was a suspicion of a previously unreported infectious disease. Cases of spotted typhus required an obligatory quarantine together with the treatment of the dwelling with insecticides. Eventually, however, almost all the cases of suspected infectious disease were hospitalized. Given the nightmarish sanitary conditions prevailing in the ghetto, such cases were relatively few. The unusually violent epidemic of dysentery in the first year of the ghetto – nearly 25 per cent of the population had succumbed to it – was prevailed over in a relatively short time, which was an unusual feat. The fact that infectious diseases had not decimated the ghetto population almost bordered on a miracle. To some extent this was due to the ghetto health service.

For the third or fourth time, the sharp sound of the bell penetrated his brain. He covered his head with the blanket as if this could help him to return to the sleep interrupted by someone's early morning visit. He still felt a fatigue in his bones, and primarily under his eyelids, after the night shift at the first-aid service ... His wife went to the hallway and after a while returned.

'It's for you. The little Gutman girl again.'

'With a death certificate?'

His wife nodded her head affirmatively.

'Ask her to wait. I've just got to get dressed ...'

As two other medical officers did, he filled out the death certificates on the spot. At least this way, the people who took care of the last ghetto affairs of the deceased would be spared additional trouble. In the beginning the names he entered in those cards had not meant anything. Typical Jewish names ending in berg, sohn, blatt, blum, names that he had not associated with any person he knew. However, after a certain time, names of people he knew began to appear – colleagues or friends from the previous, normal life. By an unusual coincidence, he signed the death certificates of three of his friends with whom he had started school and with whom he had finished the gymnasium. At that time, he still was not so indifferent to death, so intimate with it, as not to reflect for a while on the violence inflicted by this war on the human fate. He even tried to persuade himself that it did not actually make any difference if someone at the age of twenty-five, actually at the threshold of life, finished it in the forts of Verdun or behind the barbed wires of the ghetto; from gangrene or from hunger ... later he gave up this kind of philosophizing.

As the second ghetto year began, he filled out the first death certificate on which his own family name appeared. This was the beginning of a long series. One after another relatives came to visit, members of his father's numerous family – less often about some medication or a referral to the hospital, more often with a form to be filled out and signed. In the third month of the occupation, his parents had fled to Warsaw. At that time he had already worked at the first-aid service and decided to remain in Łódź. His father's brothers and sisters found themselves in the ghetto with their families. Very large families.

To tell the truth, he never felt particularly close to his father's family. Actually, he had no occasion to reflect on family bonds. They were one of those matters that he had relegated to somewhere in the distant background as matters of little importance. He had compartmentalized his life in an orderly fashion and deluded himself that the correct, that is the scientific, outlook would automatically divide matters into grand and small, faraway and near. And the grand and important matters were those on the front pages of the newspapers, not in the family chronicles. He had no doubts about the correctness of such compartmentalization. He was convinced that he was only obliged to digest the political or ideological problems of the contemporary world, that the rest was only something secondary, of little importance. In short, he was convinced that in the mechanism that regulated the pulse of life, there were wheels of greater importance and wheels of less importance. The family belonged to the latter. This attitude was all the more convenient since only a few representatives of the numerous crowd of aunts, uncles and cousins of both sexes created in him cordial, well, let us say, warm feelings. What is there to say? His family, the one on his father's side, was a world completely alien to him. Only here, in the ghetto, when those people one after another began to disappear into non-existence, and he bid them farewell by signing his name on the bottom of the death certificate, had he vaguely become aware that an entity of which he too was a part was crumbling away, that the wheels of little importance in the mechanism of life had their meaning.

The matter was not that he had suddenly discovered the existence of consanguinity. It was something else. Besides, many of those people he hardly knew or knew very little of. He used to meet most of them on Saturday afternoons at his grandmother's on Śródmiejska Street; actually at father's youngest sister's who took care of grandmother. Even those meetings became sporadic when he went to France to study and returned to Poland only for the two or three summer months. He also used to meet them on some special occasions:

54

someone's funeral, someone's wedding or bar-mitzvah celebration, or when someone unnecessarily came into the world.

The custom of the Saturday gatherings was his earliest family memory. Against their background moved about and gesticulated single puppets in which he recognized his father's sisters, brothers, brothers-in-law, sisters-in-law and numerous cousins of both sexes. He attended those gatherings as a polite, well-brought-up, well-scrubbed boy, and somehow never advanced to the role of an equal participant in them.

It was grandmother who drew the family to Śródmiejska Street. As far as he could remember, she had always been old, wasted and … absent. Non-existent. Although it was she who had been the reason they were all meeting there, she never left the kitchen. Because, in spite of everything, this was not her world. She had left her world behind in Krośniewice. In Łódź where she had lived for a quarter of a century, she never opened the gate of the house onto the narrow pavement, the deep gutter and the cobblestones of Śródmiejska Street. She thought that the threat on the part of the enemies of Israel always lay in wait for her. Here, in the big city, the anti-Semites could do anything – direct the horse of a *droshky* at her or arrange for her to be knocked over by a wild cyclist when she was crossing the street, not to mention already those cursed automobiles. They could also drop a brick from the roof, and pour water on the pavement for her to fall and break a leg in the winter-time. In Krośniewice she had been the respected owner of a little vegetable store. In the big city she was a lost, scared old Jewish woman.

Most of the time she was silent. He could not even recall her voice, let alone any remarks or sentences. For her he himself was probably another element of the alien world in which her youngest son had found himself.

Strange was that building on Śródmiejska Street. Its two floors contained one- or two-room apartments primitively equipped. By coincidence, that building was taken over by his family. On the main floor at the right side lived in two rooms his father's youngest sister with her husband, two sons and her mother. This sister, to whom his father felt the greatest attachment, was a seamstress. She employed two apprentices. The layout of her apartment was such that when a client came to fit a dress, the husband and the sons either sat shut in the kitchen or went out to the courtyard. The aunt's husband did not work: he had lost his job shortly after he had married. Grandmother lived in the kitchen, and there stood her iron bed. In the same wing, also on the main floor but on the other side of the stairs, lived grandmother's brother and his wife, son and countless daughters. The whole family lived off a small grocery store that shortly before the war they had to close after all ... On the first floor of the same wing lived father's oldest brother Felix. He lived with his wife, a little, chatterbox of a woman, and two children – a son and a daughter. Felix had been by occupation a bookkeeper but he probably never held a steady job. It was difficult to know from what he lived, but he must have earned a living after all since he had educated his daughter as a Polish teacher and his son as a pharmacist. The daughter was always looking for work and the son, a Communist, was dismissed several times from the pharmacies that had given him a job. Uncle Felix himself was fanatically religious and even prayed at the synagogue located on Śródmiejska Street, two buildings closer to Gdańska Street.

An entire legend was connected to that synagogue. Apparently, the owner of the building, a certain Nasielski, consented to give two apartments on the main floor to the synagogue since he wanted this way to improve in the eyes of God the family reputation that had been damaged by the sins of his son. Because the son had been an actor! He appeared in numerous cabarets and, what was even worse, in films, and at that not in Jewish films but in *goyish* ones. While it was true that he had changed his name to Sielański, and was known to all Polish film-goers under this name, God could not be deceived. He knew of course that Sielański had been the degenerate descendant of a good, Orthodox Jewish family. Whether the present given to God in the form of renouncing the decent rent from two apartments on the main floor was sufficient to redeem the son's sins, we will find out only on the day of the Last Judgment.

Uncle Felix had been the first for whom he had filled out a death certificate. His tearful daughter came for it. This was still the time when one cried after a death. Felix died suddenly. Shortly after, his wife died. The daughter still managed to take care of the formalities in connection with her mother's death. A few weeks later she herself succumbed to a virulent form of tuberculosis and died as well. Neighbours picked up her death certificate ... Her brother had been carried off somewhere by the vortex of war.

On the main floor of the front wing of the house at Śródmiejska Street lived father's other sister. In one room without sanitary facilities and bathroom, she lived with her husband, two daughters and a son. This cousin was the same age as him and probably the only relative on his father's side to whom he had any affinity and with whom he had been friends. This aunt was also a seamstress and until the children grew up had supported the whole family. Her husband was also always looking for work. That was the constant element appearing in the pictures from the past: the men chasing in vain for work, looking in vain for a place in a world that had no need for them. On the first floor of the front wing, directly above father's sister's apartment, lived two of grandmother's sisters on mother's side. Two old spinsters who were tormented by their mother, his great-grandmother. They too were seamstresses. He could never understand what client would use their services. The smell of urine always filled the apartment – his great-grandmother was incontinent. Besides, she was always laughing and shouting various insults at the clients.

In sequence he filled out death certificates for his father's sisters and their husbands. Later for his grandmother's unfortunate sisters then for his father's second brother, the umbrella maker, and his wife, then for several cousins ... Still, despite everything, considering the war and the situation of he Jews, those were normal deaths. All those relatives, uncles, their wives and children died in bed, surrounded by family, if they had still been alive. Yet more often news of a different kind of death began arriving in the ghetto, a death thought up by the Germans in which there was no one with whom to share the fear of crossing the last threshold and in which each of the thousands of dying could rely only on himself ... He felt the most pity for those young girls for whom he filled out death certificates, girls he had known well, to whom life had seldom handed out joy, and who had been dying away in the ghetto without knowing a man's embrace, a man's tenderness, a man's care ...

'Apologize to her and tell her I shall be ready in a minute, explain to her that I was on night duty.'

'I told her already. She is waiting quietly, as always.'

On Saturdays at his grandmother's, actually at his aunt Rose's, his father, though the youngest of the siblings, sat in the place of honour at the table. His words were listened to with respect and it was to him that grandmother first served the plate of peppered hot chickpeas, waiting for his opinion on how this rare dish came out this time. Her youngest son was the one who had succeeded best in life, and indeed was the only one who had succeeded, not counting the one brother who at the beginning of the century had emigrated to America and had never been heard from since. Yes, father had succeeded in life. Was it because he was lucky? And perhaps because he really was talented? Indeed, luck played not a small part in father's life. He was able to take advantage of it and squeeze out from it whatever he could. He was a handsome man and liked by women, which had been more important for him than for a bookkeeper or umbrella maker. At the end of the last century, as a young teenager, he came from Krośniewice to Łódź. Here he worked at first as an errand boy, then as a junior salesman. The basis of his education in Krośniewice had been the *cheder*. In Łódź, like the hero of a positivistic novel, he studied at night in a dark room and matriculated as an external student. This by itself was an unusual feat. At that time he joined the PPS (Polish Socialist Party) and played an undetermined part in the events of 1905. Later, or perhaps still earlier, he moved to Warsaw where he intended to study law …

He was, however, primarily fascinated by the theatre and everything connected to it. He was a superb interpreter of literature. He wrote poetry and newspaper columns. He found himself in the circle of Yiddish writers grouped around Peretz, and he became friendly with Sholem Aleichem[5] with whom he travelled across the country reciting his work and, as the writer stressed in one of his letters, 'he knew Sholem Aleichem's work better than Sholem Aleichem himself.' He also became friendly with the 'mother of the Yiddish theatre' Esther Rochl Kaminska, and even acted with her daughter in 'The Live Corpse.' He would have probably dedicated his life to the theatre if a Łódź matchmaker who knew his trade had not found him a pretty lady with a big dowry, the daughter of the most popular assistant surgeon in the city. However, once he had a family, he had to think about a more stable existence – one could not count on that in the theatre, particularly in the Yiddish theatre. He had to find a more steady and secure source of income.

Father then returned to the textile wholesaler with whom he had started out in Łódź. There he became a sales manager with quite a handsome salary. When the circumstances seemed favourable, and this was already after the First World War, he recognized that he could achieve greater independence. He opened a store with textile materials. This was not, however, a decision of which he would be proud. For a time he had his name on a sign on the Piotrkowska Street, but it was clear that he would have preferred to have seen it on a theatre billboard. The textile store and the hopes associated with it fizzled out, and at the end of the 1920s he again took a job. He had high qualifications and was trustworthy, therefore he was a well-paid employee. At the same time he was writing: articles, skits. At that time, together with the Yiddish poet Broderson, he established a Yiddish theatre studio from which later emerged the famous 'Ararat' theatre. He had been a co-founder of the choral society 'Hazomir' and its eternal vice-president, since the position of president was reserved for someone of greater wealth. At the 'Hazomir' he founded a theatre group that became famous country-wide. There he staged and directed plays by Sholem Aleichem, Peretz and Mendele Mocher Sforim[6] and even *Bury the Dead* by Irving Shaw. For staging this play he had been called to the censorship office and threatened with the closure of the theatre and of the 'Hazomir' if similar attempts to spread Communism were repeated. So he staged 'The Good Hope' by Heijermans ...

Together with the depression of 1931 had come the liquidation of mighty wholesale firms, and father suddenly found himself without work. At home money had become tight and then dawned a new opportunity an opportunity skilfully taken advantage of. People in the industry persuaded my father to work out a method of producing different varieties of canvas by simultaneous weaving and finishing, to replace on the domestic market canvas imported from Czechoslovakia. His own idea, along with someone else's money, again found my father on the top. It became possible for him to send his son to France for studies, to devote all his free time to writing articles or directing plays, to participate in honourary committees and to be a member of a variety of organizations.

No, it was not surprising that father had been seated at the place of honour at aunt Rose's and everyone listened attentively to his opinions on topics ranging from grand cultural matters to small everyday problems. How else! It was his name after all one could find in the *Folksblat* or the *Tageblat* for whom he regularly wrote Friday columns. He later read them out aloud, and he was an excellent reader. The family audience was friendly, though objective. He was easily persuaded during the Saturday gatherings to imitate well-known Yiddish actors, and had no equal in that. How remarkably well he imitated the great Yiddish actor Morewski in *The Dybbuk* or the Yiddish actor Samberg in *Yoshe Kalb*. It is remarkable that although Yiddish literature and theatre had been very close to his heart, as it appeared from the letters to his son when there still was communication between the ghettos of Warsaw and Łódź, he became an actor in Warsaw in the Polish theatre of Andrzej Marek. He performed a lot and in principal roles at that, alongside such celebrities as Michal Znicz! He still appeared here and there giving recitations. Even mother, who had treated this aspect of her husband's interests with suspicion and dislike, wrote of his success. What an irony of fate! War had to come, the Germans had to undertake the realization of their crazy plans, so father could realize the dream of his life. To devote himself exclusively to the theatre and support himself by acting on the stage.

He went into the hallway. There stood Gutman's oldest daughter wrapped in a gray shawl and wearing an old man's jacket: cousin Gutman's. She reminded him of the classical illustration to 'The Little Match Girl'. She was no more than eleven or twelve years old. In her hand she held a gray form.

'Father?' he asked.

She only nodded her head.

The Gutmans did not come to the Saturday family gatherings. The house where they took place was not religious enough for them. It smelled of *goyish* apostasy. Gutman's wife was father's oldest sister. Between them there was a gap of sixteen years and several epochs. It was difficult to imagine someone more principled in regard to observing religious rituals. She wore a wig, of course. She ate only strictly kosher food and therefore even her mother's home had been too liberal for her. Father, delighting in the peppered chickpeas or some other delicacy of his mother's, did not cover his head with a hat, and this already was an unforgivable sin. Gutman, her husband, a tall thin man with a long, magnificent beard, had not dirtied his hands with work his whole life. From morning until evening he pored over wise religious texts and, engrossed in the teachings of the forefathers, he left the worry of making a living to his wife. The son followed in his father's footsteps, and the daughter-in-law was too busy giving birth to earn a living. Their source of income was a little coal yard that brought in pennies. Old Gutman's wife carried on the business, overcoming in unbelievable ways the obstacles and dangers that threatened it from everywhere. Between births, the daughter-in-law helped her. In ten years of marriage she managed to give birth to six children – five daughters and one son. If not for the war, this activity would have continued.

He knew the young Gutman better. True, he would not show up at the Śródmiejska Street gatherings either, but he occasionally used to visit the home of his youngest uncle. It was probably his mother who sent him when she had been overwhelmed with financial troubles. The young Gutman passed for a follower of the Alexandrov *tsadik*.[7] He transferred his allegiance to the Alexandrov *tsadik,* after the demise of the famous Radoszyc *tsadik* whose funeral in Łódź at that time attracted over one hundred thousand followers. Whoever had been a follower of the Alexandrov *tsadik* was at the same time an opponent of the *tsadik* of Góra Kalwarii – that much at least he gathered from listening to the Saturday conversations at Śródmiejska Street. It was difficult to establish in what ways the two dynastic courts had differed.

The elder Gutman died several years before the war. The young one, together with his whole family and the mother, found themselves in the ghetto. Of course, here too he did not work. What else could he do besides study the Talmud? To him the Germans were just a worse variety of the world of the *goys,* and this world never needed his knowledge of the views of Rashi[8] on the meaning of the Song of Songs or of the fourteen books of Maimonides's *Yad ha-Chazaka.*[9] The only one who worked in the ghetto was the oldest daughter, the one who now waited in the hallway, and for the pennies she earned the family redeemed their food rations. The elder Gutman woman

61

had died in the first ghetto year – he only learned that, however, a few months later. The resettlement of the Jews to the ghetto and the locking them up behind a barbed-wire fence, instead of bringing the father's family members together, had set them apart. The increasing anxiety, hunger and sicknesses forced everyone to busy themselves desperately with his own and his family's affairs. The busyness had not done much good. One after another uncles, aunts and cousins were departing.

'When did father die?'

'Last night.'

'Had you called first aid?'

The little one shrugged her shoulders.

'What for? Well, Uncle saw for himself.'

She called him 'Uncle' because she probably thought this form of address to be more respectful. And he had indeed seen the young Gutman. Two days earlier, in the early morning, the little one came to him. That time not with a death certificate for one of her siblings who had just died.

'Father asked Uncle to come to him as soon as he can.'

'Is Father ill?'

'He does not get up from the bed. But he asks Uncle to examine him still today.'

He was surprised. He did not think that Gutman would believe in medical help when God had tested him like Job by taking away from him one child after another.

The same day he found himself on Zawisza Street, where the Gutmans had lived. The room they occupied was no better or worse than the thousands of other ghetto dwellings. At the beginning there had been nine of them who lived in that dark cell. After the elder Gutman woman and three children had died, only five remained. But even for the five the room was too small. The children slept together on a mattress or a straw mattress on the floor near the wall. On the narrow bed, the only normal piece of furniture in the room slept the Gutmans. The other furniture had probably been used for heating during the past two winters. Now an old man, whom he could barely recognize as his cousin, lay on the bed. Gutman was covered with a torn blanket and a worn-out coat. The long, dishevelled, thick beard covered almost his entire face. On one side, near his bed, stood his wife and on the other his oldest daughter. In silence they looked now at the lying man and now at him … However, Gutman did not let them say a word. With a gesture he ordered his wife and daughter to move away from the bed, making them understand that he wanted to talk with him without witnesses. He lifted himself on his elbow, asked him with a finger to bend down, and in a gasping whisper said:

'Listen, matters are not good with me … I … cannot any more.'

'What can you not?'

'You do not understand? With the wife I cannot …'

His wife either heard his whisper or guessed what his complaint was, enough that she nodded her head with pity. He did not know what to say.

'Unbutton your shirt. I shall examine you.'

He put the stethoscope to the sick person's chest and was appalled. He swiftly removed the blanket covering the man. On the dirty sheet lay lifeless, horribly swollen legs. The skin on the legs and the scrotum was so tightened by the swelling that it was reminiscent of shiny bluish tissue paper …

'I'll give you a referral to the hospital.'

On a slip of paper, he wrote the referral and a little note to the doctor on duty in emergency with the request that the sick man be taken in right away … He gave the slip of paper to his wife who, as well as the children, had not said a word. The children. Well intimate with death, assembled near the mother, they formed a hopelessly pathetic group … Behind the door his wife asked:

'How is he?'

'You can see yourself. The first-aid ambulance should still take him away today.'

The nature of his cousin's anxiety became clear to him only on the stairs on the way back. It was not the matter of some male pride as he had, surprised, suspected in the beginning. This was anxiety caused by the inability to perform the duty prescribed by the ritual, discussed by the sages, commanded by tradition. Possibly until recently, barely breathing, dragging with difficulty, his legs swollen from hunger, he was performing this ritual. Now he was unable to perform it any more, and that was why he called a doctor … In other matters his help was not needed, but in that so important …

'Had the first-aid ambulance come?'

'They came but there was no room at the hospital. They were supposed to come again today, but they would not have helped father anyway ...'

'Had he suffered?'

'No, no ... But suddenly he could not breathe and ...'

He asked her into the room. She sat down on the edge of the chair. While filling out the death certificate he realized that he did not know the first name of his cousin, his aunt's son ... He copied it from the identity card ... Dawid Majer Gutman. Age ... Thirty-nine years! Unbelievable! He was only twelve years younger than Gutman... Cause of death? He should have written: the Germans. He wrote in the names of several trite diseases: exhaustion, weakening of the heart, swelling of the lungs ... What difference did it make?

He handed in the filled-out card to the little one. They looked at each other without words. He had not detected any sorrow in her eyes. Rather fatigue. Endless fatigue. And this was only the second year of the ghetto era.

Notes

1. In Greek mythology, the river in the Underworld over which departed souls were ferried to Hades, the place inhabited by departed souls.
2. Rumkowski, the chairman of the Jewish council.
3. On being incorporated into the Reich, Łódź had been renamed after the German General Karl Litzmann, who fell while conquering Łódź in the First World War.
4. The administrative unit established by the Germans on 26 October 1939 and comprising those parts of Poland not incorporated into the Reich.
5. Peretz and Sholem Aleichem were important Yiddish writers at the end of the nineteenth and beginning of the twentieth centuries.
6. Considered the 'grandfather' of modern Yiddish literature.
7. The head of a Hasidic dynasty.
8. Rashi – Rabbi Shlomo Itshaki – (1040–1105), a Jewish scholar in Troyes (France), wrote comments on the Bible and Talmud.
9. Rambam – Rabbi Moshe ben Maimun (1135–1204), a Jewish scholar and philosopher in Spain. Author of *Yad ha-Chazaka* (The Strong Hand) – the code of Jewish law according to the Talmud.

5 The True End of the Łódź Dintoyre[1]

The beginning of what I am about to describe to you, sir, goes back to the very distant past. We Jews, you know, have become so used to being whipped by history that we have divided our past into sections according to the defeats with which the Jewish God put His chosen people to the test. Starting with slavery in Egypt, the milestones of our history only seldom indicate periods of relative peace or even more relative well-being. Most of those milestones are adorned with a torn prayer shawl or a bloody pillowcase after a pogrom. During my child-hood, when the whole family had been gathering on Saturday afternoons at my grandmother's, the talk was about the slaughters by Petlura's Cossacks[2] or Denikin's White Guards,[3] as if they had still been current events – events reported in the newspaper. Those events, you know, were accepted by many Jews as something that makes the course of their history credi-ble. Without them it would have been unreal. The years of my youth were marked by other slaughters and pogroms. And then the Jews were crucified by a nation that they came to love while the civilized world, with its institutions and churches, played the role of Pilate ... no, no ... do not interrupt me, sir. Indeed, there is nothing to argue about. I would agree with you that I began the story ringing too powerful a bell, after all this is neither the Hagaddah nor the Book of Esther. And besides, of what importance could my view be on those matters? It is less important than the speck of dust on the lapel of your jacket ... oh, here, allow me to shake it off. I only wanted to emphasize that the story that I intend to tell you take place in the period after the Cossack pogroms and before the Nazi slaughter. Compared to what went on before and after that period, those were idyllic times. At the most the *Mały Dziennik*[4] was teaching society anti-Semitism, Goebbels came to Poland to lecture at the invitation of some groups of professors,[5] and Przytyk[6] and other little towns reminded the Jews not to become dizzy from an excess of calm. Even a tear spins in my eye …

In short, what I intend to tell you, sir, concerns a very small fragment of Jewish life between the two wars and at the beginning of the occupation. And this small fragment compared with the great events of history at that time is like the fortune of a little shopkeeper on Nowomiejska Street compared with the fortune of Rothschild. I have the impression that God himself did not have the time to notice this fragment, although in any event He shows too much interest in everything connected with the fate of His people … I see, sir, that you are becoming impatient. And rightly so. I am unnecessarily philosophizing. But please forgive me, I had to begin this story about the end of the Łódź *dintoyre* somehow.

It was a very strange city, this Łódź, which at that time was loved by no one. Perhaps by its inhabitants and even of that I am not certain. Łódź was three, what am I saying – four cities, and perhaps even more. Certainly more. There was the Łódź of the Poles, the Łódź of the Jews, the Łódź of the Germans. There was the Łódź of Bałuty, the Łódź of Chojny, the Łódź of downtown. In my memory, because after all this is to what you are referring, there remains the Łódź of the streets and quarters where the majority of the noisy, nervous, extremely busy, restless Jewish poor lived. Those Jews existed from one Saturday to the other, from the Yom Kippur of one year to the Yom Kippur of the next. On Nowomiejska and Wschodnia Streets, on Kamienna and Peiper Streets, on Południowa and Żydowska Street, indeed this kaftan-wearing artisan-trader poverty had been the calling card of that part of the city. The gloomy, gray, dirty little apartments in gloomy, gray, dirty buildings were crammed with old furniture and children, and always smelled of onions and washing. It was in those apartments, during Friday–Saturday gatherings, that the talk was about Poznański's[7] fortune, about the wisdom and influence of one *tsadik* or another, about the latest role of Molly Picon,[8] about children's ailments and about the taxes that were suffocating the Jews, about Palestine and about Trotsky. Here also the legend of the Łódź *dintoyre* and of its heroes: Fajwel Bucik,

Szaja Magnat and above all Ślepy Maks (Maks the Blind) was born and passed on from mouth to mouth

Dintoyre … You probably know, sir, where this term comes from. Literally, it means a court based on the Torah. Such courts used to be conducted by rabbis. Later this term was used to designate all arbitration courts, that means courts that allowed one to avoid the ordinary, official government courts which represented the authorities and the administrative practices of the *goys*. The experience over many centuries had taught the Jews to be wary of those courts because they represented the legal order of the societies among which the Jews lived. Nothing inspired confidence in them – neither the protracted procedures, nor the decisions or sentences that were influenced by enigmatic forces and more often than not hostility toward the Jew. The *dintoyre* was a guarantee that the verdict would be impartial, the more so since both parties had agreed on the composition of the court and committed themselves to obeying its decisions. Do you understand sir? Only later had the term come to mean the courts and sentences of the criminal world that was resolving disputes in accordance with the unwritten laws, customs or principles of the criminal milieu. Very important was the fact that according to the established prototype, the verdicts of the *dintoyre* had been sacred and could not be retracted – Please do not drag me by the tongue. I am not a specialist in these matters and cannot expand on that topic which I see interests you. But believe me, sir, the *dintoyre* had been an important factor in the creation of the specific norms of behaviour obeyed in the Jewish criminal world, and not only in the Jewish one. Due to the *dintoyre* certain new rules of the game had evolved, creating better organization, and primarily discipline in that milieu. I probably do not have to convince you how important this was … I told you, sir, that I do not intend to expand on that topic but I would still like to share with you a certain observation that would take us in a moment, with your permission, beyond the ocean, and in time to the 1920s and the 1930s.

The 1930s in the United States were the golden years of prohibition. Golden – for all kinds of bands, gangs, powerful organizations with a turnover of hundreds of millions of dollars, organizations that employed thousands of people, controlled the production, transportation and trade of alcohol, controlled hundreds of brothels, thousands of gambling houses and night clubs. It had also been golden for rackets that governed the syndicates, and above all for Tammany Hall – the Democratic Party of New York. In connection with this mighty, one could say splendid, growth of the power of the criminal world, whose names were at that time on everyone's lips, and were certainly not disappearing from the newspaper pages? You sir obviously cannot remember or know that. Those names were almost exclusively names of Italians and Jews. As far as the Italians were concerned, this seems to be understandable: they transferred the rules of the Mafia, and above all the Mafia organization, to New York, Chicago and Los Angeles. Still at the beginning of the century a certain Ignazio Saiette brought over the first Mafiosi to New York and Chicago. Later Joe Masseria, Ciro Terranova, Alberto Anastasia, Vito Genovese and above all Al Capone and Lucky Luciano climbed to the highest ranks of the criminal world's hierarchy. Yet they were not the only heroes of the golden legend of those times. If you are ever in New York, speak with old barmen and pensioners who are living off the profits from bootlegging. Speak with the journalists who remember the times of the most corrupt institution in the history of politics of the United States, and perhaps the whole history of politics – Tammany Hall. You may question them all and they will tell you that the golden legend would have been only a collection of newspaper reports if not for such figures as the genius Arnold Rothstein, Lubu Rozenkrantz, Abe Landau, Abbadabba Berman, Mendy Weiss, Jack Zelig, Gurrah Shapiro. And also Bo Weinberg and Lepke Buchalter – the chiefs of Murder Inc., which had been founded by Lucky Luciano. Both ended in the electric chair, as befitted such professionals. Why so many Jews there? You may say, sir, that the Italians and the Jews were the most numerous, and at the same time the most disinherited, ethnic groups. You may say so, but everyone will remind you that by no means a smaller group of the poor were the Irish in New York, the Poles in Chicago, and everywhere the Puerto Ricans. And besides, a man like Arnold Rothstein was the son of a rich entrepreneur, and a man like Lucky Luciano was the son of the owner of a racehorse stable. Do not look to economics for an answer to that question. The truth of the matter was that the laws and traditions of the *dintoyre* complemented the laws and customs of the Mafia. And perhaps even the other way around? Those efficient gangster organizations, which today are legendary, would not have arisen if it were not for the unwritten laws of the *dintoyre* and the Mafia. Only on that foundation had the organizational talent of Lucky Luciano, the financial wizardry of Arnold Rothstein and Al Capone, and the drive of Lepke Buchalter been able to develop. In those organizations, Sicily and the cities of Eastern Europe joined hands. A man like Arnold Rothstein used to boast that he had never appealed to the police for help, although this could have been useful to him in his various businesses. And when he was fatally shot in some hotel, he had not divulged to the police the name of the shooter and had taken it with him to his grave. Isn't it magnificent? Do you think sir that I am going a little too far in my enthusiasm? Possibly so. But do not think that some national pride speaks out of me. This is just admiration and, at the same time, also a certain grudge against God who as usual remembers His chosen people not when it is necessary. The Italian Mafiosi, after years of ups and downs, lived to see glory, such as, for instance Lucky Luciano who settled in his native Sicily, or Vito Genovese and Alberto Anastasia who, after having accumulated respectable millions, were received with open arms by the exclusive society of the New York rich. But men like Buchalter, Weiss or Weinberg finished in the electric chair, and Arnold Rothstein, Abbadabba Berman or 'Dutch' Schultz (the only Jew not from Eastern Europe) became the victims of personal vendettas.

Well, now I can continue in peace the story interrupted by the excursion across the ocean. You will excuse, sir, an old man. When he starts talking … In any case, to whom and when will I have another opportunity to talk about those matters? At least you listen to me patiently. So please remember, sir, that what had become legendary was born not only in the villages of Sicily but also in the dirty little Jewish towns. And in the Jewish beerhouses of Warsaw and Łódź, in the seaport saloons of Odessa, in the cellars of Nalewki Street, in the slums of Bałuty, and in the police stations and jails – everywhere where the unwritten laws of the *dintoyre* ruled. The laws of the *dintoyre* grew out of the ghetto conditions and the illusions created by the stormy rebellion against the laws of the state of the *goys*. That common genealogy links Lepke Buchalter from New York with Maks the Blind from Łódź and Benya Krik, the king of the Odessa Moldavanka.

Of course you are right, sir, Łódź is not New York and not even Odessa, and Maks the Blind … But I must say that if one were to believe everything Maks the Blind told about himself, one could fill many a volume with his stories and supply film scriptwriters with topics for many, many years. But unfortunately, and let it remain between ourselves, Maks the Blind was a mythomaniac, though it was mainly due to him that the Łódź *dintoyre* had a specific colouring … Rumour had it that in the triumvirate that ruled the Łódź *dintoyre*, Fajwel Bucik was the smartest, and Szaja Magnat, actually Szaja Zylberszac, was without doubt the richest. Szaja owed his nickname to the fact that he really had been the owner of a building in Bałuty, and such a property in such a location counted for very much.

War came and even the *dintoyre* collapsed like a house of cards. Fajwel Bucik disappeared somewhere without a trace in the vortex of war. He probably died namelessly as did many of his brothers. Szaja Magnat, about whom there will be more to say in this story, wound up in the Łódź ghetto, and Maks the Blind walked out from Łódź on 6 September 1939 and stopped only when he got to Kazakhstan. He survived the war, returned to his native city and, having realistically assessed the new power relationships, came to the conclusion that the days of the *dintoyre* were over. He became an honest merchant. After a few years, he died a respectable Jew and at his grave *El mole rachamimi*[9] was sung. How his soul was received in the next world, I do not know. Perhaps one day I shall find out but I am not at all in a great hurry for that. You may think that the end of the *dintoyre* came on 1 September, 1939, the day the war broke out. Well, no. If that were the case, I would not bother you with the whole story.

But let us return to the times of the distant past when the Jews of Łódź, not prescient of the experiences awaiting them, were chasing after a piece of bread and after their dreams and longings, which they had harnessed to the daily treadmill of worries. As I already told you, sir, on the Jewish street, the names of Fajwel Bucik, Szaja Magnat or Maks the Blind were being mentioned with reverence. Above all that of Maks the Blind. Not only because he succeeded in rising above mediocrity and grayness, with his name appearing in the press, (though not together with the names of Uszer Kohn of Widzew Textile Manufacturing or of the boxer Szapsi Rotholc who gave it to the Germans), but above all because for many Jews distressed with worry he became a legendary Janosik or Robin Hood figure. Although I can swear to you, sir, that in the Jewish street it would have been difficult to find many who knew who Janosik and Robin Hood were. In addition to this, you must take into account that we do not really know whether both those legendary heroes ever existed, while Maks the Blind was a man of flesh and blood who, in the sad times of the Łódź reality between the wars, in his way regulated the way the poor and weak of this world were devoured by the rich and ruthless sharks.

The matters that the *dintoyre* was solving seldom left the circle of the interested parties. As you yourself understand, nothing was put on record, and those affected by the decisions of the *dintoyre* heard the decisions directly, albeit in a variety of ways: orally or, though only rarely, by a bullet. There is no one left who could give you precise information on that. The earth has swallowed the dust of those who issued the sentences or decisions as well as those who were affected by them. Memoirs, diaries, you say, sir? I do not believe that Maks the Blind, as the respectable Maks Borensztajn, wrote any memoirs. I do not believe it because Maks never liked to write, and the malicious even claim that he never knew how. And even if he had left something behind, who knows what would be true and what would be fictitious in his reports? On the other hand, I can explain to you, sir, what part of Maks the Blind's activities earned him fame as a defender of the wronged. This was a part of his activities that was absolutely legal, or rather, it took place in the narrow area that separates legality from activities not entirely in accordance with the law … If you would ask me

71

what induced Maks to engage in that kind of activity – whether it was the desire to make easy money while respecting the law, or should I say, skirting it in a small way, or it was the admirable desire to help his fellow man – I could not answer you. In any event, why dwell on it? When we admire a beautiful church built at the expense of some rich philanthropist, we do not stop to think which part of our admiration we owe to the benefactor's calculation that with this church he would bribe God, and which part we owe to his disinterested desire to build a monument to the glory of the Almighty. Let us leave such considerations aside but pay attention, with your permission, to another significant fact. Because it turns out that the ethical norms of the world in which Maks the Blind ruled were equally applicable when he was deciding matters of the *dintoyre* or executing its sentences, and when he was defending the little people from the bigwigs.

Officially and legally Maks the Blind operated an office for writing applications. It was located at 9 Sieńkiewicza Street. In the pre-war telephone book you can find, sir, the above address as well as the corresponding telephone number. I shall try to explain to you what functions such an office performed because to you, it seems, the details of the past are interesting only when they emerge from the story in the rich palette of colours, like a decal picture when the paper is rubbed with a finger.

Applications were the only way for the little people to reach the distant authorities. They were the bridge between the governed society and the governing administration, a bridge, of course, on which the traffic went only in one direction. An application could contain a request for work, for a reduction of taxes or for dividing them into installments, as well as requests for the postponement of a court case, for relief from army service, for delaying an eviction or for the acceptance to a school … What? In a certain way you are right, sir. In the main, the world had not changed. But you see, today there are considerably fewer people unable to write themselves such an application, and there are none for whom the Polish language would be an obstacle they could not overcome in drafting such a document. In short, the numerous offices for writing applications were at that time often the last resort for poor people in general, and for poor Jewish people in particular, because to them the authorities of that time were certainly not kind. Applications drafted by a specialist from an office like that of Maks the Blind probably gave those poor people a similar illusion of efficacy as the notes with requests wrapped in blades of grass that grew on the graves of *tsadiks* or as the notes inserted between the stones of the Wailing Wall in Jerusalem. The only difference was that the authorities had eventually to reply to the applications of the citizens, even to Jews, whereas the dead *tsadiks* ...

As I said, Maks had an application office, although the very appearance of the place indicated that the office functions were of secondary importance. It was an office, but at the same time, a residence. True, some girl typists sat there, and a lawyer was regularly on duty, but the main feature of that place – and one could say its executive arm, always on duty in the hallway – had been a group of five or six thugs, gangsters, the kind I would not wish for you to meet on a dark street even in a dream. Because Maks the Blind's application office took care of the problems and matters of clients whom other such offices would rather not help. Now, Maks the Blind had in his own way been helping the slow-moving law. He did not act against the law – God forbid! Rather in the spirit of the law. If some young man promised a decent Jewish maiden to marry her, and before that absconded with her dowry (and, God forbid, picked her cherry), where would such a maiden then look for justice? To the police? In the courts with the help of an expensive lawyer? She did not have the money for that, not to mention that the young lover would have managed to disappear 100 times over in the time it would take, and had an equal number of occasions to squander the dowry. To look for him with the help of the authorities who had other things on their mind would have had the same effect as a prayer that God return the lost virginity. On the other hand, at Sieńkiewicza Street, at Maks the Blind's office, they immediately set to work. For a small fee, the executive team on duty in the hallway would soon find the young scoundrel. Before they talked to him, they would give him such a beating that he would lose the desire to grab the dowry and the virginity of a decent Jewish girl again. This was the deposit. Next, depending on the client's wishes, the scoundrel would be forced either to return the money with proper interest on top, or would be dragged to the *chuppa*. On this occasion the delinquent would learn that Maks the Blind was interested in the case, and the fists of the employees of the application office and Maks' reputation acted faster and more effectively than all the institutions that stood on guard of the law.

For the sake of historical accuracy, it should still be noted that of the matters with which Maks the Blind's application office concerned itself the most important ones were matters, let us say, of the life of commerce, and among them the complicated problems of transactions in promissory notes. I see this surprises you, sir. So, I shall tell you something. You may read not one but 50 books on the economic relations of that time, on commerce or credit, but you certainly would not find any information on the role promissory notes played in maintaining thousands of small middlemen on the surface of life. Regardless of who issued or endorsed it, a promissory note started its voyage through life, and believe me, sir, it was a very interesting voyage. Of course, the better known and reliable the signature of the person who issued the note, the more luxurious was its voyage. The note changed hands like the gold in the aria of the 'Gypsy Baron.' It was the paper substitute of that gold, and a lot more easily acquired than money. The first owner of the note held it until the moment he realized that he needed cash. And since cash was expensive and always needed, he usually kept it for a short time in order to surrender it, let us say, for 80 per cent of its value. This was called discounting. You would be surprised, sir, how many people could make a living discounting promissory notes.

After a certain time, since the date of its maturity became closer, the second owner surrendered that note for let us say 85 per cent. That five per cent was his clear profit. The third discounter of the note, that means its third owner, acted in a similar fashion, and so did the subsequent owners. The number of discounters and the discount rate depended of course on the reputation of the issuer as well as on the maturity date. The pure profit was constantly diminishing but it still existed as it would in any normal commercial middleman transaction, since the promissory note was simply merchandise. Only that not all merchandise was equal, the same way that Łódź woollens could not compare to Bielsko woollens, and Bielsko woollens to English woollens. Obviously … And promissory notes of the quality of English woollens, issued by the powers of the commercial world, seldom appeared here. Transactions in them were already the domain of credit institutions and banking houses.

How many small Jewish middlemen – merchants barely able to keep body and soul together, artisans trying to mend their business – made a living from discounting notes, I could not tell you, sir; and even at that time no one could have told you. At any rate, you can figure out for yourself that the earnings were minuscule. Even more so because there were also notes in circulation that were of dubious quality and risky. Often the profit on a discount transaction would be no more than two or three *złoty*. And even that profit could easily evaporate if the person issuing the note did not buy it back on time, which brought to the protest of the note. Then the profit of a few *złoty* would turn into a loss of several tens or hundreds of *złoty*. And this was happening often. There were also often cases when the issuer of the note knew ahead of time that he would not buy it back, and no one could do anything to him because he intended to declare bankruptcy in order later to settle his debt for 20 or 30 per cent. Of course, the creditor could claim his rights through the court; he could resort to the help of a sheriff or receiver or who knows whom, but this would mean, as I have already told you, you had to give yourself over to the hands of a justice that was perverse and slow and, in the case of bankruptcy, helpless. What remained? There remained Maks the Blind's application office. I already told you that the *dintoyre* was a kind of arbitration court. Maks Borensztajn's application office would summon the issuer of the protested promissory note – most frequently a crook, a swindler, or a specialist in dishonest bankruptcies – and 'suggest' to him that he voluntarily pay to the last owner of the note, that is the creditor, who most frequently was a small merchant or trader barely making ends meet, its full amount. In general, such a summons signed by Maks the Blind's application office was immediately effective. If it was not, the executive apparatus of the office, in the persons of several thugs, went to the home of the debtor and for starters turned it upside down, including the furniture and its content. There was usually no need for further persuasion. If the issuer of the protested promissory note somehow did not know who Maks the Blind was, friendly souls would quickly enlighten him and advise him to settle the matter if he valued his life.

Now you already understand, sir, why Maks the Blind's name was mentioned with gratitude in hundreds of Jewish homes, little stores, tailor or shoemaker workshops. Broken marriage commitments, defaulted loans, and above all notes, notes, notes – those were the matters in which Maks the Blind replaced the law, and acted in its spirit while not concerning himself with its letter. It was he who decided which side was right. It seems to me, although I am not imposing this opinion on you, that by his activity Maks the Blind had narrowed the eyes of the net of justice of that time through which various crooks and swindlers were too easily slipping through. Particularly those who had enough money to extricate themselves from that justice ...

Returning to Maks the Blind, I would not want you to have the impression, sir, that his activity was limited to the range of matters mentioned above. This would have been unjust and he himself, had he been alive, would have certainly protested against such an opinion. Unfortunately, the chronicles are silent about most of the matters he condescended to take care of. They were surrounded equally by legend and secrecy, and both were so indispensable for efficient action. Only occasionally were they revealed. For instance, when Maks executed a sentence of the *dintoyre* and shot an underworld boss (if my memory is correct, his name was Balberman) on the corner of Wschodnia and Kamienna Streets. The press then gave Maks publicity that was a pleasure to behold. You understand, sir ... This was a feat that elevated the rank of Łódź to that of a second New York. In a sense, the court seemed to have recognized the *dintoyre*'s sentence as legitimate since it gave Maks only three years in jail. He left it after not even two.

As I am saying, most of the cases in which Maks or anyone of the ruling triumvirate of the *dintoyre* was involved will remain forever a secret. Nevertheless, I still must mention to you, sir, two of Maks the Blind's feats, even though this might prolong my story. The hero of one was none other than Bronisław Huberman. Huberman, a Jew from Częstochowa, as you may recall, had been, in the inter-war period, one of the greatest violinists in the world. He often came to Łódź because you should know that at that time Łódź boasted an excellent symphony orchestra and also a great public that was much appreciated by the most famous virtuosi. Sometime in the 1930s, during Huberman's visit to Łódź, his violin was stolen (probably still at the railway station). Not all violins are equal. The one stolen from Huberman was no more and no less than the creation of Stradivarius. That was enough, wasn't it? The whole police force of Łódź, and not only of Łódź, was set in motion. The violin disappeared as if behind the smoky veil of the Łódź chimneys. After two weeks the authorities suggested that Huberman turn to Max the Blind to deal with this matter, and the police would provide the necessary help in making the contact. Huberman was somewhat surprised but had no other choice. The summit meeting took place at the Grand Hotel. When Maks learned what the matter was, he became extremely enraged. He took it as a personal insult that in his kingdom there was a thief who stole the violin of the best violinist in the world who in addition was a Jew. It is unknown what springs he put in motion, on whom and where he put pressure, it is enough that after 12 hours the Stradivarius returned to its rightful owner. A neat ending, isn't it? But listen further, sir, because now the best part of the story begins. Huberman of course wanted to reward Maks the Blind appropriately. Everyone would have accepted such reward but not Maks who even felt somewhat offended. This was after all a good turn rendered by one master of his trade to another, by one Jew to another ... Maks the Blind did not want a reward. He only had a small request of the great violinist. He and his family would be happy if Huberman would agree to accept an invitation to his home. Friday evening they could eat together carp cooked the Jewish way – his kitchen was famous for it. And what do you know? Huberman accepted the invitation. During supper, Maks the Blind raised a glass to the health of the pride of the Jewish people, the great violinist Huberman. The toast was accompanied by a request that the great violinist be good enough to play a piece for him and his family only. And Huberman indeed played. And on the Stradivarius. Only it is not known what he played. Perhaps it was Sarasate, or perhaps Paganini – this was not reported in the chronicles. In any event, Maks cried, the rest of the family too, and Bronisław Huberman himself, apparently, was also very moved.

This story is of course authentic, although different versions of it reached our materialistic times. But this does not change its essence. For you, sir, to have a full picture of the man Maks the Blind was, I will relate one more incident. You will delight in this story no less than Huberman delighted in the carp cooked the Jewish way during Friday's supper at the chief of the *dintoyre*. Now, sir, listen carefully.

In the 1930s, and perhaps a little before that, the devil knows, two commanders of the Łódź police had quarrelled. The name of one was Weyer, of the other, Elsesser-Niedzielski. Precisely what they had quarrelled about was difficult to say. Probably about the extremely measurable profit from bribes given to them because of the positions they nurtured. Apparently, there was no room for two suns in the firmament of the Łódź police. They accused each other of taking bribes for so long until one of them wound up on the bench of the accused, although without doubt both of them belonged there. Which of them was finally tripped I do not remember today, and in this case it is not essential. What is essential is that the main witness for the prosecution was ... Maks the Blind.

Can you imagine that? Maks the Blind as a witness before the court in a case in which one commander of the police accuses another of taking bribes! So the prosecutor asks the stereotypical question: What does the witness Borensztajn know regarding this case?

Witness Borensztajn knew a lot. Because it was he himself, not knowing what dirty task he had undertaken, who was handing over bribe money to the accused. Where did he do it? In the home of the accused. Does he have proof of it? He has no material proof but he could describe the room in the home of the accused where the transaction took place – every picture, stick of furniture and carpet ... The defence lawyer could not bear it. He stated that such proof is no proof. After all someone could have described the said room to the witness Borensztajn, the witness could have found himself there by accident on some other business, and the accused would certainly confirm that this was the case. The accused did. Maks had been waiting just for that.

Clearly, the defence lawyer's argument is reasonable. Indeed, someone could have described the room to him or he could have found himself in it by accident on some other matter. But he, Maks Borensztajn, gave an oath, and he was not used to lying before the honourable court. Yet, if the court still had some doubts, perhaps the honourable court would be willing to go to the home of the accused. And there, in the room in question, stood a table. On the reverse side of the table-top he, Maks Borensztajn, had cut out with a knife a suitable mark whenever he had been at the home of the accused with a bribe. There were as many marks on the reverse side of the table-top as the number of times Borensztajn visited the accused for that purpose. The honourable court sent specialists to examine the table-top, and they confirmed that indeed many marks had been carved there, exactly corresponding to the number of bribes that, according to his deposition Maks handed over to the accused. So, what do you say to that? All the judges of Łódź delighted in telling each other what had happened. Whether that was what really happened, or whether someone had helped Maks the Blind, no one would know today. In any event, Maks the Blind as well as the whole *dintoyre* was assured of the best relations with the police for many years. Besides – I probably do not have to explain to you, sir – without the kindly support of the police, the *dintoyre* would not have been able to function properly. Note that this only reflects positively on the police. It should be in the interest of all police forces that tolerable order should reign in the criminal world. In case of anything happening, there would be rules how to proceed. The police preferred to deal with a criminal organization that operated according to an unwritten, but still real, moral–professional code rather than with numerous dilettantes acting on their own whims. And at the same time the underworld – the consummate burglars, the famous all over

Europe safe-crackers, the quite outstanding craftsmen-forgers – were defending themselves against the invasion of irresponsible and erratic amateurs. As you see, sir, at all times similar rules are operating. When defending themselves in situations where the professional deficiencies of the amateurs had been compensated for with a knife, knuckles or a revolver, the *dintoyre* were helping the police. How many murderers the police found thanks to the *dintoyre*, no one will ever know. This is how it was, and perhaps was not, but I will tell you another story about Maks the Blind. It will give you an idea how the *dintoyre* operated.

Sometime at the beginning of the 1930s a certain respectable Jew came to Maks the Blind with a request for help. To cut it short, I will tell you only that this application office client had his mind occupied with the Yiddish theatre, literature, music and writing columns – in one word, matters that would not provide him and his family with a piece of bread and delicatessen from Dyszkin's.[10] To support his family he worked at a job for many years. He was a specialist salesman. For different wholesale firms, selling the product that Łódź produced – textiles – and for many years earned quite a good salary. Then the lean years came, which were not kind to people engaged in textiles in general, and in particular to those who were just selling them. During the depression, he lost his job. He found himself in a difficult situation and who knows how this would have ended if not for a chance ... This chance put him in touch with someone who was at that time importing canvas to Poland. Do you know, sir, what canvas is? This is a material on which our mothers, grandmothers and the mothers of those grandmothers embroidered various designs. From the embroideries of deer, hunters, and dancing girls, tablecloths, cushions and even pictures for framing were created. Canvas was a web of thread and weft arranged in squares. The squares, however, were of a special kind, alternately larger and smaller. At the time when there was no television and decent women stayed home in the evenings, every other woman was engaged in embroidering some design, and there was a great market for canvas. But all the canvas was imported from Czechoslovakia because in Poland no one had succeeded in stiffening the webbed material to prevent the squares from losing their dimensions. Do you understand sir? If someone could produce such canvas, his business would be booming ...

So, this theatre dreamer and specialist in selling cheviot and percale started experimenting on his own. After several months, with the help of some masters from the Łódź factories, he succeeded in producing canvas that would satisfy the most demanding female taste. But now, in order to start production, he needed cash. Now it is called 'capital', at that time it was called 'cash'. And cash this inventor did not have. He looked for it here, he looked there, and in the end, it turned out that in the building where he lived there was a rich Jew willing to help him. Let us say that his name was Orkin. This Orkin sensed that canvas could be a gold-mine, and since he had a head for business, not for the theatre, after three months his inventor–partner found himself on the street. Without money, without the right to produce canvas, and without a list even of prospective buyers in all of Poland. And all because his mind was at that time preoccupied with the staging of Mendele Mocher Sforim's *The Travels of Benjamin the Third* and not with drafting an agreement that would protect him from a hyena like Orkin ...

You see the situation, sir? A friend advised him to seek the protection of Maks the Blind ... I will not take up your time with details. In any event, what is most interesting is how Maks the Blind proceeded in this case.

And so ... One day, let us say a Monday, two gentlemen presented themselves at lunch-time to Orkin. They wore tight jackets padded in the shoulders, wide trousers and caps. They politely requested a short confidential chat with Orkin. Well, they had come on behalf of Mr Maks Borensztajn, the proprietor of an application office. Mr Borensztajn would be greatly obliged if Mr Orkin would within three days sign a document in which it would be stated in black and white that he would never engage in any business related to canvas. Neither he, nor his son, and so on up to the tenth generation ... Let us say ... he should deliver this document to the gentleman whom he kicked out from the partnership and who lived on the third floor.

So Orkin did, as you may guess, what everyone in his place

would have done: he kicked out the two gentlemen from his home. Before leaving the inhospitable home both gentlemen asked Orkin not to upset their chief who unfortunately (such was his nature) lost his self-control quickly.

Orkin did not even think of renouncing the booty that came his way so easily. On the fourth day, the same two gentlemen appeared again at Orkin's home. And again at lunch-time. They politely removed everymember of the household from the table and before anyone could grasp what was going on, the table-cloth and everything on it were on the floor. Then on top of the mess they overturned the table and the cabinet with all its contents ... When the police came and obtained from Orkin the details of what had happened, they advised himto meet the request of Mr Borensztajn as soon as possible. Because against Mr Borensztajn – that is Maks the Blind – he certainly would not win. And if Mr Orkin had any doubts, it would be best if he consulted his acquaintances ...

It is probable that those acquaintances explained graphi-cally to Mr Orkin why he should draft and sign what was required of him in a hurry. That very same day the proper document was in the hands of his aggrieved ex-partner on the third floor ... After a few weeks, he in turn found a rich fellow that in exchange for the joint exploitation of the production method of canvas paid him a handsome salary. This way thanks to Maks the Blind Poland was not obliged to import canvas any more, and the Łódź Yiddish theatre was enriched by a performance that became part of its history.

And that was how things were until the outbreak of the war. The Germans marched into Łódź and the whole empire of the *dintoyre* collapsed. Perhaps one or another of the *dintoyre* chiefs hoped that the *dintoyre* would be able to rely on its experience during the previous war, but very soon this turned out to be only an illusion. The Germans of those times differed from the Germans of Hitler's time as a sick man hallucinating in fever differs from a madman with whom one cannot cope without a strait-jacket. In any event, Maks the Blind escaped from Łódź early in the war and went to the east, from where he returned only after seven years. Does this mean that with the beginning of the occupation the history of the Łódź *dintoyre* ended? No, sir. True, Fajwel Bucik perished somewhere, but Szaja Zylberszac, alias Szaja Magnat, remained, and he remained in the Łódź ghetto. So, it is he who is now the hero of the continuation of this story. And this story is very enlightening. Since, despite everything, so little is known about our Łódź, yours and mine. And I have in mind the story of that part of its people whose ashes one cannot even look for. Every seemingly unimportant contribution to the story of those who perished has the value of a precious document. The wind knocking about the streets at night, streets that at one time brimmed with Jewish folklore or Hasidic optimism, cannot give to the present inhabitants of Łódź any information about the times from which we are separated by only two generations. So let the story about the greatness and fall of Szaja Magnat remind us of something of those times.

I mentioned that Szaja Magnat found himself in the Łódź ghetto. This is rather imprecise because he had always lived there. Marysińska Street,[11] where the building that he owned was located, remained almost entirely within the ghetto boundaries. And then Szaja Zylberszac was not just any inhabitant of Bałuty, he was its uncrowned prince. The nickname Magnat, with the stress on the last syllable (and you should not forget that, sir), came from the fact that just owning a building in Bałuty was a proof of wealth, though it should be understood this was not the only reason for that nickname.

Do you know, sir, what Bałuty in Łódź was before the war? It was a mixture of misery and crime. For a few pennies one could buy everything there: a spring knife, a diamond ring belonging to the czar's family, a girl, cream to remove corns, the goodwill of an official, and the conscience of a policeman. For a few pennies one could also get a knife in the back, be hit with a club over the head, or with a fist in the eye. Dickens and Balzac could have invented Bałuty, but there was no Fagin or Vautrin to bring fame to that Łódź district. No one would tell you today how the majority of the Bałuty inhabitants made a living, and no one knew it at that time either. No one looked into anyone else's pot or pocket, but it was known that the Bałuty pots were often lean and the pockets empty.

So Szaja Zylberszac was like the *dintoyre's* representative for this forbidding district. His posture resembled that of Maks the Blind. But in contrast to his friend, his eyes were sharp. Maks the Blind had lost one eye. When and how he had lost it no one knew. Maks himself frequently changed the story of how this happened. The last one stated that a czarist gendarme had knocked out that eye, but as I said Maks had been such a bluffer that many an inhabitant of Marseilles would be envious of him.

But let us return to Szaja because otherwise we will never finish this story. Tall and balding, Szaja Zylberszac was very strong, and that in Bałuty was a great asset because without physical strength one could not maintain one's authority. Just like Maks, Szaja spoke Polish poorly, but in Bałuty that had not mattered because everyone there spoke something like a local dialect. One need not delve into the mysteries of psychology to guess what Szaja felt after the ghetto had been established. He had been at home here, and then the whole of Jewish Łódź, or rather what remained of it after the escapes and deportations, was squeezed into his territory, into Bałuty. What was more, on the territory over which he felt he had been the ruler, there came into existence without his consent an entire new state – with Jewish authorities, Jewish officials and a Jewish police. His – his! – world had not mattered any more. Note, sir, that due to his connections and cunning, Szaja Magnat could have probably survived in his Bałuty several years in circumstances no worse, and perhaps even better, than the 150,000 other Jews. Only that Szaja Magnat did not have in him anything of a martyr. He could not accept being a tortured, starving, sickly and beaten Jew like the others did. It is entirely possible that his ambition and a kind of bitterness motivated his later actions. No one needed him here! Worse, he who had been a specialist in all matters to do with law-breaking, he the old conman for whom no facet of thievery had any secrets, had to look on how all around him, in this grotesque little state, thieves – *nouveaux riches* – amateurs who held their positions thanks to the benevolence of crazed old Rumkowski – were the bosses. And finally, I also think that some feeling of solidarity was born in him. He must have realized that, when confronted with an enemy like the

Germans, Jews were obliged to solidarity, and in such a situation, stealing from each other was shameful.

That was one aspect of Szaja's problems. The other was of an entirely different nature. As I already told you, the *dintoyre* had been helped by the police and the police had been helped by the *dintoyre*. The question Szaja posed to himself was not trifling: will the German authorities, on taking over all the documents from the Polish police, demand of him, on the basis of continuity, any concrete services? From what his friends told later, one could conclude that he expected at any time to be called to the Kripo or Gestapo. Szaja held ordinary informers in hearty contempt. And certainly those who worked for the German authorities. I cannot tell you much about this, but there were indications that the German police used the services of people who had previously worked for the Polish police. Several of them were in the ghetto. Those were informers about whom everyone knew, and everyone knew what they had been doing. Fingers were pointed at various Wajlands, Berkowiczes and Grynbergs whom everyone remembered from before the occupation. It is possible that at the beginning the German authorities were using them. However, one day all three of them suddenly disappeared. Every trace disappeared of two of them – Wajland and Grynberg, and the massacred body of Berkowicz was removed from the Kripo on Kościelny Square and brought to the cemetery by the ghetto ambulance … And Szaja, full of misgivings, waited. He considered himself superior to the others and he would have probably considered his cooperation with the police to be an understanding between two equal powers.

Several months passed and, luckily, no one showed any interest in Szaja Magnat. Szaja himself of course had not been working because thank God the time had not come yet, at least that was how he saw it that Szaja Magnat from Baluty should work for his bread. He was looking around. He was looking around and waiting … You will ask, sir, how do I know all this? Because at one time I was somewhat interested in the fate of Szaja Magnat, a chief of the *dintoyre*. I talked to people here and there, and the rest I figured out. Had I figured it out correctly? The further developments will prove to you, sir, that I was not mistaken.

At last Szaja became bored with his idleness. He began searching for something to do ... Obviously he was not interested in doing some work for a few ghetto pennies and a hunger ration of food. Such work Szaja would probably have considered shameful. The former boss of the *dintoyre* started to look for possibilities of earnings on a grander scale, as would befit his past and his reputation. The master of all specialties in thievery could earn in one way only. I'm sure you understand that, sir. He could probably obtain a management position without difficulty and steal to his heart's content – and he would have done it with greater skill and elegance than others. But Szaja dreamt of something considerably bigger and more lucrative. You will understand Szaja's aversion to stealing from the Jewish population and to the dirty little deals that mostly involved stealing food products and selling them.

In short, Szaja Magnat decided that if he had to steal from someone, it would be the Germans. He reckoned that this way he would distinguish himself from those low fellows who by stealing a loaf of bread, a potato or a turnip were robbing the ghetto population. Perhaps he had the vague notion that by stealing from the Germans he would be fighting against the enemy of the Jewish people, though I am not certain that his reasoning went this way. You will say, sir that in the final analysis this did not matter much. During the occupation, half of Poland lived by stealing from the Germans. Yes, this is true. But do not forget that this was considerably easier to do it outside the ghetto than inside. It was like being in prison and planning to steal from the guards. Szaja figured that by the time the Germans discovered that someone was stealing from them and found the culprit, the war would be long over. So it appears that Szaja shared the same foolish optimist as millions of other Jews. On the other hand, I would like to know what else but foolish optimism remained for them at that time?

Before Szaja set about to act, he tried to thoroughly explore the situation. So he sat in his residence on Marysińska Street and made calculations. What and how he calculated I could not tell you, sir. He was visited by a variety of people whom he questioned on a great variety of matters. Soon he knew more about the various ghetto arrangements than the ghetto authorities on the Bałuty Market. He knew everything that could be known about each ghetto dignitary – sfrom the lowest to the highest rank. He even had an idea about the political panorama of the ghetto, although this was too unimportant a factor to be of great concern to the Germans. In short, from the height of his residence on Marysińska Street he obtained an almost perfect perspective on the ghetto affairs.

At any rate, he made a decision. He recognized that the merchandise that was the most profitable and the least dangerous to steal would be leather. A great deal of leather came to the ghetto, a very great deal. It was being delivered to the shoemaker workshops, the so-called *ressorts*[12] which produced shoes, primarily for the army … You would not think, sir, that they had the ghetto inhabitants in mind, would you? Pardon me, I had no intention of offending you … The theft of leather destined for shoes for the army was therefore morally justified, but even with the greatest sympathy for Szaja Magnat it is doubtful that he was much concerned with this aspect of the matter. That the Jewish shoemakers would be ever more needed by the Germans, Szaja Magnat probably knew earlier than the ghetto authorities. The experience of generations teaches that during a war the most needed persons are generals, sergeants and shoemakers. The Germans had an abundance generals and sergeants but of shoemakers they were always short. Particularly of Jewish shoemakers!

Believe me, sir, those were artists, miracle-makers, geniuses of twine and awl. Just for the sake of the Jewish shoemakers and their *ressorts,* the Germans were ready to maintain the ghetto – that was what Szaja figured and probably this really had been the case if you add to it the Jewish tailors! Well, what he figured, he figured. In short, to everyone's surprise, after a certain time Szaja began to work at a shoemaker *ressort*, and he would not have been Szaja Magnat from Bałuty if he had not succeeded in obtaining work at the warehouse. I do not have to explain to you, sir, that in the shoemaker workshops, where the work was manual, the warehouse from which raw materials were issued and where the product ready for delivery was stored, was the vital point, one could say the heart of the enterprise. The rest was easy. While he decided to take personal charge of his scheme, he still needed help. He easily bought off the warehouse manager. Then came the turn of the chief accountant, and at last of the *ressort* director himself whom Szaja apparently held firmly under his thumb. How did he hold him? I have no idea. But as things were, it was probably possible to blackmail every *ressort* director. Having the required team, Szaja worked out a method by which the theft of the raw materials would come to light only after two or three years. By that time there should be no trace left of Hitler or the *Gettoverwaltung*.

Experience had also taught Szaja Magnat that before beginning such an undertaking one must secure the help of the police, and not in the person of some lowly officer. His choice fell on the commander of the jail at that time whose name was ... Well, in the final analysis what does it matter what his name was? In the whole story, he plays a rather marginal role. Let us say that this commander was a known figure in the ghetto. Why had the choice fallen precisely on him? As in many matters in this affair, here too we can only speculate. I think that this commander was an acquaintance from before the war and he was indebted to Szaja for something. In any event, Szaja's choice could not have been better, and although the whole story did not develop as he imagined, still it must be said that in the choice of the people he showed uncommon flair. One could wish the same for everyone ...

From the first moment, the business began to develop excellently. Everyone with an interest in it subordinated himself without a word to Szaja whose reputation from the *dintoyre* days had not after all been extinguished. The largest part of the stolen leather Szaja decided to store and hide in the ghetto area so that it could be used immediately after the war when the Germans would be no more and the store of leather could be accessed. A small portion, however, Szaja allocated to current needs. The footwear the people brought into the ghetto did not last long. It needed mending and supplementing. Szaja made the mending possible and Szaja made the supplementing possible. For this people had to pay. Even if they paid in useless *rumki*,[13] Szaja managed to convert the *rumki* into considerably more valuable things. How he did it, this I cannot tell you sir, I do not know. He could have been helped by the experience from the time of the *dintoyre*. Szaja Magnat knew who among the Jewish police had taken part in house searches and confiscation and who had acquired the most booty. Szaja exchanged the *rumki,* and with part of the valuables acquired he paid his collaborators. The rest Szaja Magnat hid away. Like the leather. Apparently at one time he declared that what he accumulated was not his and that he would return it to whom it had belonged. I have difficulty believing that, though who knows, perhaps a book about Robin Hood had somehow fallen into his hands? All this is of course speculation, and if you intend at some point to write about these matters, you should emphasize that we are forced to speculate, even more so because in contrast to Maks the Blind, Szaja Magnat was certainly tight-lipped.

As I already said, anticipating in a sense the end of the story, everything took a different turn than Szaja had expected. Today, in hindsight, we can say that indeed he had little chance of bringing his plans to fruition. Looking from the perspective of today at how the former boss of the *dintoyre* proceeded, I must say there was a lot of the incorrigible romantic in him, and he was perhaps even an idealist. His methods and way of thinking were anachronistic. The rules of the game – obsolete. In his fight against the Hitler machine, he was a *priori* condemned.

The enterprise started to crumble when, to the surprise of the ghetto population, the Gestapo arrested the jail comman-der, the pillar of Szaja's scheme. In those times one arrest more or one arrest less had not been significant but in this case it involved someone who in the eyes of the ghetto population had been a power to whom everything was permitted. Szaja Magnat, it appears, not only understood that this was the end of his wide-ranging plans, but also that in the conditions of the Nazi occupation there were certain rules that he had not taken into account when he made his game plan. And one of those rules was that this occupation could not be defined by any precise rules: this already exceeded the limits of the experience encoded in the tradition of a people that had been beaten and persecuted for generations. In any event, Szaja Magnat, as can be surmised today examining his actions at that time, decided to liquidate his prospering business as quickly a possible. And this of course did not prove easy.

Permit me now to interrupt my story for a while and introduce you to some aspects of ghetto life. You could live to be a hundred-and-twenty not knowing a thing about them, and be not less happy than those who know about them, but I would not have a clear conscience if I did not enlighten you about them, sir. To understand a more detailed account of what happened next, is necessary to know exactly what the functions of the various German institutions and authorities in the ghetto had been. And particularly to know where the authority of the Kripo ended and where the authority of the Gestapo began. Unfortunately, I cannot be your guide here. My knowledge of this is non-existent, and the subtle differences between the particular uniformed German formations are for me just the different intensities of torture and persecution they could apply. In regard to this the Gestapo as you know was supreme. The Gestapo was in charge of all the institutions that ruled over the ghetto on behalf of the Germans and extracted unbelievable profits from the ghetto. One does not have to be an economist to figure them out. It is enough to check how much it would cost to sustain a 100,000 people on the narrow border between life and death and how much value their slave labour would produce. No, no, this has no connection with the Szaja case, but you know sir, when an old man gets the floor ... Well, in short, at the same time when the above-mentioned jail commander was arrested, a new figure appeared in the ghetto. This figure was a certain Dawid Gertler. At the beginning it was not clear, to say the least, what his functions were. But from the start he appeared to be someone with limitless authority, or rather potentialities. At the same time an institution came into existence whose functions were as unclear as suspect, but whose name was plainly ominous. This institution was called the Sonderkommando, and it shared its name with the SS units whose functions included the liquidation of Jews, deportations and pacification. So Gertler became the chief of the Sonderkommando and his friend Marek Kligier his assistant.

Gertler, a short, dark man, was a boor, a gangster type from old films. On the other hand, Kligier was the Gary Cooper type. Tall, with a dark complexion, and a faultless presence, he could easily be taken for a provincial ballroom dancer. In the ghetto where the lot of the inhabitant was never certain and depended on the whims of people in the hierarchy of authority, Gertler and Kligier played the role of defenders of the oppressed. From time to time, here and there they indeed threw a pittance of help to some people, and this sufficed to create around them a kind of legend that did not cost them anything.

There was no doubt that both were connected, and that very closely, to not just anybody but the Gestapo ... What? You say that for such an accusation evidence is needed? You are right. Now listen to me carefully, sir. What I am telling you now, I know from a certain doctor. I assure you that he can be fully trusted. In any event, this doctor is still alive, to a hundred-and-twenty, and if you ask him, he will certainly confirm my words. In this whole case that doctor becomes one could say the chief witness.

There are of course those who would think it is not befitting after so many years to write that there were Jews who collaborated with the Gestapo. Why is it not befitting if it is true? And I take the liberty to ask in what sense is the good name of the over a 100,000 Łódź Jews being besmirched by the fact that there were two villains among them? (There could have been more, but what of it?).

The father of the doctor to whom I am referring found himself in Warsaw during the war. In the Warsaw ghetto, he appeared on the stage as an actor. One day the doctor, at the time still a young man, was summoned to the Sonderkommando. Such a summons always created a certain anxiety, but it turned out that Gertler's assistant, Kligier, brought this doctor a letter from his father. Just listen and note that this was in the summer of 1942 – two weeks before the liquidation of the Warsaw ghetto had begun! Indeed, the father of that doctor was taken off the stage during a performance on the first day of the liquidation campaign. So pay attention sir, just before the liquidation of the ghetto in Warsaw began, Kligier had been there! As if nothing had been in the offing! How did he get there? For what reason? Was it an excursion to visit the city? He certainly did not travel there to bring a letter from a father to his son in Łódź. It is worth noting that in response to the doctor's question about the situation in the Warsaw ghetto, Kligier replied that it looked as if the Warsaw Jews could expect difficult times. In other words, he knew that the liquidation of the Warsaw ghetto was being prepared two months before it had begun.

Two weeks later, in September, the Germans set out to do the same in the Łódź ghetto. But here they limited themselves to deporting, that is sending to their death, all those who had not worked – children, the sick and the elderly. For this purpose, they announced a *Sperre*, which means a prohibition for people to leave their homes. Can you imagine sir what atmosphere took over the ghetto? No one was certain what would happen from one day to the next. But the *Sperre* was announced during a raging epidemic of abdominal typhus. And it so happened that Kligier himself had also succumbed to typhus – it appears the germ was not afraid of the Gestapo. For a patient like Kligier one doctor had not sufficed. The most eminent ghetto physicians appeared at the sick-bed of the chief of the Sonderkommando, and they decided that such an important and esteemed person could not be taken to the hospital. So, Kligier was treated at home. And it was decided that, just in case, the patient should be under constant – that means 24 hour, medical care. Gertler demanded that the Health Department send the best person for that task. And by chance, sir, the then director of the Health Department sent to Kligier the very doctor to whom Kligier had brought the letter from his father in Warsaw two months earlier ... I shall tell you sir for the sake of accuracy that initially the doctor refused to go, although he had been tempted with an additional daily ration of bread. He refused not for any moral reasons: at that time morality weighed less than the daily bread ration. And besides, at that time the doctor was not thinking about the connection between Gertler and Kligier with the Gestapo. He refused because he wanted to stay with his young wife and her family during the *Sperre*. But here Gertler himself intervened. He came to the doctor at night and threatened him with such consequences that the doctor had no choice but to take a tooth-brush and pyjamas and to move into the home of the typhus patient Kligier ... Pardon me sir for telling you all this in such detail, but I want to convince you that I am not sharing with you some fables that have no foundation in fact.

In short, this young doctor lived with Kligier for two weeks. He was not allowed even for a second to leave the patient in whose home a team of physicians would gather every day for consultation, although the patient's state of health did not require it. Also, Gertler hardly ever left his friend. And when Kligier finally felt completely better, both of them talked for hours one on one. The talks were private but not completely for their own ears, because this young doctor did everything to eavesdrop on the content of those talks. You will say sir this was not nice. You are right. So said also the male nurse, a Sonderkommando employee assigned to take care of Kligier, who caught this doctor in the act of eaves-dropping ... Luckily, he kept this fact to himself.

What interested this young doctor was, first of all, how a Jew, even one of the chiefs of the mighty Sonderkommando, could travel so freely between Łódź and Warsaw. He was astounded by this even more because a few months earlier a certain Skosowski came from the Warsaw ghetto to the Łódź ghetto ... Perhaps you have heard, sir? This Skosowski, who was originally from Łódź, boasted to his Łódź friends that he worked for the Gestapo and benefited from all the rights of an Aryan. This Skosowski was later killed in Warsaw according to a sentence of the AK.[14] You understand, sir, that intuitively a parallel between Skosowski and Kligier suggested itself. And so imagine sir a young well-brought-up doctor with his ear at the keyhole attempting to fish out the content of the unfortu-nately very quietly conducted conversations, and at the same time watching out not to be caught by the male nurse.

What the young doctor heard, or rather overheard, was unbelievable. And I remind you sir that I heard this informa-tion directly from him, and not second- or third-hand. Only parts of the sentences, snippets of conversation had reached his ears. The names of such cities as Kiev, Charkov, Lwow, Odessa and Poltava were mentioned. From the conversation, one could conclude that Gertler had been sent to those cities either by the Gestapo or by some other German organization or institution. One of his functions was to help find concealed stocks of goods, hidden supplies and lastly private belongings. It seemed that G. and K. had been no mean specialists in those matters and had rendered great services to the Nazis. You probably noticed sir that the cities mentioned in those conversations had large Jewish communities.

The matter was therefore clear and could be called by its name. Gertler and Kligier were helping the Germans to finish off the plunder of the occupied territories, and did it in areas as far from Łódź as the Ukraine. What do you say to that sir? Some writer once said that there are matters of which philosophers have not even dreamed ... Why philosophers? I too have the right to dream and you sir have the right to dream, and I am asking you, which Jew would have dreamt of something like that?

You will ask what connection is there between that and the case of Szaja Magnat? Well, I told you sir, after the arrest of his police protector, Szaja set out to liquidate his enterprise. Such large enterprises cannot be easily liquidated. Rothschild as well as the heirs of Onassis would tell you that. This was particularly true in the ghetto. In the meantime, Gertler came to the forefront of the whole affair. Szaja Magnat was summoned several times to the Sonderkommando, Gertler paid Szaja several visits at his residence. What did they talk about? What could Gertler propose to Szaja? This nobody knows and nobody will ever know, and even more so because today, after so many years, this does not have the least shred of importance. Szaja Magnat most certainly faced perhaps for the first time in his life dilemmas that he could not resolve by relying on his past experience. It may be guessed that even in Szaja, who had seen and heard many things, a Gestapo collaborator like Gertler must have caused disgust.

And finally it happened. Szaja Magnat was summoned to the Kripo, where several SS officers interrogated him. Szaja returned home from this first interrogation but never told anyone what had happened during it. As a trustworthy person told me, Szaja had attempted suicide. But someone in his household cut him off from the rope ... Why? Several days later Szaja was called to Kościelny Square for the second time. This time he did not return home. Other inmates who had been arrested at that time by the Kripo maintained that Szaja Magnat was interrogated for ten hours at a time, without interruption. He had been beaten and tortured but they did not get out anything from him. He had not betrayed any of his partners. He had not revealed where he had hidden what he had succeeded to steal from the Germans in that short time, and what jewellery or gold he had succeeded in buying. A search of many hours was conducted in Szaja's home. All the methods of torture invented by the German mind to satisfy German sadism were tried out on him. Nothing helped … After three or four days, in the traditional manner, the first-aid ambulance was called to Kościelny Square. The doctor was handed a bag with a note attached that stated that the remains of Szaja Zylberszac were inside. The cause of death, according to the Kripo, was a heart attack … You may look at it as preordained, but the person who picked up the earthly remains of Szaja Magnat from the *Kripo* was the same doctor for whom Kligier had brought his father's letter from Warsaw and who had eavesdropped in Gertler's partner's residence on their conversations during the September *Sperre* …

That was how the existence of the Łódź *dintoyre* came to an end. Not with the outbreak of the war, not with the return of Maks the Blind, but with the death of Szaja Magnat who had been tortured to death by the Kripo.

I can supplement this story with another detail, sir. When more than ten years after the war, they began to demolish the old Bałuty in Łódź in order to build ugly apartment blocks in place of the demolished hovels, they found, during digging, a huge store of leather. Apparently leather of the highest quality and at that excellently preserved. Was this part of the treasure Szaja Magnat intended to put away for after the war? I think so. I think that when more demolition work is carried out in Bałuty, more hiding places will be found. I could not tell you whether Szaja Magnat thought at all how those treasures would be used in the future. But thank God the working classes are now the rulers, there are no rich people and exploiters, and those treasures finally came into the hands of the people, don't you agree?

You are asking me, sir, what happened to Gertler and Kligier. This is also an interesting facet of the story. So, one year before the liquidation of the Łódź ghetto, Gertler disappeared. Rumour had it he that had been arrested and sent to a camp. Arrested or not, he ended the war in a state of health we could both wish to be in. This is interesting only because no one had ever survived an arrest by the German authorities. The entire family normally would also be finished off, just in case, as the case was with that jail commander. Kligier became the chief of the Sonderkommando until the end of the ghetto, and he too finished the war in excellent health. Both friends met after the war in West Germany. There they made big money very quickly. But there were envious people who reminded themselves of the suspect contacts Gertler and Kligier had had with the German authorities and the Gestapo. They thought that Jews should decide such a matter amongst themselves. Kligier apparently hid somewhere in Australia. Gertler however appeared before a Jewish community arbitration court in the German Federal Republic. He had enough presence of mind to find himself witnesses who swore that he had been an exceedingly decent man. After a long investigation, the interrogation of witnesses and of the accused, the Jewish community arbitration court cleared Gertler of all charges. I understand that it was not easy to take the decision to condemn a Jew for collaborating with the Gestapo, but do you not think sir that if courts in all occupied countries took such decisions in regard to their own citizens, a Jewish community court could have done likewise? Dawid Gertler died esteemed and respected, although I hope that in the next world Szaja Magnat will be waiting for him behind a bend in the road ...

I see you begin to understand sir why I told this whole long story. Yes, yes, you are right. My intention was to tell that scoundrels like Gertler and Kligier wriggled themselves away from justice ... You remember sir what the *dintoyre* meant in practice. It was indeed to be an arbitration court, and if you want a court of honour ... But as you see sir one court is not equal to the other and one *dintoyre* is not like the other ... There are different kinds of justice and morality. At times, it is worth shedding a tear for the justice of the sentences pronounced by Fajwel Bucik, Szaja Magnat and Maks the Blind.

The True End of the Łódź Dintoyre

1. Yiddish 'rabbinical court'.
2. Semyon Petlura, a Cossack chief, supreme commander of the army of the short-lived independent Ukraine in 1918–20. His troops made pogroms against the Jews in the Ukraine during which great numbers were killed.
3. Anton Denikin, a White Guard general whose troops in the course of fighting against the Bolsheviks made pogroms against the Jews.
4. *Mały Dziennik* – the 'Little Daily' – a Catholic newspaper founded by Maxymilian Kolbe, in which the religious message was united with nationalism and anti-Semitism.
5. Goebbels, the Nazi minister of propaganda, visited Poland in July of 1934 and lectured at the University of Warsaw. Many dignitaries attended the lecture, which dealt among other things with the Nazi attitude toward the Jews.
6. A little town south of Warsaw where on 9 March 1936 there was a pogrom against Jews during which several Jews were killed.
7. Poznański – a Jewish textile manufacturer and philanthropist in Łódź.
8. An American Yiddish actress.
9. A Jewish prayer for the dead.
10. A delicatessen store famous in Łódź in the 1930s.
11. According to *The Chronicle of the Łódź Ghetto* (ed. Lucjan Dobroszycki, New Haven, CT: Yale University Press, 1984), he lived at 14 Młynarska Street.
12. Abbreviation of the German *Arbeitsressort*.
13. The ghetto money.
14. Armia Krajowa – the Home Army – the Polish underground army that was subordinated to the Polish government in exile in London.

6 The Second Last

'Just two more, doctor,' the policeman touched the visor of his cap lightly with two fingers in the nonchalant salute clearly reserved for someone outside the prison authorities.

'Bring them in one by one,' he said. He was completely exhausted, physically and emotionally. Instinctively he looked at his watch. Three o'clock. Three o'clock in the morning. From noon of the previous day, he had already expended a full 15 hours of hopelessly idiotic effort. The Germans had ordered that a physician examine every person designated for deportation. Some tried to find an optimistic prognosis in this fact. He knew that such optimism was not justified by anything. What could he have said to all those unfortunates who looked into his eyes begging silently for a decision that could mean life for them? The Germans had perhaps three times lately ordered the ghetto authorities to provide for deportation only people who were healthy and physically fit. As it later turned out, those groups of Jews had been sent to work somewhere outside the city, and even far from Łódź. On the other hand, the German authorities every so often declared that only those who were capable of working in the workshops would remain in the ghetto. So, when new decisions on deportations from the ghetto were constantly announced, it was not known anymore whom the German authorities had in mind: whether people capable of working outside the ghetto or people incapable of working inside the ghetto. The Germans were not eager to make their intentions clear, but it was easy to guess what had been the fate of the deportees in the second category. To have physicians assist in the deportations by assessing the state of health and fitness of those designated for them was just a deception. Besides, the physicians themselves had often not known whether by

1 One of the bridges that connected the three sections of the Łódź Ghetto

2 The Eldest of the Jews, M. C. Rumkowski, speaks to 'the people'

3   Lódź ghetto money

4   The infamous 'red house' –
the Łódź headquarters of
the Kripo, the German
criminal police

5   The deportation of the Łódź Ghetto Jews with the participation of the Jewish police in 1942

6   One of the many warnings issued by the Eldest of the Jews, M. C. Rumkowski, about the penalties to be meted out to those who avoided his orders to report for deportation

7   Deportation to Auschwitz in August 1944

8   Arnold Mostowicz (photograph: DP)

qualifying an examinee as not capable of physical work or sick, they were saving him from being sent for some hard labour outside the ghetto or were condemning him to deportation, which meant to death. Only after a transport had departed, did it become known whom the Germans had chosen and whom they had left behind, although they were by no means meticulous about that. What mattered most to them was to fill the insides of their trucks with deportees whose number had been determined in advance. What mattered was that the numbers should agree. The quality of the deportees was of secondary importance. Besides, the ghetto population was easily submitting to this method. It defended itself from the truth about the fate of the great majority of the deportees with the help of rumours and gossip about the existence somewhere in the Reich near Cracow, or somewhere in Russia, of labour camps to which all the deportees were taken. It was not impossible that the Germans were planting those rumours themselves, not wanting to run the risk of desperate acts of self-defence on the part of the deportees. Besides, such acts were out of the question. Between the executioners and their victims existed a strange unwritten agreement. Calm in the ghetto, which had been bringing tremendous profits to the Germans without special fear, was the pretext for maintaining one of the last aggregations of Jews in Poland for the ruling German ghetto authorities. And only that mattered to the Jews. Calm gave them the chance to endure. It gave them the chance to count on a miracle ...

Luckily, the organization to which he belonged had its own sources of precise information. It knew the destination of each deportation, and therefore of this particular one too. And that was why he found himself here. In other words, someone had somewhere arranged that someone somewhere assign precisely him and that other doctor for this disgusting work. They were to save from deportation some persons from among those whom the ghetto authorities had designated to be deported by qualifying them as capable of working inside the ghetto. But the others ... He did not want to admit even in his mind exactly what this meant for them. Though he could at least justify himself to himself by the fact that regardless of whether he was there or not, in any event 800 people were destined for death in the trucks …

He had not heard the door open, when the policeman brought someone into the prison cell that had been converted into a doctor's office.

'Good morning,' said the man who stood at the door in German.

'Good morning. Please come closer. Your family name?'

'Cohen.'

'Your first name?'

'Albert.'

Mechanically he filled in the columns of the duplicated questionnaire.

'Age?'

'Forty-eight.'

'From which transport are you, sir?'

He used the terminology applied to the people who had been deported to the ghetto from the West.

'From the Prague one.'

'Undress, sir.'

When the man had removed the worn-out jacket of good woollen cloth, the shirt and trousers, he put the stethoscope to his chest. He did not even have to look at the examined man to imagine the wasted, emaciated body, a spot-covered skin, wilted muscles, a collapsed chest and probably legs swollen from hunger.

'Excuse me, doctor …' The man's voice sounded soft and had a pleasant, sonorous ring to it.

'It is starting,' he thought. He put away the stethoscope in order nevertheless to have a closer look at the man who stood in front of him. He was clean-shaven and wore glasses. From behind the lenses big, black, thoughtful eyes stared at him which absolutely, but absolutely, did not befit his completely shaved head.

'I am listening to you.'

'Can you give me an honest answer?'

'What does that mean?' he asked impatiently.

'That means, do you have it in you to tell me the truth?'

This was provoking. He intended to reply sharply but controlled himself.

'I shall try.'

For a while, silence reigned in the cell. They looked at each other without saying a word. Those big, black, disquieting eyes. 'Doctor Mabuse' – he recalled for no reason a film from years ago. No, 'The Student from Prague' – with Conrad Veidt. From Prague …

'Are we being sent to work or to death?'

He shuddered. For a few moments he was silent, looking for the right words.

'I do not know. I really do not know.'

'You do know, doctor. Indeed you do know who the Germans will deport and whom they will leave in the ghetto. After all they rely on the physicians' opinion.'

'So what about it?' he burst out arrogantly and immediately regretted it.

'You see, doctor, I know. This whole transport is destined for death. Perhaps it is strange, but I wanted to hear it from you.'

'Why is it so important to you that I …' When he began to talk he realized that by this he confirmed the supposition of the man that stood before him. This was for many reasons imprudent, and even dangerous. In such cases the Germans had not hesitated and already had many times announced that they would include in the transport anyone that infringed on the regulations established by them. He therefore added quickly:

'If the whole transport were destined for death, they would not distribute among those assigned for departure' (he stressed the word 'departure') 'the additional ration of bread and sausage.'

'That is convincing. Forty decagram of bread and five decagram of sausage.' An obvious irony was heard in the man's voice.

'Yes … If you would permit me, I would now like in turn to ask you something.'

'Please do.'

'What is your occupation?'

'My occupation? Until yesterday, I was a garbage man. Before that… Once upon a time, if that time existed at all, I held the position of assistant professor at the Prague University. I am a doctor of philosophy.'

101

'Have you published any scientific papers?'

The man looked around.

'You are asking me strange things, sir ... In these circumstances. What importance does it have? But if you need it for some reason ... I have always respected someone else's interests. I have published several works on Schopenhauer. And my doctorate was supervised by Max Nordau.'

He did not know how he should formulate what he wanted to say.

'If ... in the event ... well, if you are anxious to stay in the ghetto and possibly avoid deportation ...' He immediately felt that he had formulated it badly. That he had in general involved himself in an unnecessary conversation.

'I do not want to remain here ... I do not want to avoid deportation ...'

'I do not understand ... What are you up to? After all, it was you who started this conversation. Do you have a family in the ghetto? A wife? Children?'

'I have no family. I am alone. My mother committed suicide at the time of the deportation from Prague ...'

This conversation was upsetting him ever more. He was tired. He was angry at the man sitting opposite him and even more angry at himself. He stood up and made a few steps from one dirty wall to another, near which stood an oilcloth-covered couch, which was supposed to give the cell the character of a doctor's office... The jail was called 'Central.' Perhaps someone's megalomania had been satisfied that way ... He sat down again. It was the man who broke the silence.

'You think that my question does not make sense? And does your sitting here and sending people to death make sense?'

'You know well, sir, that I am not sending people to death!'

'If you please ... And are you not sending me to death?'

'Do I have to explain to you that it is the Germans who establish the list of persons designated for deportation?'

'Depending on the conclusions of a physician.'

'If you know that much, you probably understand that regardless of the physician's conclusions or assessment, the Germans will deport a definite number of ghetto inhabitants.

Besides, I have after all proposed to you that I would assess you as capable of physical work but you refused ...'

'One could say that I am sending myself for deportation and death. Did you not wonder, doctor, why I rejected your proposal?'

'How could I know?'

'Listen, sir. I rejected it for two reasons. You see, here, in the ghetto, I shall croak – from typhus, from hunger, from tuberculosis ... Each of those is loathsome. I have observed them all. I prefer to die from gassing. I shall be fully in control of my will to the end, to the last moment ... At the last moment I shall do what my mother did. I am prepared for that. And the loathsome death in the ghetto may make such a conscious act impossible. Are you a believer?'

'No.'

'Neither am I ... But I am curious as to what happens ... Therefore, instead of dying in some hole, rotting from filth, spitting out my decaying lungs, I shall try as long as possible to have my Jewish eyes open so that the transition into nothingness that the Germans have planned for Albert Cohen from Prague occurs in the most dignified manner. I concluded a long time ago that this is more dignified than succumbing to that death which is on duty here in the ghetto.'

The man fell silent. It was obvious that he regretted flying into passion.

'And the second reason?'

'I am surprised that you have not guessed it from the course of our conversation. After all, if you do not send me, someone else will have to take my place. The trucks will not leave empty. How many of us are required to fill them? Five hundred? A thousand? I do not want, I do not wish someone else to die for me.'

'You probably did not learn that from Schopenhauer,' he said sarcastically, and again immediately regretted it.

'No, doctor, from the Greeks ... But at the time I studied them it did not occur to me in what circumstances I should have use of their teachings.'

Silence. Quiet. The dull noise of people gathered in other parts of the building could be heard through the walls of the cell.

'Let us end this conversation,' he said quietly as if admitting defeat.

'Indeed, this depends on you … But still, one more thing … Do you know, sir, why I asked you if this transport is destined for death? I wanted from your answer, from the tone of your voice, or perhaps from your eyes, to see clearly whether you are doing what you are doing consciously… You know that the transport is doomed … But I beg you, only do not say, sir, that we are all doomed.' That was exactly what he intended to say. 'That is too banal … It does not befit you. You received a recommendation, and perhaps even an order. An order is an order. I wish you never in your life to be forced to execute similar orders. But even such a recommendation does not justify you. The fact that you, knowing what fate awaits the people deported, are letting some stay in the ghetto and sending others to death, this is unforgivable! …

Silence. 'I shall drop here from fatigue,' he thought, but aloud he said:

'How do you know this?'

'One knows those things … And perhaps,' he burst out laughing, 'at their death people have the ability to see better and understand better than when alive … No, no, speaking seriously, there in the waiting room sat a few of yours … A few members of your organization, whatever its name is. They were so sure of themselves that from their conversation one could guess everything. Well, they were young … Besides that, indeed very pleasant and likable …'

He coughed lightly and wanted to interrupt him.

'Calm down. I shall not denounce you. If I did do it, I would it only for the pleasure of doing so… I would not have any benefit from it … You are like God. To one person life, to the other death … According to a list.'

He jumped up.

'You are impudent! All this is not true! Besides …'

'What do you mean not true? After all you proposed it also to me …'

Silence. Sand under the eyelids. A loud conversation in German from behind the cell window. His head is heavy as if pressed to his neck by the ceiling.

'Mister Cohen … Doctor Cohen,' he corrected himself. 'Has

it not happened to you that you have acted in the name of some higher reasons which dictated that different rules of morality be applied?'

'Higher reasons for sending people to death?'

'No, my God, no! Reasons that dictate to leave people of special value in the ghetto.'

This sounded dull and false. Particularly in the face of the man's attitude.

'Is it you who evaluates it, sir?'

'No, not I. But I am relying on the judgment of people, on opinions that I have no reason to doubt.'

'I am curious to know how this is evaluated. With the help of what criteria does one determine the value of people that you have to save with your certificate, and how does their value compare with the value of those whom you send to death instead? ... I do not know if you will survive the war, the Germans, the ghetto, but I do not envy you. You seem to me to be an honest person. To the end of your life you will wonder if you did not make a mistake by saving some at the expense of others ... Because to justify yourself by the infallibility of the others who made up the list ...'

The door opened and there stood the policeman reporting dutifully, sprightly as if after a pleasant nap.

'May I lead out the examinee?'

'Please wait a while.'

The policeman, who was somewhat surprised, gave a glance at the still undressed man and left the cell shrugging his shoulders. Now he too noticed that the man was almost naked. He was naked and as if proud of his miserable nudity, ready to meet the fate that he himself had chosen.

'You know, I am certain of my reasons, otherwise I would not be sitting here. But I do not have the strength to ... Besides, you as a philosopher are better prepared for such a discussion.'

'Perhaps. However, I know with absolute certainty that the correctness of my arguments is supported by thousands of years of culture and civilization.'

Suddenly he perceived his chance.

'Do you not think that everything that is happening around us is evidence that the thousands of years of culture and

civilization were cheapened and dirtied ... That in the struggle
to survive they are as useful as a spear in modern warfare?'

'Perhaps you are right, but what do you propose instead of
the culture that has not defended Europe from savagery?'

'I think that another morality ... Different values. No,
perhaps the same values but differently defended ...'

'Let us leave it alone. Do you not see that the verbal duel in
this place in this situation is comical? May I get dressed?'

'Yes, yes, of course.'

He looked at the questionnaire in front of him. He could
either save this man in spite of his wishes, or send him to his
death in spite of himself. Before he did the second, he looked
at the man who was quickly getting dressed. The man noticed
that and something like a request for forgiveness lighted up in
his eyes.

'Goodbye, doctor.'

'One moment ... I have one more question and would be
very grateful if you would answer me ... Do you not have any
doubts as to the fate of the whole ghetto?'

The man felt a trap. From the door he returned to the table
and weighing every word said:

'I understand. If you want to hear it from me ... You want
me to tell you that I have no doubt about the end of this
spectacle ... This would mean that I am certain that the same
fate as mine and this transport of deportees waits for everyone here. Then my decision would be only a hastening of the
inevitable. No, I will not relieve you from the burden of
responsibility for what you are doing here, doctor. It is possible the Germans will not liquidate this ghetto. Perhaps they
will not have the time. Perhaps they will want to preserve it
for some reason. After all you can count only on that' – he
repeated clearly the expression 'you can count' implying that
this already did not concern him ...

He interrupted him.

'If you found yourself in the ghetto at the time when ...
when the moment of its liquidation arrives, how would you
act? Would you try to escape? Would you attack the SS men
with your bare hands?'

Silence.

'I do not know ... Most likely, neither one nor the other.

After all, I am assured of a fast death thanks to one small, easy-to-hide pill ...'

'And perhaps those whom I have saved today at the expense of others would indeed attack, with bare hands. And perhaps, if the ghetto endures, if they in some way survive ... then in the future, in future circumstances, they would be needed more?'

Silence. Prolonged silence.

'I'll tell you the truth, doctor ... You will be shocked by it, but I am completely indifferent to that. Perhaps this is the most important difference between us. You divide people according to some criteria ... You are giving them grades. As far as I am concerned, nothing would free me from the burden of knowing that someone was sent to death instead of me ... The garbage man Albert Cohen from the ghetto and the capable philosopher Albert Cohen from Prague are equally undeserving that someone should die for them ...'

It seemed to him that he could still throw something onto the scale of his reasons.

'Do you not think, sir, that our arguments are the two sides of the same spiritual inheritance?'

This sounded false. He did not raise his eyes from the questionnaire in front of him. He heard the man open the door and still say something at the threshold. It reached him like a voice from another world, from another space.

'Let us say you survive the ghetto ... That would be a miracle ... And the decisions you made today and perhaps not only today, are praised... Perhaps even one of those whom you saved at the expense of others survives ... He will worship you ... You will hear compliments ... And those who were deported to die instead of the others will not voice any reproach, any reproach, any reproach ...'

He raised his head. There was no one in the cell. 'Not good,' he thought, 'I am hallucinating.'

In the door stood the policeman. As nonchalantly as before, he raised two fingers to the visor of his cap.

'Well, the last one today, doctor ... Thank God!'

7 The Hauptsturmführer at Work

Three officers in black gloves and high boots that shone with indecent cleanliness were chatting with friendly interest to an elderly man who stood near them. The man was above average height. He stood erect, almost as if on duty. On his gray head he wore a navy-blue cap with a visor. Above the visor, the sign of a red cross cut out from material was visible. This indicated that the man was a doctor. The officers' interest was doubtlessly triggered by his appearance. He stood out from the crowd of gray figures with yellow stars, which the row of freight wagons had spat out. A few steps away stood a young man, wearing a similar doctor's cap, who was listening to the lively free-flowing conversation for a short while. The conversation was of course conducted in German, and the German tongue of the civilian with the cap with the red cross distinguished itself with unusual elegance.

'In Dorpat, you say,' said the highest-ranking officer. 'That was an excellent university.'

'Yes, 48 years ago,' stated the man with some pride.

'The lecturer in pathology was at that time I think the great Runge himself,' said the officer.

However, before the man could answer, a violent tumult reached the group. It came from behind, from the ramp where the train stood. One could distinguish in it the shouts of soldiers and the enraged barking of dogs. Actually the tumult had been going on all the time. It was coming in waves – at times it rose, at others it subsided, depending on how fast and how efficiently the people were forming in a column. One of the officers glanced with slight impatience in the direction of the ramp, and at that moment, as if under the influence of his gaze, the noise subsided somewhat.

'In Dorpat, pathology stood on an unusually high level.

Perhaps nowhere in Germany could one hear such excellent lectures in pathology. Particularly on internal diseases ...'

'And what is your specialty?' interrupted the officer who stood to the left of the one with the highest rank.

'Skin diseases ... I specialized in skin diseases.'

'And of course in venereal diseases,' laughed the officer. 'The two after all went together, did they not?'

'But no,' interrupted the highest-ranking officer, 'a good specialist in skin diseases did not have to deal with venereal diseases at all.'

'You were certainly a good physician,' said the one officer who until now had been silent, 'so many years of experience.'

'After my studies I specialized in Berlin and in Leipzig. In Berlin at ...' The noise again interrupted the man's words. But after a while he continued. 'at the university clinic there. I have very pleasant memories from that period.'

'You speak excellent German,' praised the officer with the highest rank. (Only now did the young man with the doctor's cap notice a riding-whip in the hands of that officer.) 'You owe the Germans a lot.'

Now the tumult broke out with such force as if a conductor of some orchestra from hell had ordered all the instruments to play *forte*. To the barking of the dogs, the screams of the soldiers and the appeals of mothers to their crying children was added the locomotive's rhythmic and loud letting out of steam. It was preparing to depart, leaving the empty wagons and their former passengers on the railway ramp.

The column of people was already formed and it looked relatively neat.

'Time for us to go,' remarked the officer who stood near the highest-ranking officer. He was stepping impatiently from one foot to the other like a horse before a race.

'Yes, indeed,' said the highest-ranking officer. He turned around and went swiftly in the direction of the formed column.

With some boredom, he began an activity that had become his routine for a number of months. Skilfully holding the riding-whip between the thumb and the palm of his hand, he divided the column into two unequal parts with a slight movement of his hand in the elegant black glove. The larger part he directed to the left, the smaller one to the right.

One of the other two officers called something out loudly, indicating with a questioning look the older man with the cap with the red cross.

'Normally, normally!' shouted back the highest-ranking officer, not interupting his mechanical and, one must admit, not very attentively performed activity.

The third officer, the least loquacious one, politely indicated to the old man a spot in the column that was already marching to the left in a long black ribbon. The man bowed lightly and took his place near a woman with two children. Slowly he moved in the direction of his destination, in the direction of the showers where the faucets, like the previous smiles of the officers, were only snares.

Following the permissive gesture of the officer, the young man with the same doctor's cap, assured of his barely thirty years, ran to join the column moving to the right.

It was August 1944, and this was one of the last selections that Josef Mengele had carried out in Auschwitz.

8 There Once was a King …

He closed the book. He was thinking. While leafing through it – he did not have to read it since he knew its content only too well – he reflected on what he would say if someone had proposed to him to discussing that book.

What he would say and what he would want to say.

The title of the book was *The Chronicle of the Łódź Ghetto.*[1] It had been published in English in the United States. More than ten years earlier, the first two volumes of the *Chronicle* appeared in Poland. They did not arouse any great interest at that time. It was as if the topic was shameful. And besides, strictly speaking, who would care about the daily record of events and information relating to the ghetto and the 170,000 Łódź Jews? Even their memory was drowned in oblivion. Another almost 20 years had to pass and several considerable shocks had to ensue for that topic to become timely. Or perhaps it had just become fashionable?

The historian who had begun preparing the book was forced to leave Poland in the 1960s. Now he published the *Chronicle* in its entirety in the United States where it had apparently stirred up people's minds and had become a real bestseller. Was it the case that the report about the descent into hell, and life in hell, written down in English, appealed more to the imagination than the same report in Polish? Or perhaps it was the case that with the passage of time the interest in the affairs of a condemned people had increased as the result of a vague feeling of guilt?

The history of four years of life in the ghetto. The record of affairs and events that our magnificent twentieth century had swallowed without choking. The *Chronicle* of the times … of contempt – as those times had once been described by a great French writer; of furnaces – as they had been described by a Polish colleague of his. It is rather a chronicle of the times of indifference. The spectacle of the murder of an entire people was displayed at that time before the eyes of Europe and of America, which is now so passionately interested in the *Chronicle*. That spectacle had not aroused anything but the banal emotions provided by similar spectacles in previous centuries ... After all, the Christian morality that at one time had sanctioned such spectacles had not changed that much. Perhaps the complications of the era of colonialism had made that morality more sensitive. And of course this was after all the twentieth century – the slave trade, the conquests of the conquistadors and the Inquisition belonged, thank God, to the past. Nonetheless, the victorious Caesar's finger pointing downward still indicated someone who had never been loved, who could not find himself in the well-bred European society, and whom it was difficult to get rid of. During that spectacle, the public that had been sitting in the luxurious loges above the European stage could also be fascinated by the technique of the staging and by the masterful performance. There was no booing. Even discreet applause bestowed on the direction could be heard here and there ...

The Chronicle of the Łódź Ghetto – a chronicle of extermination. If he had to write some remarks on the topic of the book, he would have put two of its heroes to the forefront. One of them would have been Mordecai Chaim Rumkowski, on whom the Germans bestowed the title of *Älteste der Juden*, which had been clumsily translated into Polish as the Chief of the Elders of the Jews. The other one would have been he himself, the reader of that *Chronicle,* and at the same time one of those who had survived all the events recorded by the chroniclers. He – one of those 170,000 or 180,000 Jews who had been put behind the barbed wire of the ghetto, one of the 70,000 deported to Auschwitz, one of the few 1000s whom the gears of Hitler's camp machine did not have the time to crush. One of those about whom no one cared during the war, finally one of the last who 40 years after the war's end was still alive. And who could bear witness.

The two heroes of that book. He felt unclearly the relationship between the two. In whose name should he stand up to

112

speak: In that of a victim? Of an accuser? Of a witness? Perhaps he should stand up to speak in the name of all three at the same time?

The actual author of this chronicle is Hitlerism. Only that to Hitlerism, the bill had been presented a long time ago, although not everyone had accepted it. And Rumkowski? After all, he had for many people figured as an accused equally guilty in the list of the Łódź ghetto cases to be tried by history. Oh, he too had been presented with a bill. A bitter one. A severe one ... Most often, he had been condemned. Like a bad student, he was being compared to a model student, who in this case had been Adam Czerniaków, the Chairman of the Warsaw *Judenrat*.[2] Czerniaków committed suicide because he did not want to sign the death sentence for his people. Rumkowski had not mustered such courage, and to this day he is being reproached for it. Together with Rumkowski were accused all the *Beirats*,[3] all the *Judenrats*. And this in spite of the fact that the passage of years and the growing knowledge about the Holocaust times should have made historians aware that in situation that history had not known until that time, all the models and rules of behaviour were worth less than a single Jewish life.

Not only had Rumkowski not committed suicide, but he was giving his consent, and signing, and signing, and signing. Another consent for 10,000 to be gassed in Chełmno. And another death sentence for the elderly and the children. And also for those who, out of hunger, stole a can of preserves, and for those who took a bribe in the form of a piece of bread ... My God! He had indeed been signing. After all, there could be no doubt about this accusation. But are there not perhaps any gaps in it? And if so, how can one look for them?

The last day of August of the year before the end of the war. Between the barracks and on the *Lagerstrasse* of the former Gypsy camp at Brzezinka[4] swarmed the lucky people from the Łódź ghetto who had passed the selection. They swarmed waiting to get bread, soup, to be sent to other camps. That day the condemned swarmed rejoicing about something. Some of them – and this is unbelievable – even smiled, if a smile could cross the wires of the camp at all ... Well, among the Łódź Jews the news spread that to Auschwitz had been brought – Rumkowski. The report is apparently reliable and is being spiced up with ever more details. Here the Jewish king of the ghetto fell into the hands of those who over the years had been deported from the ghetto. After having during those years passed through the hell of camp torture, through the constant selections, through hunger, frost, and murderous work, they had in the course of the months and often even years of camp university, worked out plans of revenge. And here the charitable Jewish God, or perhaps the God of Revenge of Sholem Ash's play of that name, permitted them to realize those plans exactly as they had hoped. What fortunate person succeeds in bringing his dreams to reality? Here in Auschwitz *they* were the kings. They had to have the health of a devil and perhaps the soul of Satan in order to survive what they had survived. And finally, on the Auschwitz railway ramp, they caught up with Rumkowski. Or perhaps they succeeded in obtaining him from the SS men by entreaties – today who would know? They greeted him politely, not to say cordially. First they let him observe, through the cleverly constructed little windows of the gas chamber, how his, the Łódź ghetto king's, subjects perished, how they twisted and suffocated in the fumes of Zyklon B. And when they decided that he had satisfied his eyes with this view, they pushed him alive into the abyss of the crematorium furnace …

That was the reason for the satisfied smile on the lips of those who now filled the Auschwitz barracks that the Gypsies had vacated … The king got what was coming to him! They paid him back! For their wives and children who were now in the crematorium, over there, from where a column of black smoke rose … For the children he had sent out from the ghetto to their deaths! And in general for the shitty martyr's life that had been their lot for years. On him, on Rumkowski, their hatred had become concentrated. His death brought them the satisfaction of revenge.

Curiously, no one managed to find out in what way, and primarily why indeed he, Mordecai Chaim Rumkowski, had been appointed that 'Eldest' of the Jews – *Der Älteste der Juden*? Why indeed had this actually insignificant figure in the Łódź Jewish community been pushed to the forefront to play such a significant role in those most important and most tragic five years for the Łódź Jews? All the versions regarding this event, that is the appointment of Rumkowski, declare that dubbing him the 'eldest' had been absolutely accidental. That means that it had been the unintended result of his accidental participation in some delegation that conducted one of the first meetings with the occupation authorities on behalf of the community. The person who had been the chairman of the community council until then succeeded in escaping Łódź. The Germans therefore decided to appoint a new chairman, that is an 'Eldest.' And their choice for this function fell on Rumkowski because his appearance fitted ideally that function and suited its content exactly.

In 1939, Rumkowski was sixty-two years old. He was as gray as St Nicholas on folk pictures, but without a beard. His round wrinkled though vigorous face was surrounded by a halo of bushy white hair. Apparently, this was sufficient. A man with such an appearance fitted like a miracle the position of the Eldest of the Jews that the Germans had invented. The Germans were not blessed with an excess of imagination, but in this case, the symbolic title suited their notion of the role Rumkowski had to play in the nearest future. Regardless of the stages that were to bring about what shortly obtained the ominous codename 'the final solution.'

Rumkowski received the appointment in the middle of October 1939. Two days later he completed forming the Council of the Elders or *Beirat*. Its members were forced to accept their positions under the threat of the direst consequences. Three weeks later, on 11 November, when the whole occupied country passed through a wave of bloody terror, the members of the council were arrested. They had been incarcerated in Radogoszcz and the majority of them were shortly exterminated. Rumkowski then formed a new *Beirat*. That one was on a considerably smaller scale. If the first *Beirat* was still composed of people with whom Rumkowski would have had to reckon, at least in the beginning, the second one amounted to nothing ...

It is quite probable that Rumkowski was appointed as the 'Eldest' only on the grounds of his appearance because it is difficult to find other motives that could have justified such an appointment, as was the case even with the chairman of the Warsaw Jewish community council. After all, Czerniaków had amounted to something ... In Łódź Rumkowski had amounted to nothing or to very little. He had been the chairman of the Jewish orphanage in Helenówek and one of the councillors of the Jewish community council. That was all.

His education had been less than poor. Four, five grades in some *gimnasia* in Czarist Russia. By occupation he was ... It is curious that of those who wrote about him hardly anyone attempted to verify how he made a living. He had not been a 'Łódź merchant,' he had not been a manufacturer, as some maintained. He had simply been an insurance agent and this, if one was smart enough, allowed one to earn a piece of bread ...

He had never enjoyed much respect among the activists of the Łódź Jewish community council, and there were various rumours about his management of the orphanage. He was a primitive man but doubtlessly a shrewd one. Some experience in communal affairs was sufficient for him to rapidly put on a new skin. It fitted him perfectly and he felt excellent in it. With this, he recompensed himself for the lowly position he held in the pre-war period. If previously no one had thought him to be exceedingly ambitious, now it soon became obvious that he was exploding with ambition. When he spoke before a large audience, the awareness of his power and perhaps, perhaps responsibility, gave him wings. How he loved to speak in public ...

The Chronicle of the Ghetto reports precisely the content of the speeches of the Chairman (that was his official title). Reading those reports, he recalled the circumstances in which he had the opportunity to listen to those speeches. Every time they were an important event in the dreary ghetto life. Rumkowski thought himself a good speaker, and since he was the child of the commercial Łódź, he knew how to sell what he had to offer – news of some new decision, some demand of the ghetto's uniformed or civilian German authorities.

Since he knew the content of the various German circulars of greater or lesser secrecy, or some shreds of the Nazi plans for the near future, Rumkowski probably understood from the beginning that no good news could actually be expected for the Jews who found themselves at the favour or disfavour of the Germans. He met with the hangmen every day and he had enough intelligence to grasp that the fate which they were preparing for the ghetto was written not only in their books and circulars but above all in their psyche.

He exaggerated the importance of whatever good news there was for the ghetto, because he rightly understood that if it proved correct he would earn the gratitude of his subjects, and if not, the fault would lie with the Germans. But more often he exaggerated the bad news, news that announced new worries and new persecutions. With the only purpose being to be able to claim that it was he, and only he, who deserved the credit if the calamities proved smaller than expected. He would then travel from *ressort* to *ressort* in his *droshky* and joyously announce that the food rations would be cut by less than was threatened, or that the number of Jews designated for deportation would not be as large as anticipated … It could have appeared that he had known the art of winning the love of his subjects to perfection. Unfortunately, this was only a theoretical knowledge.

He was a believer and very religious. Before the war, the prominent social activists had treated him with disdain. It was not out of the question that, as he increasingly realized that he possessed unlimited power in the *Litzmannstadt-Getto*, he began to get vague notions of an authentic theocracy. He had certainly not been familiar with that term, but he probably remembered that at one time in their history the Jews had a régime that had resembled it … On Yom Kippur, as he stood beside other clergy, he would bless the congregation with fingers of both hands arranged in the traditional way and with a prayer shawl covering his head. Indeed! He performed marriages and usurped for himself the authority of rabbis. He probably would have gladly seen himself in the attire of a high priest so precisely described in the Old Testament. Then he would have been the master and the high priest that ruled over his somewhat unhappy and unruly people on behalf of the German executioner and of the Jewish God …

The longer he ruled over the ghetto and the longer the war lasted, the more he believed in his charisma. After all, he knew – but perhaps he did not want to acknowledge it in such detail – that the ghettos of Poland were disappearing one after

117

the other in the gas chambers and the crematoria. He knew what the fate of the largest of them was, the one in Warsaw, which in the person of the proud Czerniaków did not want to listen to his advice. The last Jewish communities were disappearing, but the ghetto in Łódź endured.

Is there any wonder then that he was ever more convinced of his infallibility? In every respect: in making his own decisions, in consenting to the demands of the Germans, in assessing people. Only *he* knew what was bad, what good, what to praise and reward and what to punish ... He was a boor. Boorishness was the moral code that guided him. He constantly changed the team of people on whom he bestowed his favour, a favour that after all was riding on the motley horse of his changeable caprices. He held most of the flatterers that surrounded him in contempt, not only because they deserved it but also because he had not trusted anyone but his brother ...

All Rumkowski's people.

The Chronicle of the Łódź Ghetto begins with January 1941. It does not cover the year 1940 and the first months of the existence of the ghetto. At that time, he had had frequent opportunities to have contacts with the Chairman's close collaborators. They were a mediocre crowd. How many of them delighted in the new power they possessed and retaliated for all the past failures in their lives! How many of them were home-grown dictators who, if it were in their power, would have prolonged the German occupation and their power! How many of them had, in the shadow of the one chosen by the Germans, suddenly become transformed like he himself from ordinary zeroes into masters over the life and death of the unfortunates incarcerated in the ghetto!

This happened in April of the first year of the ghetto era. The ghetto at that time was the terrain of numerous actions by the starving ghetto inhabitants. On the large square located at the then Lutomierska Street, behind the emergency clinic, a meeting called by the remnants of the workers' groups took place. He was on duty at that time at the emergency clinic and the details of the events he witnessed became well engraved in his memory. What had he actually witnessed? The most authentic provocation whose consequences would have been frightful ...

The premises of the emergency clinic were taken over by the commissioner of the ghetto police, a certain Hanemann, as his headquarters. He directed the operation to disperse that meeting from the premises of the emergency clinic. Every few minutes he telephoned Rumkowski with information on the situation on the square – like Ludendorff informing Hindenburg on the course of the Tannenberg battle ... Only that Hanneman's information was constantly increasingly alarmist and, what was worse, deceitful.

As the physician on duty, he had recognized that to use the premises of the emergency clinic for this kind of activity by the police was inadmissible. He told this to Hanneman, who was not much moved by his protest. When he saw that Hanneman and his people were not even considering leaving the premises, he turned to the chief physician of the emergency clinic, Dr W., who was present during those events, and asked him to do what he should do. Doctor W., an unfortunate cripple (he had an artificial leg) who was afraid of his own shadow, had no intention of seeking a quarrel with the influential commissioner of the ghetto police. And Hanneman was actually informing Rumkowski on the telephone that the situation was already so threatening that he would not be able to deal with it by himself, and that it was necessary to summon the Gestapo.

In the meantime, the meeting on the square was ending and those assembled there did not even have a more serious demonstration in mind.

However Hanneman, in anticipation of the Gestapo's arrival, closed the exit from the square and also blocked the back door of the emergency clinic that led to the square...

Later he often wondered many times, what motivated the behaviour of that man. Hanneman must have realized after all that there would have been a blood bath; that the Gestapo would be only too pleased to slaughter several hundred Jews in order to report to its superiors and to the Łódź German population how successful they were in liquidating the danger that threatened – a Jewish revolt! Perhaps the ambitious commissioner dreamt that he would gain the favour of the Germans for himself and would replace old man Rumkowski on the ghetto throne? Perhaps he imagined that this way he would establish something like a partnership of both police forces? In any event, regardless of the motives guiding the commissioner with the yellow star and the arm-band of the ghetto police, the provocation process had been put in motion. Rumkowski called the Gestapo for help.

That was too much. Since Dr W. did not open his mouth, he said aloud what he thought of it all. He took off from his sleeve the arm-band with the red cross (the dressy caps were given to the doctors much later), threw it to the ground in front of Hanneman and went out from the emergency clinic to inform the demonstrators of the danger from the Gestapo. In any event, he achieved his goal. The people on the square scattered in all directions, some by jumping over the wall that surrounded the square, others by forcing their way to the street through the back door of the emergency clinic. When a truck with around 40 armed SS men arrived at Lutomierska Street a few minutes later, the square was empty.

The event though had a sequel of which he was partially the hero. That same evening he was arrested on Rumkowki's orders. This was the only case in the ghetto where a doctor was arrested. He was released after 24 hours thanks to the then director of the Health Department, one of the few figures who stood above the norms of the time and place. A further result of those events was that he succeeded in establishing contacts with the left-wing activists who had remained in Łódź ... But this was an altogether different story, and it related to the first attempts at organizing a trade union movement and something like a resistance movement in the ghetto ... About all this the *Chronicle* is silent (except in the introduction). Perhaps at some point in time it would be worth returning to this story as well.

Rumkowski had gathered around him people just like Hanneman. True, he did not have much to choose from, and he was being deceived by his instinct like an old bloodhound by his smell. If in his opinion someone had disappointed him, he got rid of him like of a useless rag. Often he meted out justice like a stern father – with a few slaps or kicks. He must have guessed that such behaviour had not added to his popularity but he was so convinced of his mission that he believed that sooner or later everyone would understand him, come to love him and be grateful to him ...

How mistaken he was! For those who survived, for those who after many years dedicated any works or books to the Łódź ghetto and to its ruler, the Eldest of the Jews had become over time an increasingly abhorrent figure. He was painted exclusively in black. He had become the personification of evil: Lady Macbeth and Richard III rolled into one. Such a portrait, the result of the fascination with the real and imaginary wrongdoings handed out to individuals as well as to the Jewish population incarcerated in the ghetto at large, makes it impossible to arrive at a different truth; a truth possibly more important and more complicated than the one used as a guide until now.

The American edition of *The Chronicle of the Łódź Ghetto* lies nearby and caresses the eye with its elegant appearance. The reader will not find in the *Chronicle* an answer to the question that today, after many years, has to be asked at last. If he had to discuss the *Chronicle*, he would formulate that question approximately this way: What kind of action would have been the appropriate one at that time, at the time of unpunished genocide? That means action that took into account the consistent realization of the German plans and the hopelessness of any resistance in a ghetto like the one in Łódź, which was closed in, surrounded by a mostly German population and in which there was not even a single weapon? Action that took into consideration the hunger that paralyzed people's will and the indifference of the world to their fate? In other words, what was it necessary to do, how was it necessary to act in order to save as many Jews as possible? Formulated this way, the question in a sense rejects another question, namely, what was it necessary to do to die with dignity? No one wants to die. We all had – he would write – the hope to be saved, even in the most tragic, the most hopeless moments. Because such hope originates in the instinct to live. To conquer that instinct is heroic, but only individuals happen to be heroic, not masses. The Nazis knew that mass murder produces a smaller threat of resistance than the murder of individual people, and therefore they acted as they did ...

But those starved, terrorized Jews incarcerated in the ghetto were not thinking of the high self-esteem of their future religious–spiritual heirs. They thought about how to save themselves, how to survive. All the more so because even if they had known what Czerniaków or Rumkowski had known about the Nazi plans, they did not want to accept this knowledge. The question therefore of how one was to act at that time pertained less to each of those condemned to extermination than it pertained primarily to such people as Czerniaków or Rumkowski. How were they supposed to act and behave having known what they knew?

A trifle ...

One does not have to be an historian to be aware that probably, in the history of mankind, no leader ever stood before a dilemma such as the one that confronted the German-appointed leaders of those two Jewish communities. Never yet had history charged any person alive with a similar burden. That means, with the consciousness of the lot that could befall the hundreds of thousands of people for whom they were responsible, as well as with the moral duty – not feasible to fulfill in practice – of saving those condemned from the fate to which the crazy Nazis had designed for them. Unfortunately, the Jews of the Polish ghettos were separated from their persecutors by barbed wire and not by a sea that would open up for the persecuted but drown the persecutors.

On what could Czerniaków and Rumkowski count at that time?

When writing about the *Chronicle,* he would have asked that question differently: On what did they have the right to count? Of course, on the reaction of the civilized world, even disregarding the fact that Hitlerism had been its pampered child. They had the right to count on the reaction of the Vatican, the international institution that even in the world of blond-haired and blue-eyed Aryans possessed great authority. They had the right to count on such reaction because the civilized world and the Vatican were very well informed about the sentence passed on the Jews. They were also informed that the Nazis were executing that sentence with scientific consistency.

This is how the question could have been presented. The problem arose at the moment when both Czerniaków and Rumkowski realized that there would be no reaction from the world's secular and spiritual powers. Those powers had other matters on their mind than the possibility of saving from death a few million Jews with whom there had been nothing but trouble for 2,000 years. Neither Jewish king could count on any help from this quarter.

So, what remained for them? The answer was simple. And how simple! They could only count on a miracle … Indeed, that was what he would write in discussing the *Chronicle*. When counting on the conscience of the world had been an illusion, counting on a miracle was becoming realistic thinking.

Honourable court of history! You have to pass judgment in the case of two people, two people who were so very different in regard to the dimension of their morality and intellect. But two people on whose shoulders had fallen the necessity to count on a miracle if they wanted to save from extermination hundreds of thousands of people entrusted to their power and care. And let the court take into consideration: there could have been only one miracle – that the Germans would not have the time to bring their plans to life. In other words, that the Allies would succeed in sending the Nazis to hell sooner than the Nazis would succeed in sending the remnants of the Polish Jews to the gas chambers. But two approaches are possible in the case of counting on miracles, as illustrated by an old Jewish anecdote.

A poor Jew had a complaint against God for not performing a miracle and helping him win the lottery. The complaints were ever more bitter and vehement, until the Jew heard a voice from heaven that said to him: 'Well, I shall perform a miracle and you will win the lottery but on condition that you in turn help me. That you buy a ticket …'

Czerniaków had not done anything to help the miracle, or had done very little. When in July 1942 it had become clear that the miracle would not occur, that the defeat of Germany had been far away but the defeat of the Jews had already been signed, he chose death – a most dignified one. But before that? Should he not have heeded the advice of the boor from Łódź? Indeed no one, honourable court, had heeded his advice. No one knows what Rumkowski and Czerniaków had to say to each other when they met in Warsaw.

Because the boor from Łódź decided to help the miracle. Not for nothing did he learn as a child to make calculations.

He knew what he was doing when he tried for any price – for any price meant the highest price – to convert the whole ghetto into a camp working for the occupant. Thousands of Germans enriched themselves greatly from the ghetto slave labour, and hundreds of other Germans had saved themselves from being sent to the front thanks to the existence of the ghetto.

As can be seen, the calculation was not complicated. But once the gamble of survival, the gamble for a miracle, had begun, it was necessary to conduct it to the end and not to give up easily. And that was, honourable court of history, what the Jewish king of Łódź probably had decided. He had not paid much attention to Czerniaków's disdain. He was probably somewhat more concerned about his subjects' opinions of him. He was obsessed however with his mission, and avowed that even if he had the ghetto population against him, he could not take this into account. He could not after all ride over the streets of the Jewish quarter and proclaim from the podium of his *droshky* that God had passed a sentence on his chosen people through the intermediary of Hitler and that only he, Mordecai Rumkowski, knew how to turn around God's verdicts.

He would have written all this in discussing the *Chronicle*. And he would supplement his appeal to the honourable court of history with a few more facts. Because after all the Łódź ghetto was liquidated only in August 1944. A conscientious historian would look into a calendar. Then he could consider what would have happened if the Soviet offensive had not stopped at the Vistula. If the historian is a fatalist, he will answer that in any case the Germans would have had enough time to liquidate the Łódź ghetto. It is not out of the question that such a fatalistic view would be justified. However, that historian could also notice another event in the calendar. In July of that year, the attempt on Hitler's life took place. If that attempt had succeeded, the Łódź ghetto under Rumkowski's leadership would with all certainty have been the only Jewish community that was saved from slaughter ...

So, when no power in the world was thinking of stopping the hand decorated with a swastika and armed with *Zyklon* – he would have written in discussing the *Chronicle* –

Rumkowski's tactic of counting on a miracle could have resulted in success. What would have happened then? Would Rumkowski have been declared a national hero? No! Most certainly not! The miserable Jewish king of Łódź would have been hanged or torn to pieces by those who thanks to him had survived, by those who rejoiced in Brzezinka about the news of his dark end. He would be held responsible for the death of more than 100,000 ghetto inhabitants – who had been sentenced to death by starvation, epidemics, gassing in the gas chambers of Chełmno. He would be held responsible for all the abuses, bribes and thefts by his subordinates. He would be reminded of all the slaps and kicks he had been distributing right and left, and also of the food ration coupons with which he was buying himself those on whom he depended at the moment. And perhaps – oh, irony of fate! – before he was hanged, he would have been reminded of the example he should have followed – that of Czerniaków ...

He would have certainly written all that if he had had to discuss the chronicle of the ghetto hell. But he would not fail to remind the court of history that the Łódź ghetto outlasted the Warsaw ghetto by 18 or 20 months of military struggle. And every day of that struggle could have decided the fate of those Jewish communities, the life and death of hundreds of thousands of Jews ... And he would also have added that the streets of Bałuty had not for one minute been the arena of the chaos that resulted from the dark confrontation of horrible misery and helpless hunger with the rich speculators – smugglers, as was the case in the Warsaw ghetto on Nalewki or Dzika Street. Because this too was the truth of the Warsaw ghetto. The last heroic chord of its history that had been the uprising – an act of desperation when the execution of the sentence of the Warsaw Jews was nearing its end – belongs to an entirely different category and demands totally different considerations.

And yes, and he would still write that in the final summation it would be necessary to take into consideration also the fact that from the Łódź ghetto after all there remained alive more than 10,000 Jews whom death in the camps had not had the time to swallow. Almost no one survived from the Warsaw ghetto, except those few who found shelter on the 'Aryan side.' This bookkeeping is of course terrible. If the second fact is clearly not a debit for Czerniaków, the first fact is a kind of posthumous credit for Rumkowski ...

Yes, this bookkeeping is terrible. Even more so, because it does not take into account the magnitude of the wager that brought in the end such meagre winnings... only that this dark account of loss and benefit was the deed of Hitler's racism and the racism of the whole civilized world that had endorsed it.

That is how he would end the discussion of the book that encloses the history of four years of the Łódź ghetto, and the *res gestae* of its king ...

Notes

1. *The Chronicle of the Łódź Ghetto*, ed. Lucjan Dobroszycki, New Haven, CT: Yale University Press, 1984.
2. Jewish council, appointed by the German authorities.
3. Jewish council of 'advisers'.
4. In Brzezinka (Birkenau=Auschwitz II) there was a section for Gypsies, who were gradually exterminated to make room for the Jews from Łódź.

9 The Most Important Conversation of his Life

Before him lay both of the letters. The one that he had received a few weeks ago and the one that contained his ready-to-be-sent-off reply. He had started that reply many times, but each time something held him back ... Embarrassment? Unease about how his letter would be received? Still, he had surmounted that unease, though his letter's final version had not pleased him. But since he had already decided to write it, another reply was not possible.

'This is not however the main reason why I decided to write to you. By accident, rumours reached me here that during the war you had met my brother, that you had chanced to encounter him in altogether unusual circumstances. The news shocked me: I could not believe that this was true! After all, you never mentioned that fact to me, although there were many occasions when you could have done, when I still lived in Warsaw and our contacts were frequent and cordial. I do not believe that in general you would hide something from me. What is the secret here? I do not understand your silence. But, first of all, was it true? Had you really met Jerzy? Why do I learn this only now and here, far from Poland? Why, why ...'

He could not dismiss those questions with silence. Silence would be simple cowardice. Lying was out of the question. And the truth?

'My dear! How glad I was to receive your letter. For the life of me, I had not expected it. So much time went by from the moment when your work as a doctor was taken away from you and you were hounded out of our homeland! When you had to leave the country because you were reckoned to be among the wrong kind of "Zionists" or "cosmopolitans". Twenty years were needed to replace the old anti-Semitic epithets discredited by Hitlerism with new ones, compatible with the spirit of the new times. Have you noticed how these two designations agree exactly in their spirit and sense with the previous "Judeo-Communist"?

... Yes, yes. How much time has passed from those days when each of us, the shipwrecked from the boat of our hopes and dreams, had been forced to find our own ways of rescue? You allowed the waves of events to carry your raft ever farther and farther. As for me, hanging on to one of the wrecked boat's boards, I reached the nearest shore. Rescued? Saved? I do not know...

We had not looked for an opportunity anywhere or anytime to jointly pour out our grievances against history. Nor to talk about matters about which we would have so much to tell each other. At one time, while abroad, I obtained your telephone number. I did not call. I flinched before the fear of a disappointment that might destroy the remnants of our joint memories.

And now this letter from you! Beside the common courtesies, it contains a request. Seemingly on the margin of the letter, how easy it is to guess that it was this request that was the main reason why you broke your silence and are attempting to return to matters from almost half a century ago. You write that rumours had reached you about some encounter of mine with your brother, and that this encounter apparently had taken place in altogether unusual circumstances. You are asking if that was true and how I could justify my silence until now.

I shall meet your request, although I took the decision to explain the matter completely after long reflection. Why I hesitated so long, you will easily guess after you read this letter. On the other hand, I think that you too knew about Jerzy more than one could infer from your behaviour, but it would be ridiculous for us to reproach each other for that now. That would be somewhat like spouses reproaching each other for their mutual infidelities 20 years after their divorce ...

In any case, your request for an account of my encounter with Jerzy acted like a trigger that stimulated a cascade – indeed an avalanche – of reminiscences connected equally with the last period of our pre-war stay in France as well as with the war.

When I was a young boy, I listened intently to the colourful memories of both my father and my grandmother about the time that they nostalgically called "before the war." This of course referred to the years before the First World War, and for me they were as distant as the Napoleonic wars or the discovery of America. Well, now I am a lot older than my father was when he was weaving his memories from before that war, and even older than my grandmother. While their memories reached to a period of twenty years or let us say of a quarter of a century back, mine – ours – reach times and matters of half a century back. And so I think that for young people who at some point in time might perhaps reach for those memories, the problems they deal with will be as distant and strange as the concerns of cavemen ...

However, when writing about your brother I cannot avoid dealing with the years of our youth. Even more so because you, your brother and I had chosen studies in the same area, and had almost at the same time become involved, with all our youthful temperament, in political matters. The catalyst for our political maturation at that time had been the civil war in Spain, a war that had reached out to us in each of its most minute episodes and that had sensitized us to all the important world issues. We took care of the volunteers who on the road to Spain stopped over at Toulouse, which had been at that time the base from which they were being dispatched to the Pyrenean Peninsula. Later we took care of the fighters of the international brigades who looked for shelter in France after the defeat of the republic.

I wrote "our political maturation" ... How many times have I reflected whether it had really been maturation or only the manifestation of some kind of tropism genetic to all of us, our generation of the Jewish intelligentsia: the need to direct our aspirations and hopes to the same ideological goal.

Your brother belonged to those who were the most imbued with politics and, as we talked about it enviously, to those who were the most militant. From that period, I always recall two episodes that were so characteristic of Toulouse in those years, and also so characteristic of Jerzy. The first took place in the huge hall of one of the Toulouse movie houses. After the showing of a film about Spain (and perhaps it was the *Marseillaise* by Renoir), we were collecting, together with your brother, donations to help the republic, in a stretched out Spanish flag. With what passion your brother called for sacrifices to help the cause of the struggle in Spain. With what fire, as he stood on an improvised podium, did he persuade the audience that the Spanish republicans were fighting not only for their freedom, but also for the freedom of Europe from fascism.

The second episode had the university hospital for a background. Some soldiers from the international brigades lay in it. After the defeat of the republic, they crossed the Pyrenean Mountains into France during the harsh winter. Many of them had severely frozen limbs which at times required amputation. The students and even the doctors treated those soldiers very meanly – with contempt and hostility. Once, during a round with a professor, we stopped near the bed of a Pole from the Dąbrowski brigade. He had severely frozen feet which would perhaps require an amputation and, moreover, he had tuberculosis. One of the students loudly made some ironic remark about the *métèques*[1] who were looking for shelter in France when in need. Upon hearing this, Jerzy hit that student in the snout with his entire might. The fellow was covered with blood, and Jerzy was barred from the hospital grounds. Luckily, he had already done all the clinical examinations ...

There is no doubt that Jerzy had been our spiritual leader at that time. Everyone predicted a great future for him – when our time came ... He finished his studies as one of the most promising physicians of the younger generation. However, he had no desire to return to Poland. He intended to remain in France and to obtain the right to practise there. His command of French was excellent, he knew English and Spanish, and had in general become a Frenchman in his habits and customs. And then there was Gabri ... Gabri – his wife. I think that her influence on him was greater than you, his sister, could notice. I remember how amazed we had been by the fact that Jerzy was marrying an authentic Lebanese woman, an authentic Maronite and an authentic millionaire! I must admit that Gabri as a woman had greatly appealed to me, and she impressed us all with her life-style which was so different from our own. Not the least important reason that influenced Jerzy's decision was the fact that Gabri had French citizenship. This induced him to legalize their liaison.

That is how it was. This period of life ended for me in July

1939. You all accompanied me to the train station when I returned to Poland.

Then came the war. You remained in France, and so did Jerzy. You were in the Resistance and had performed magnificently. Indeed, I looked many times at the picture in which you are seen being decorated with the Cross of Bravery by De Gaulle himself! France did not exactly reciprocated when, forced to leave Poland, you wanted to settle and practise medicine in the country for which you had fought. You were categorically refused that privilege ... Actually, the country that you were forced to leave had not exactly clasped you to its bosom either ...

The war meant for me, in sequence, the flight from Łódź, work at the Baby Jesus hospital during the siege of Warsaw, the return to Łódź, parting with my parents, the ghetto ... The Łódź ghetto was liquidated in August of 1944. After having been fortunate enough to pass the sieve of selection, I found myself in Auschwitz, actually at Brzezinka ...

(I wonder if everything I have written until now is not superfluous – I am recalling matters you know well. Still, it seems to me that such a procedure makes sense. It will prepare us better – you to receive and me to transmit the account you requested in your letter.)

If in the ghetto each Jew had been at the most a particle of a cost-free labour force, a mass of slaves from which the Germans were able to derive enormous profits, here, in the Auschwitz death factory, each of us became a nobody. We were an anonymous crowd composed of anonymous units whose numbers had to tally during roll call. All I had been left from my possessions were my trouser belt and my shoes. I received for clothing some torn breeches and a threadbare jacket – both of them too narrow and too short for me. I mention this because it is not irrelevant to my account about Jerzy.

In the attire in which I had been outfitted, I looked like a caricature, a circus clown. Perhaps that was intentional: to make the inmate look ridiculous. But I soon realized that such attire was a disaster in Brzezinka. On the *Lagerstrasse*, in the block, during the handing out of bread or soup, in the latrine and during roll call, every *Kapo*, every *Blokälteste*[2] felt that it was his duty to give a person with such an appearance a kick, a slap, or at least a shove. The experience of the first two days convinced me that my external appearance could be among the most important reasons for making me a *muselmann*,[3] that is, a candidate for a speedy end in the crematorium oven. Luckily, I met an inmate – also a Jew from Łódź – who had received on the other hand trousers and a jacket much too large for him. I offered to swap clothes with him, and the bread ration I had added to the offer closed the deal. And so I looked more or less decent. I was not exposed anymore to kicks and shoves, and when I walked with a brisk and self-confident stride, I gave the impression of being a camp somebody. In short, I could move around freely, so to speak.

However, at the very beginning of the Auschwitz chapter of my biography, on the first day of my new experiences before I made that deal that was so advantageous to me, I had been put to a test, which taught me that the world in which I now found myself could, beside its menacing face, also show a mug altogether grotesque. True, this matter is not at all connected with Jerzy, but I would still like to describe it to you.

Our whole transport, strictly speaking the close to a thousand inmates that remained of its male component after the selection, was made to assemble in one of the barracks in the part of Brzezinka called the Gypsy camp. We were sitting on the stone floor squeezed together like sardines in a can. The brick facing of a furnace ran along the barrack wall. On the furnace sat several SS men and an inmate, a trusty with some undetermined powers. And it was indeed that inmate who made the speech whose purpose was to clarify for us our new situation, and to instruct us on what would threaten us if we did not observe the Auschwitz discipline. During his lecture, the gold-lipped speaker was walking along the furnace gesticulating with the skill of a high-class orator. Could it be that he had been an actor by profession? He spoke neither in Yiddish nor in German but in the peculiar mixture, a sample of which I had the occasion to hear many times in the ghetto when representatives of the Jewish authorities talked to the Germans. The content of this speech was approximately as follows:

'Pay attention to what the German authorities have to say to you through me. You must know that you are now in the world's largest concentration camp. None of you will come out from here alive. Only those who behave well will prolong their stay in the camp and may count on the goodwill of the authorities. So far as your wives and children are concerned, look in the direction of the chimneys. That is where they are now burning. What remains of them is only that smoke. You too will end up in those ovens. For each act of disobedience – the death penalty. And therefore the authorities are giving you now one last chance. If anyone succeeded in bringing any jewellery, gold or dollars into the camp let him hand them over to us now and nothing will happen to him. In the camp, there are extraordinary machines that will in any case detect everything. But if the machines detect those things, nothing will protect you from the death penalty."

All this was said with great eloquence. In any case, the last words of the speech had made the proper impression. Several inmates stood up and, pushing their way through the sitting crowd to give single dollar banknotes to the speaker. As it turned out, the result of the appeal had not satisfied the authorities who sat on the furnace. The Nazis whispered something into the ear of the gold-lipped speaker, and he called out in a loud voice: "Let all the doctors stand up!" It so happened that there were perhaps eight of us in the group. Initially I had not intended to respond to his call – after all those who sat on the furnace did not have to know who I was. But I soon changed my mind because I felt on me the gaze of several of my close neighbours. I understood that if I did not respond to the call myself, someone would point a finger at me ... I stood up. The speaker summoned us to stand near him on the brick facing of the furnace. When we carried out the order, he looked at us carefully and he chose me for his further experiments (perhaps because I had been the last to respond to his call).

"Where do you have the gold and the dollars?"

"I don't have anything."

His fist hit my face.

"Admit."

"I don't have anything."

"Well, we will soon check ..."

I had a smashed lip and was prepared for the worst. It appeared that my inquisitor was the machine that looked for the gold and the dollars. To begin with, he ordered me to open wide my mouth and verified whether I had a goldmine in there. Then he looked into my ears. Then he ordered me to let down my trousers and with his own hand checked closely the content of my anus. From the height of the furnace I shone down with my emaciated nudity and felt on me the gaze of the thousand inmates who looked on, not with any sympathy but rather with the hope that something would be found in my ass that would pacify the Germans. Nothing of the kind was found. The other doctors were not examined after that. When we returned to the stone floor, one of them whispered into my ear:

"You see what a high opinion they have of us?"

After this meeting, with me in the starring role, we were placed in different barracks of the camp that was the largest in the world – a fact, we were given to understand, of which we should all be proud. The usual Brzezinka days began: from roll call to roll call, from bread distribution to bread distribution, from one escape from a round-up for work to the other. It was a period of waiting. We had become for the SS profitable merchandise to be sold to factories and mines in the Reich that needed workers. Perhaps that was the reason why, in the history of the camp, this was a period of relative calm. It meant that the normal death from starvation had not been supplemented by constant selections and by the exploits of the SS and their trusties. This relative, though perhaps only temporary, calm immediately gave rise to altogether optimistic moods among the Jews deported to Auschwitz.

Once, after the morning roll call, a former patient of mine approached me and in all seriousness said: "Is it true, doctor, that this mountain climate is good for the lungs?" What could I reply to him when the black plume of smoke rising from the crematoria ovens was visible behind his head?

In the first few days or perhaps weeks – it is indeed difficult for me to place all that in time precisely – I acquired a few valuable skills. I learned for instance the art of relieving myself together with others. When I saw for the first time the cement latrines with over a dozen openings, I was reminded of a fragment of a book by Céline in which he described his impressions of a trip to the United States. He saw there for the first time public latrines for several people. Their users often encouraged each other in an activity that at times required considerable effort by backslapping … Here there was no question of backslapping. At the most, one could be pushed down from the cement structure by an impatient inmate, or hit over the head with a truncheon by some Kapo who decided that your time to relieve yourself had run out already ... I also learned how to overcome collectively the sharp chill of the autumn mornings and evenings. A row of inmates, standing with their backs to each other, formed something like a snail that was growing in length as more and more willing inmates joined in. Together with the warmth, they also shared their lice. They too needed to be warm. Under the influence of the warmth, they became nimble and aggressive. I later learned that macaques were overcoming the cold in a similar manner.

And, as I said before, I learned to walk through the camp with my head held high and with a long, energetic stride. On occasion, I even gave a shove to a *muselmann* who was in my way. That made an impression. And indeed, sometime at the beginning of the second month of my camp life, during one of such walks (I was looking for my cousin, who was a nurse, in the part of the camp where the hospital had been located), I ran into Jerzy.

As you certainly know, it was forbidden to come too close to the wire fence. An SS man who stood in the watchtower would swiftly take aim at anyone who disregarded that rule. I therefore walked at a certain distance from the wire fence. I hoped to notice my cousin on the other side. Then I caught sight of a group of inmates who were pulling a sanitation wagon, or perhaps it was a mighty barrel into which the camp latrines had been emptied. At first, I paid no attention to the inmates harnessed to the barrel, but one silhouette seemed vaguely familiar to me. I came closer in order to have a better look. And that inmate had also noticed me. What was more – he signalled something to me. We were at a distance of eight or ten metres from each other but with the wire fence between us. After a while I recognized him and was astounded. It was Jerzy! When he saw that I had noticed him, he called out to me in French the number of his block and, before the SS man who guarded the inmates kicked him, he managed to shout for me to look him up.

You must understand that my amazement resulted also from the fact that I had no idea at all of what had been

135

happening in France during the Nazi occupation. I knew of course that at that time France had already been liberated, but what had been happening there during the four years of occupation was a mystery to me.

That same day I decided to look up the block that Jerzy had indicated to me. This was somewhat risky, but the clothes I wore gave me courage.

I located the block with little trouble. I had not realized immediately that this had been a block assigned to the privileged inmates who formed the so-called "Canada." Those inmates were performing specific functions: for instance they searched the baggage that belonged to those who arrived with the transports, burned the corpses pulled out from the gas chambers, and so on. It turned out that the inmates who cleaned the latrines also lived there.

If my memory does not mislead me today, and to the extent that I am able after 40 years to reconstruct all those events, the ordinary camp pariahs were forbidden entry to the "Canada" block. In any case, somehow no one had stopped me (always my appearance) and I found myself ... How can I describe it to you exactly? In short, I found myself in the land of fairytale. Obviously, a camp-occupation fairytale, a fairytale that embodied the dreams of beings who for years had been starving. The entry to this fairytale enchantment was ... the aroma. One could have assumed that the block where the inmates cleaning the camp latrines had lived would simply smell of excrement. Well, no! The inside of the block was redolent of the most marvellous, most wonderful aroma for an inmate like me, the aroma of fried onions, fried sausage, fried eggs, fried bacon. At least one sausage ring hung above each plank-bed, and onions were hanging everywhere. On lines under the ceiling, laundry was drying as well as various items of men's clothing. The plank-beds were covered with real covers or woollen blankets. All this came of course from the transports of Jews that constantly arrived at the Brzezinka railway platform. From Hungary, Greece and of course from Poland, which at that time was being cleansed of the Jews. Against a background of concentration camp conditions, the insides of that barrack glittered and overwhelmed one with its riches, and its residents looked excellent. When preparing their meals, they laughed and joked like army recruits telling obscene jokes ...

I walked slowly between two rows of plank-beds. At last, I noticed him. He stood near his plank-bed, which was deep inside.

We stood one opposite the other and actually did not know how to act. We were clearly embarrassed, one could say like a pair of lovers who met after many years. Today, as I reflect on that encounter, I think that we were unconsciously tormented by a feeling of shame. Shame because of the bankruptcy of our visions or expectations that were based, as it had appeared to us, on the unshakeable foundation of science ... Because we found ourselves in a situation that no theory had envisaged and no imagination could envisage. It had always seemed to us that the future could not let us down – and yet it did. It had always seemed to us that the road we took was leading us directly to our goal and yet ...

We did not even fall into each other's arms as should have happened in similar circumstances, and as it would have happened in a story ... Was it because such behaviour seemed to us to be too pompous? Later I understood that Jerzy's reaction at the moment of our encounter in Auschwitz could have been influenced by other motives. Besides, today I cannot describe all this with the details that may have caught my attention at that time. I cannot recreate all this, even only because from the first moment I had been made as if giddy by the aroma that attacked not only my smell but also my palate and my stomach, believe me, in a paralyzing way ... Here in Brzezinka I felt hunger considerably more acutely than in the ghetto where in spite of everything the food had been better ...

But, to continue. Jerzy sat me down near him on the plank-bed. He immediately began treating me to sausage, chunks of bread and pieces of bacon. He was doing it as discreetly as possible so that no one would notice. I immediately began to eat ...

So we passed a few minutes in silence, during which I just gorged and gorged myself. Later, Jerzy began to question me about Łódź, the ghetto, the transport to Auschwitz. His questions followed one after the other. He was curious about everything. I was answering in monosyllables, and he, not waiting for my answer to one question, put a new one to me. Today I understand that he clearly wanted to delay my putting questions to him. But he could not avoid them. So, without being asked, he began to talk of his own accord.

If, my dear, I never told you about this encounter, if I never tried to refer to what Jerzy confided to me in Auschwitz, it has been for several reasons. The most important one was that I was convinced that in this matter both of us were guided by a mutually accepted silent agreement. I did not know and did not want to know what you knew about Jerzy's lot during the war. I could believe you knew much or guessed as much. After all, the two of you had not been at two different ends of the world during the war and occupation. True, the northern part of France was separated from the southern part by a border, but it was not a border that it was difficult to pass, and it was even easier for various rumours or gossip to get through. This had not even been rendered impossible – though it was perhaps harder – if one was involved in a clandestine activity. Moreover, Jerzy had not only been a person with whom one participated in meetings and demonstrations; he was, for God's sake, your brother, in whose affairs it was your duty to take an interest. Since in your letter you are asking me to tell you everything, everything about my encounter with Jerzy in Auschwitz, I have the right to conclude that you yourself do no know everything. Or that you did not want to know until now ... I also understand that you want to drink to the end this cup of sorrow. You want to seal the history of two defeats. His and yours ...

The second reason I never mentioned this encounter to you was of an entirely different nature. In short: there were so many gaps in Jerzy's account that it seemed to me difficult to make a whole out of it. Today is the first time that I am trying to do it.

His account (it lasted for several hours!) contained many details through which I could not easily find my way, even if I had been concentrating the whole time. But it was becoming ever more difficult for me to concentrate on his words. At moments, I could not do it.

His account, or confession, was not only filled with many minute details but also with many insinuations. If I had to report his account faithfully, I would have to use dozens of ellipses, exclamation marks and question marks. Some sentences would not connect, others would refer to matters completely alien to me, for instance those regarding his personal life.

He was talking ever more passionately, as if he had before him God knows how large an audience. On the other hand, I, his actual audience, was dozing off and eating, eating, and dozing off. Later I understood why this had been for him the most important conversation of his life. He actually said: "Believe me, this is the most important conversation of my life." This was the confession that he had been waiting to make. For me it was a stream of words that barely reached my brain, and a wonderful, splendid, and only chance to sate my hunger.

He began by saying that he wanted to disillusion me if I thought that he found himself in the concentration camp because of his political convictions or activities in the Resistance (this was the first time I encountered that term). As I understood from his narrative, several reasons had contributed to his "desertion" (he himself used this term, so I am repeating it). Those reasons included my departure for Poland (I think he added this reason later), your and Tadeusz's departure for Paris, and above all the outlawing of the party and its political position in the first months of the war. If the first two reasons had probably been the product of his defensive imagination, I can understand the other two. He had intended to settle in France, and the membership of a Pole in the outlawed Communist party ruled out the possibility of naturalization.

He was bitter about the political position of the party. In his opinion, at least that was how he tried to explain it to me at that time, in the "Canada" block, in the aroma of fried sausage, that the party should not have subordinated itself to the Soviet–Nazi pact so unconditionally. That absolute support for Stalin's policy, he said, had even moved the party leadership to demand that France should conclude a peace with Germany after the capitulation of Poland. And this would have left after all our country, he meant of course Poland, in the paws of the Nazis.

I hardly interrupted his monologue. I was so content that I

would not have anything against it if it had dragged on into infinity... And he, as if he thought that he did not accuse himself severely enough, that he did not discredit himself sufficiently in my eyes, began to tell me that he had been increasingly seized by fear as time went by. Panicky fear. He justified himself that this feeling had been the result of the fact that he never had the experience of political work in underground conditions. As you must remember, this was an old complex of his.

He continued his monologue by saying that since participation in meetings threatened being arrested, and the hanging of billboards or the handing out of leaflets threatened the most severe penalty, he completely removed himself. He removed himself not only from the party. He was even hiding from friends, who had been mostly party comrades. All this had gradually lowered him in the opinion of all those who had mattered to him ...

Even though I was half dazed during that confession, I realized that a reference to Gabri was missing. It was as if he had read my thoughts. Suddenly he began to talk only about her. Sometimes as about a tender lover, sometimes as about a shrew, though always, that was at least how I perceived it, with some affection as about the woman in his life, as about a person who will forever remain the closest to him. Nevertheless "everything became complicated" (that was how he had formulated it) with Gabri. Gabri became increasingly bigoted. A Maronite, a bigot! Today I can somehow say to myself that the Arabic-European mixture flowing in her veins provided excellent nourishment for such vehement religiosity which, what was worse, became fused with French nationalism.

Apparently Gabri urged him at that time to convert to Catholicism, and he clearly, out of spite, felt ever more Jewish. One can imagine what became of the conjugal life of those two people who without doubt continued to love each other, who in previous times and at each opportunity emphasized their love for each other with rather exhibitionist freedom. Besides, after all, he depended completely on her for his livelihood ...

Jerzy divulged all this to me probably in an attempt to

explain to me by means of all the possible reasons of a psychological and sociological nature the confusing course of his conflict with Gabri. (I am using the word "probably" which is in this case perhaps inappropriate because I am trying to recreate the details of the conversation only while I am writing.) After all, only a small part of his confession had reached me.

When the Germans became the rulers of France and the French subordinated their life to the conqueror's rules in total submission and with masochistic satisfaction, his fear of what could happen to him became a mania. He stopped leaving the house at all, he began to hide from stranger and friend alike, he even thought of suicide ... He talked and talked and talked about it, from time to time interrupting his confession to check if I followed him on the inclined plane of his ruin ...

And I did not stop eating. I was of course making an effort to understand him in order to become aware what had become of him before he began to empty the Auschwitz latrines, but this was becoming for me increasingly difficult. He talked about himself in self-accusing despair, while I was happy to be able to eat my fill ... I do not know if you can visualize the situation. I do not know if anyone could visualize it dozens of years after the camp hell.

Initially, people still tried to influence him, to persuade him, but very soon they left him alone. There were at that time more important matters than saving a person from himself. In his monologue, Jerzy made the remark that indeed at that time the Polish–Jewish emigration in France was not a very convenient ally for the party. But you know a lot more about it than I, and there is no reason to inform you about a matter you experienced yourself. Later, Jerzy said, party policy somehow changed (this was probably after June 1941[4]) and that emigration began to play an increasing role in the Resistance movement. But at that time, he had not been in Toulouse in any case. He and Gabri moved to Saint Gaudens. It seems Gabri thought Jerzy would be safer there. I think she rather wanted to remove him from the great centre of party activities that Toulouse had become at that time.

In the little town of Saint Gaudens, where he knew no one, he found himself completely at Gabri's favour and disfavour. He realized that he was increasingly becoming a burden to her. Several months of life far from Toulouse were enough for him to understand that he had become for Gabri an obstacle in the realization of some life plans of hers that were becoming crystallized as the Germans, with increasingly greater assuredness, were settling down in France. Gabri blossomed. She was exploding with religiosity and Petainist patriotism. The time for people like her had arrived. She was becoming, Jerzy claimed, ever more beautiful while he felt like an isolated, despised and spurned little Jew as depicted in the caricatures to which the French press had at that time been lavishly treating their readers.

I am not going to tell you how much bread and sausage I managed to eat until that fragment of his confession. Jerzy interrupted his monologue for a moment to bring me a cup of hot coffee. I delighted in it like in the one, you must remember, at the Maison du Café, on rue de Metz ...

So one day, he said, what was bound to happen did happen. Gabri simply declared to him that he, Jerzy, had no right to endanger her life and that he must ... help her. Help her? That meant that he had to disappear. Apparently, she had already been asked why she was harbouring a Jew in her home, and a Communist at that. In another city, he would be safer too. In short (Jerzy talked about it at much greater length), she gave him money and sent him back to Toulouse. In Toulouse, he rambled for a few days over the city. He was hiding because he did not want to endanger anyone with his person and did not want to endanger himself. At last he ran out of money and returned to Saint Gaudens. From this fragment of his story, it appeared that as he intended to enter the residence in which he had lived with Gabri, two German officers were just about to leave it. A smiling Gabri stood in the doorway, and they were elegantly saluting her. You can imagine what impression his presence made. Gabri somehow collected herself and pulled him inside. She made a terrible scene and demanded that the next morning he leave town. The Gestapo, she apparently told him, was in the possession of evidence of his pre-war Communist activities ... He was indeed supposed to leave the next day. But he did not have the time. The next morning, police came and arrested him. Gabri was well-informed ...

That part of his story I remember somewhat better. Probably because in continuing his monologue he now limited himself to bare facts and gave up his literary–theatrical self-accusation.

When he was arrested, he obviously wondered whether it had not been Gabri who had betrayed him. (I think that was probably how it must have looked.) He tried vehemently to defend her, although I had not even thought of accusing her. In prison (or was it during his arrest?) interrogations began that lasted for hours. Did he know anything? No, he knew nothing. Really nothing. Since he had not been meeting with anyone for years ... This went on for a couple of weeks. Jerzy claimed that finally two Gestapo officers began participating in the interrogations. I am not acquainted enough with the situation in southern France to know whether the Gestapo really could have participated in such interrogations. In any event, so he said, their very presence had paralyzed him. He was threatened with beatings and torture. He was once shown a prisoner after a similar interrogation... You can imagine. Nevertheless, he could not tell anything because he did not know anything. Luckily ...

One day the interrogators set to work. And they knew how to strike effectively. Well, and ...

Here – at least that was my impression – Jerzy's story began to be very confusing. In any case, from what he tried to tell me, it appeared that, unable to endure the beatings, he threw his torturers the address of a man he had met in Toulouse and who had invited him to his place. He knew with all certainty that this man was supposed to be dispatched to Spain any day. The beatings stopped and after a few days the German interrogator congratulated him, one could even say thanked him, cordially. The information he gave helped the authorities to get on the trail of an important group of Communist bandits ...

Jerzy drowned this part of his monologue in some metaphysical philosophy that it was chance that governed human fate. He reflected on the impossibility of escaping one's fate and on free will ... Not much of it remained in my memory. The world, he said, tumbled on his head, but in spite of it all he had been happy not to be threatened by beatings.

143

He had not consciously betrayed anyone, he claimed. Just the opposite, he intended after all to put the Germans on a false trail (this was an exaggerated attempt to save his dignity). But since chance had decreed for it to happen otherwise ... You understand yourself that there is no need to reflect on such reasoning. It was clear that Jerzy preferred that I should ultimately treat him as a coward rather than as a simple traitor or informer ... Because I am not certain he had not been one ...

Later he learned (he was kept in prison another four months) that at the address that he gave to the Germans, in a hideaway under the floor, some papers had been stored. And this allowed the Germans to get on the trail of what they were looking for. Jerzy maintained that, when liquidating the centre that had previously been at that location, some papers had probably been forgotten and this was how they got into the hands of the Gestapo. In any case, he was not freed. Before he was sent to a camp, the German who had interrogated him showed him a newspaper. In it was an item about cutting down several Communists from the Toulouse cell...

You can imagine, my dear, how much this confession had cost Jerzy. It might have looked as if he had been waiting for me in this Auschwitz, and I appeared before him as though I had come from the sky. The confession was made. Had a catharsis taken place? Today when I write those words, I can reflect on it. At that time, I had no inclination for such complicated mental processes. You already know what had interested me. He had probably been waiting for some sign of pity, even of pity full of contempt – I was not capable of either one or the other.

Jerzy mentioned to me that when he found himself in Auschwitz, he thought of suicide. How many times he had contemplated it! But, he admitted, he could not carry out such a step any more ... Luckily, (that was what he said: 'luckily'), after a few weeks he was put into the *Scheisskommando* (shit detachment). Although he wondered if this was not his reward for the address with which he had helped the Germans. Work carting shit around as a reward for betrayal – that is too vulgar a symbolism.

"I am doing well now, as you see," he said at the end ...

This was already more than I could endure. Ages and

cosmic distances separated me from all the other things he had told me until now, and I was able to listen to his previous confessions eating, digesting and dozing off. But Auschwitz was all around us, and we were sucked into its gears and laws. I told him, or rather screamed out what everyone in the camp knew about "Canada." He had as much grub as he wanted – of course compared to us simple, mangy inmates; he lived like a nabob, but his life was less secure than the life of any *muselmann*. Today he pulled barrels of camp excrement and benefited from privileges that only a few in the camp had – he ate bacon, he drank cognac, he slept under a blanket. But it was well known that each 'Canada' team in turn finished in the gas chamber after a couple of months.

Jerzy was listening calmly to all this. This had not been a revelation for him. The most he could be surprised at why I had reacted so vehemently to his last words. Besides, I did not know myself why they had irritated me to such an extent. His reasoning was surprisingly simple. I shall try to present it to you as accurately as possible, although it does not concern the French period of his life any more which is so important to you, to both of us. After all, you wanted to know everything about Jerzy …

So, what if they are sending us to the gas chamber from here? Everyone knows that. But how can it be explained that though everyone knows that, it is still everyone's hope to get into "Canada," or even only into the *Scheisskommando*? He advised me to try to talk about it to someone of this block. A wave with the hand was my only reply. Was there perhaps, Jerzy said, some common motive, some common reason, for such hope? So, in his opinion that common motive was the fact that before anyone got into the "Canadian rest house" he knew that he would not last in Auschwitz more than a few weeks. For everyone who had been in that barrack, "Canada" meant a prolongation of life. For a couple of months, a couple of weeks, a couple of days … And what may happen in the interval between the time set for the death of an inmate of an ordinary barrack and the time set for the death of an inmate of "Canada"? A lot might happen … And besides, he added, do not forget that everyone is guided by his own hopes, his own instincts and ingenuity. Some are deluding themselves that the Germans would not have the time to send them to the gas chamber, others have their own means to end their lives with dignity before being sent there …

And, at last, there was one more thing that Jerzy said. It sounded more or less like this: "As far as I am concerned, I … I think that I deserve it. That death. Such is certainly God's will …"

Can you imagine your Jerzy referring to God's will? That was unbelievable. I asked him since when he had become a religious fatalist. He told me that he had to believe in something and in Auschwitz only that remained since he knew that eventually he would be reduced to the same excrement he was carting in a barrel.

How could I react to all this? This was not a little student room or a café in Toulouse where we could discuss any topic at will, and at times even engage in bare-knuckled arguments. All this seemed to me untrue, it seemed like a fragment from some bad novel … After the war I reflected many times on this encounter and wondered who actually was that man whom we thought we knew so well. Was he a weakling shattered by events, or a coward, or an informer and a wretched little actor who had learned the appropriate role for the theatrical performance before the one spectator that I was? Considerably later, I abandoned the habit of readily categorizing people. I wondered how I would have performed that part of life if fate had mocked me the way it mocked him. In the last war, no pattern of behaviour had actually passed the test. The greater the distance from those events, the more we are trying to rehabilitate what so easily, it appears, became compromised in us.

At that time, at Jerzy's, I kept silent, of course. I was returning to the blissful state of being half-asleep, half-awake. Jerzy however wanted the encounter to end. Notwithstanding that I was almost asleep, that I constantly, though at a slower rate, was stuffing myself with bread, he began to explain to me why it had been so important that he unburden himself of everything. He said it was a kind of psychic healing, and that in his opinion there was in each of us something of an actor and that in each actor there was something of an exhibitionist …

I could not listen to this anymore. It sounded as if he had wanted to remind me at the end of this conversation who he

146

actually was, what he represented, whom I had before me – that he was a refined intellectual, a dialectician, a person able to coldly analyze himself and others in each situation ...

I stood up (barely so) and began to leave. I did not intend to fight for the last word. Quite coldly, I thanked him for the royal treat. I was so sated that I was as if drunk with satiety. He looked at me with his somewhat childish, somewhat beguiling gaze. He wanted to say something and then, as if he had changed his mind, he just warned me to be careful when I was going out. Because one could pay dearly for visiting this block. Well, besides I had a whole chunk of bread concealed on my bosom. Luckily, the road back was as uneventful as my intrusion into this guarded palace of the Auschwitz Croesuses.

I must add at the end that I paid dearly for this excursion and the encounter with Jerzy. As soon as I found myself back in the barrack, I ate the rest of the bread and a piece of sausage that I still had saved from the treat. That was already too much. At night I began to vomit, had a horrible diarrhea and a very high fever. When half conscious I fell asleep, someone who had been very conscious stole my shoes from under my head. Those shoes, shoes from the ghetto, had been an essential element of my appearance that, as I described to you previously, played such an important role in Brzezinka. Without the shoes, in ordinary wooden clogs, I was becoming immediately one of the ordinary pariahs. A search for the thief was of course condemned to failure in advance. When I lamented in despair the next day the loss of my shoes, the block clerk, a Hungarian Jew, advised me to look around in the barrack and see which of the dying inmates had shoes that would fit me. Or if I preferred, which of the inmates who had shoes that would fit me was in a condition that foretold his rapid end. The rest would depend only on my craftiness and, the clerk stressed this forcefully, on my physical strength since I would not be the only candidate for the inheritance. I can only tell you that the endeavour to obtain shoes had greatly enriched my camp experience. For the next two days I literally sat on the plank-bed of some Hungarian Jew and waited for his final defeat in the battle against death from starvation. At the end, I noticed that indeed I had not been the only candidate for the inheritance. Since I was afraid of being overwhelmed by superior strength, I pulled off the shoes from the dying man in the darkness of the night. Had I not done it, some competitor of mine would have done it. In the morning, the remains of the dead man were not on the plank-bed anymore.

Of course, this has little to do with Jerzy. Since however I am telling you about our encounter with all the details, its finale – even in the absence of the main protagonist of this letter – is worth mentioning.

After you read all of this, you will appreciate the reasons that did not allow me to mention this encounter to you. I thought that if you knew all of this, there was no need to remind you about it again. If on the other hand Jerzy's destiny during the war was unknown to you, there was no need to acquaint you with it. After all, your life was from your early youth no bed of roses either. Many things had conspired against you, and particularly petty human ambitions. Why therefore multiply your experiences?

What could I add to the above? Considerably later, after the war, I learned that the same month that I was sent out from Auschwitz, an uprising of the inmates servicing the Auschwitz gas chambers and crematoria ovens took place. An uprising it seems of all those who derived at that time the benefits of "Canada". Those who were supposed to be the next victims of the system of shift work organized by the Nazis … Almost all the inmates perished, but the gas chambers and crematoria ovens were rendered useless. I am always deluding myself that among those who stirred up the uprising was Jerzy. Our Jerzy. Be well.'

Notes

1. A pejorative term applied to foreigners.
2. Barrack supervisor.
3. A person in the ghetto or concentration camp so emaciated that it was obvious he would die soon.
4. When Germany attacked the Soviet Union.

10 The Interrogation

So he acted as he had been advised by the most experienced Auschwitz inmates, among them his cousin, a nurse in the hospital block.

'Avoid,' he said, 'any larger transport. The large ones in all certainty go to camps similar to Auschwitz, and that means to extermination. But the small transports are almost always directed to factories. Only there do you have a chance of surviving ...'

This was an argument as logical as it was depressing. Four times he succeeded in fleeing larger transports for which the SS men had organized a round-up. Each time he risked a beating with a truncheon or even something worse, but he was lucky. Finally, he hit on that smaller transport. Eighty inmates altogether – almost exclusively Jews from Łódź and a few from Hungary.

Of course, in this case he acted blindly; metaphorically speaking; he bet his entire fortune, that is his life, on one colour. Or rather it was a game of Russian roulette with the difference that, in its German camp system version, only one bullet was missing in the chamber.

A journey into the unknown. You flee the gas and you do not know if something worse awaits you. Although one had to admit that the beginning looked encouraging, and even led to some optimism. Before they entered the freight car, each inmate obtained a loaf of bread! This was unusual generosity on the part of the Germans. And still before that, an unexpected flash of joy: when formed in a column they passed near the women's camp and he caught a glimpse of his wife. Dressed in some rag, her hair cut off, but alive and healthy ...

Even the freight car into which they were loaded greeted

them with the comfort of a bucket in which to relieve themselves ... They stood near a little boarded-up window. Through the cracks between the boards, the last rays of the dying evening penetrated into the car. He concealed the loaf of bread in his bosom, delighting in its aroma and oval shape. He carefully broke off a small piece and ate it, chewing slowly. He knew, although it was devilishly tempting, that he must not eat it all at once. He had already had the experience of what such a lack of self-restraint resulted in.

There were around 20 of them in the freight car, and that was a luxury in itself. Among them were three doctors from the Łódź ghetto. In the next freight car, there was apparently a fourth one. A strange assortment, and at that entirely accidental. From the ghetto doctors who found themselves in Auschwitz, only one found work in accordance with his qualifications. The rest were either liquidated during the selection or designated by the SS for sale.

He squatted down in a corner and fell asleep immediately. He woke up the several times that the train suddenly slowed down with a screech or jerked suddenly forward. At one moment it appeared to him that in the darkness a hand was reaching under his head where he had hidden his bread. He woke up and placed the loaf behind his back for certainty – he now covered it with his whole body. The cracks between the boards were constantly black. From time to time the blackness was broken by the light of a single lamp that someone had not properly covered. When he woke up for the fourth or fifth time, he urgently felt the need to relieve himself. He went over to the bucket, but it was already full to the brim. In the thick darkness he noticed one of his travelling companions who, urged by the same need, simply stood near the door and relieved himself though the narrow crack. He tried to do the same. It proved to be not very difficult.

He squatted down again in a corner. He ate a piece of bread and fell asleep again. When he woke up, keen cold air, together with a pale morning light, was penetrating the freight car through the cracks in the door. The pale morning light brought out from the black background gray and extinguished human faces. Near him, with his back leaning against the wall, stood a Jew from Berlin – a doctor.

'Do you know in which direction we are going?

'As far as I can tell to the west, always to the west,' said the other.

'We must have travelled far. We've already travelled for about ten hours. At least.'

'We had long stops.'

He ate another piece of bread, then got up. His neighbours looked at him, surprised. Suddenly the train began to slow down and finally stopped. Initially nothing happened. After a few minutes, they heard the familiar noisy exhortations from the outside. The doors of the freight car opened with a rattle and after a while they were blinded by the daylight that entered. The SS men who had escorted them from Auschwitz looked in. They ordered them to get out and line up in fives. A non-commissioned SS officer counted them carefully and was pleased to assure himself that no one had run away, no one had died, and that no one had been added during the journey.

The morning was as cool as it usually is at the end of October. Another half-hour passed before they were formed in a column ready to march out. They crossed some railway tracks and suddenly found themselves in a wide-open space, and before them, far away, an extended panorama at the end of which were snow-covered mountain peaks. This was certainly not the Tatra Mountains or the Alps. He thought that the Berlin doctor who was in the same row as he was should be best oriented as to where they were.

'Where are we actually?'

'Those are the Riesengebirge.'

Riesengebirge? Giant mountains? He had never heard of them and they did not look like giants.

'Where are those mountains?'

'In the Sudeten. We are almost certainly in the Sudeten.'

It was Emil Vogel, the doctor from Prague, who marched behind them who said it. The one from Berlin was Heinz Hirschfeld. He boasted that he was a nephew of Professor Magnus Hirschfeld, a specialist in the area of sexuality whose popular scientific books bordering on pornography were in vogue after the First World War. A fourth one in this group of doctors was the dentist Loewi, also from Berlin.

They now walked along a paved road, and on the right side they noticed a sign with the inscription 'Hirschberg' nailed to a pole. So they were in Hirschberg, Jelenia Góra in Polish. That name, like the name Riesengebirge, had not meant anything to him at that time.

They marched in silence. Slowly they began to approach a city. He reached in his bosom and again broke off a piece of bread. He noticed with satisfaction that the others had no more bread left. He was proud that he could impose on himself such discipline, which was so much more difficult to do since he was stalked by hunger all the time.

After a while the uneven clatter of their steps – most inmates wore wooden clogs – resounded with an ever more prolonged echo through the clean streets framed by beautiful colourful houses with small windows like in dolls' houses. Some of the houses were green, some yellow, a few red, and the shutters were painted dark brown. No traces of the war were noticeable. It must have still been quite early because the streets were almost empty. At one moment he heard Hirschfeld, who was marching to the right of him, whisper:

'I have something to ask you. Switch places with me.'

'Of course,' he said surprised. 'What is the difference?'
They changed places, and now Hirschfeld marched to the left of him.

'I often used to come skiing here … I would not like an acquaintance to see me here …'

He was so surprised by that answer that he even stopped.

'Are you ashamed? For Heaven's sake! What are you ashamed of?'

'You know. In this striped uniform, I look like a criminal. What would they think of me?'

He wanted to say something insulting but restrained himself. He never could fathom the mentality of the German Jews. And in addition to this, he could never change it. He looked askance at Hirschfeld to see whether he was hiding his face from the side of the pavement …

They had been walking through the middle of the town for probably half an hour already. The first passers-by began to appear. Mostly women. No one paid the least attention to them. No one even turned their heads to look at them. As if nothing had been happening, as if the middle of the pavement had not been taken up by prisoners escorted by armed SS men. This had not been a lack of interest. This had been the fear of noticing something unpleasant or possibly even demonic. Disappear! The fear of an evil power, an apparition that might bring misfortune when looked at.

'We do not exist and never did,' mumbled Vogel from behind – he also had noticed the Germans' behaviour.

After marching for an hour, some of them already very tired, they at last reached the gate of a camp surrounded by barbed wire. They stopped, because a column of prisoners was passing through the gate, most likely on the way to work. That sight had not inspired optimism. The prisoners' faces were mostly emaciated, often completely black. The majority dragged their feet as if saving their energy for later, when they would have to work. The departing prisoners passed by the incoming ones with indifference. The newcomers, however, were observing the column of slaves that passed them by with curiosity and attempted to read from their faces what to expect in the immediate future.

After a while they found themselves inside the camp. Again, a roll call. Everything tallied. The Auschwitz SS men jokingly handed over the delivered merchandise to the local SS.

They were led into the first barrack on the right side, which was both a kind of canteen and an office. They were ordered to sit at long tables on which there were plates and cups. He had to admit that all this made quite a friendly impression in contrast to the appearance of the prisoners who went out to work. He sat between Vogel and Hirschfeld. He again broke off a big morsel of bread. No more than a quarter of the loaf remained for later. Two prisoners came in carrying a cauldron. With a wooden ladle, they poured each newcomer a portion of watery and tasteless soup. Pieces of turnip swam in it … But it was hot, and they ate it with reverence. A quarter of an hour had passed. Nothing happened. Apparently, they were allowed to rest. Some dozed off and smiled in their sleep … Perhaps they dreamt of a wonderful world in which everyone would get as much watery turnip soup as his heart desired.

Suddenly they heard a noise at the door. Five uniformed SS men entered the barrack. The camp inmates snapped to attention and took off their caps. One of the SS men summoned to him one of the inmates who had previously brought in the soup. He in turn addressed the new arrivals and announced to them that when representatives of the German authorities come in, they were required to stand up and take off their caps.

Swiftly, as on command, they stood up along the tables. One of the SS men generously allowed them to sit down. Together with the others, he walked slowly through the barrack and looked closely at each of them as if he wanted to memorize well all those emaciated, gray faces. When the review had ended, he said loudly:

'Let all the doctors stand up!'

He thought to himself that everything was beginning to remind him of Auschwitz.

All four of them stood up. Vogel, Hirschfeld, Loewi and he.

'Does anyone else have the title of doctor?'

Quite a strange question in those circumstances. But he did not have the time to think about it. One short, bulky, not-so-young man responded to this call. It turned out that he came from Prague, he was a doctor of laws and his name was Joachim.

The SS men exchanged some remarks among themselves. Afterwards each of them approached one of the standing doctors and ordered him to accompany him. Vogel, who resembled a shaved Don Quixote, looked the most serious of them. The Oberscharführer himself took him along with him. He, however, was approached by a short non-commissioned officer with the rank of Unterscharführer. The SS man had long arms as if to compensate him for his short legs. In general, he had in him little of the military bearing but was rather comical.

'Follow me,' he said.

He led him out of the canteen. They entered a nearby barrack. From the outside, this barrack was cleaner than the others. It struck the eyes with its fresh green colour. Several entrances led inside. The inside of the barrack was divided into many rooms. The SS man opened the door of one and let him in ahead. In the room, there was a small table, several chairs, a cabinet for paper, and that was all. On the table stood a typewriter. Heavy curtains protected the inside from indiscreet eyes. He looked around anxiously in search of the tools the Gestapo usually used in their interrogations. He did not notice anything of the kind, which made him even more anxious.

The SS man sat down at the table and loosened the belt that was squeezing him. He pushed out a second chair and ordered him to sit down across from him. After a while he pulled out a box of cigarettes.

'Do you smoke?'

He was dumbfounded. This very gesture on the part of the Unterscharführer was unusual, to say the least. And besides, the German addressed him by the polite '*Sie*'. The war was already in its sixth year. During that time he came across many SS men, and they had always addressed him by the familiar '*Du*'. His hand trembling from excitement, he reached for a cigarette. He had done it so clumsily that the rest of the bread that was concealed between the coat and the jacket fell to the floor. He bent down and swiftly picked it up, and even more swiftly he picked up the crumbs that befouled the cleanliness of the room. He collected them and stuffed them into his mouth. Afterwards, somewhat embarrassed, he glanced at the SS man who sat across from him. He had not moved and his face was absolutely expressionless. The SS man lit his own cigarette and then extended the lighted match to him. He inhaled deeply and of course choked. But the cigarette, the first one after four months, tasted very good. He inhaled again and inquiringly, or rather expectantly, glanced at the SS man. The SS man sat immersed in thought and looked around the room. Finally, he looked at him.

'I wanted to ask you something,' he said.

He spoke quite softly, and no threat or even an attempt to frighten him, as was usual with the Germans, could be detected in his voice (by screaming they excited themselves and gave themselves courage). The next sentence was thrown out slowly and thoughtfully as if the SS man had not been sure until the last moment if he should utter it.

'I wanted to ask you whether it is … that means whether all that is being said about Auschwitz is true.'

A pause. And then:

155

'You may answer in Polish if it is more convenient. I understand it ...'

He could not believe his own ears. First he inhaled once more, then he held his breath and, finally, moved clumsily on the chair. Before he had the time to say anything, the SS man added:

'I understand that you are afraid, afraid to tell the truth. But you yourself realize perfectly well that if I am asking about a thing like that it is not with the purpose, depending on your answer, to hang or shoot you. I can after all do it in any case. I am only asking you to tell me the truth ...'

He froze with the cigarette smoke in his lungs. He choked again. He did various things to delay his answer and to think. In spite of the assurances of his interlocutor, he was not at all convinced that he should tell the whole truth. Initially he tried to formulate in his thoughts some evasive answer, but suddenly he realized that he could not concentrate and formulate a few coherent sentences in German. Because he had decided to speak in German. He renewed the attempt to choke ... After a while however he calmed down enough to conclude that the German's reasoning made sense. Indeed, he could at any moment kill him regardless of what he would hear.

'What ... what do you want to know?'

'I want to know if it is true that in Auschwitz gas chambers are operating and that in them Jews are being killed with a special gas, Zyklon B.'

This was said in a dispassionate voice. As if the content of the question concerned a book just read or the latest society gossip.

'That is true.'

'How do you know?'

'In Auschwitz everyone knows about it. Even at the station, on the railway platform, your people ...' He halted and changed the formulation of the sentence. 'Even at the station a selection is made. Only those Jews who are still capable of physical work pass to the camp. It is only so lately. Previously all the Jews had been gassed. Now only the elderly people, the sick, the women with children and the children themselves are sent to the gas chambers. Later the corpses are

156

incinerated in the crematoria ovens. At times they are also burned in pits arranged in stacks ...'

The SS man stopped looking at him. Slowly he bent his head and tapped on the tabletop some rhythm with his fingers.

'The gas chambers are located in buildings that look like bath-houses,' he now talked with increasing haste. He was afraid the German would interrupt him. 'There are even shower taps there to make the gas chambers look like real bath-houses... In Auschwitz no one makes a secret of it.'

At the end of his report, he still wanted to ask if here in Hirschberg they really did not know anything about it, but restrained himself. It could have appeared that he had wanted to take over the initiative in this conversation, and even in some sense to take advantage of his superiority, the superiority of a man who had been there. That the German could possibly not forgive him ... He fell silent. Besides ... If the other one really did not know, he knows now. For a moment he was anxious because he was not the only one who had been submitted to a similar interrogation. And what if the others denied it out of fear?

'Are transports of Jews still coming to Auschwitz?'

'Sir, in Poland there are probably no more Jews left. The Łódź ghetto, the last one, was liquidated ... I think that transports of Hungarian Jews are still coming, but I do not know this for certain.'

He could still have told him how in general the life of the Auschwitz slave workers looked, how constant selections were being made in the camp itself, how the extermination system worked in all its stages, but he restrained himself from this too. Primarily because to continue his account would only weaken the impression of the first, brief report. The rest would make as much sense as to explain the punch line of a joke. And besides, he had no idea what the conditions were in this camp. The local SS men might not have known what was happening in Auschwitz, but they could have been a hundred times worse than their Auschwitz colleagues.

Silence prevailed in the room. The SS man sat immersed in thought. After a while he lit another cigarette.

'I thank you,' he said briefly and stood up from the table.

He got up also. Immediately before leaving the barrack, he extinguished his cigarette. Smoking in the company of a German could after all be interpreted as an inclination to excessive chumminess ...

In the barrack, where the other inmates of the transport had been gathered, he already found Vogel and Loewi. Both were as white as a sheet. Vogel was wiping the sweat from his forehead.

'I certainly look like them,' he thought.

He sat down at the table and did not say a word. He looked from one to the other and tried to read from their faces how their interrogation by the SS had gone.

He was still worrying whether each of them said the same thing, whether anyone had got cold feet. Finally he could not restrain himself and asked Vogel:

'Did he want to know about Auschwitz?'

Vogel just nodded.

'What did you tell him?'

'Well ... As it is ...'

After a while Joachim came in, and after a few seconds – Hirschfeld. He was the one who worried him the most. It seemed everyone told the same story as he. This fact calmed him, although it was actually difficult to explain rationally why it did so. As if the fact that their testimonies agreed with his could in any way influence the individual situation of each of them.

Joachim who was silent until now, made a comment which seemed to him very much to the point and answered their need to look into the future with confidence ...

'Could something like that have occurred a few years ago, or even a year ago? They know that this is the end.'

Vogel, who was a realist, was indignant but did not say a word.

Later they were put in various barracks. Luckily, he and Emil were put in the same barrack. That was the barrack allocated to the inmates who worked at loading and unloading coal.

In the evening when the lights in the barrack went out, he sat down at Vogel's plank-bed. He absolutely had to ask him some things.

158

'Did your German say anything about the necessity of keeping a secret?'

'No, why.'

'Neither did mine. And you know why? Because regardless of anything, we are like bedbugs so far as they are concerned. And bedbugs do not count. One does not ask bedbugs to keep a secret ...'

Vogel nodded.

'And at that bedbugs that will croak in a month or two in any case, before this whole game is finished ...'

The next day, when they were preparing to go out for the first time to the coal yard, Vogel summed up the whole incident somehow by saying:

'This is what occurred to me ... Perhaps those SS men also intended something more? It is true that they wanted to learn from us what was really happening there, but perhaps they also wanted us to know that they did not know the whole truth about Auschwitz? I'll tell you something. If at any time I had to give evidence before a court examining the crimes of the SS, I would not mention this conversation, which could be used by someone somewhere as an extenuating circumstance, although this conversation could be considered abnormal ... I give you my word ...'

They began to work at the coal yard.

In March of the last year of the war, when he and Emil found themselves somewhere else, at the camp of Cieplice (to which Joachim had been sent out before them), the Jelenia Góra camp was evacuated deep into Germany. Most of the inmates perished. Some from hunger and cold, others were shot by the SS men among who could have been the ones who had interrogated them ... During that evacuation Hirschfeld and Loewi perished. Joachim died when the Cieplice camp was evacuated. The only survivors had been he and Vogel.

Doctor Emil Vogel died several years after the end of the war. He could not carry on living when he learned that his wife, whom he adored, had been burned alive in one of the women's camps in Germany ...

And he? No one called him as a witness before a court.

However, he decided to write at some time about the interrogation at the Jelenia Góra camp. It was not because in the 40 years after the war the spark of hatred was extinguished in him. Oh no! But because he had recognized that no one was allowed to take to his grave even the least important fact that supplemented the knowledge of the times of the gas chambers and crematoria ovens. And if someone could use it as an argument in the defence of a case that was indefensible, that was too bad.

11 Maks Bejgelman[1]

The little camp hospital, or *revier*, together with the dressing-station and the doctor's residence, was a part of the wooden barrack. The rest of the barrack was used as storage space, and the stench of rotting vegetables was constantly seeping out from there. In the barrack there were also two closets which had been used as a morgue.

He had already lain in the *revier* for coming up to two weeks. From the moment that he appeared in the *revier*, holding all he possessed – the broken tin spoon – in his hand he wondered what motivated the camp doctor Neumann to pretend that he did not recognize his malingering and to take him in for observation. After all, he was without a doubt potentially a competitor for Neumann. But since he was much younger, his chances of replacing Neumann were decidedly small. The Third Reich needed young people like him for hard physical work, not for healing Jews. Healing Jewish inmates would have been a luxury in times of victory, but it was even more so in face of the troubles caused by defeat.

Whatever it was, he was there, and for over ten days he did not have to go out to the coal yard. Apparently Neumann could afford such largesse. In exchange for it, he acquired in him a nurse, an orderly, a cleaner and a messenger, all in one person …

Four light bulbs wrapped in dirty red tissue in the four corners of the ceiling threw a gloomy light onto the ward. The *revier* was submerged in semi-darkness. Grunts, moans, gasps and heavy breathing interrupted by coughing were fused into the homogeneous background noise that accompanied the last minutes of those who were departing into the dusk that was free of the Germans.

Night after night the same thing was repeating itself. Night after night he tried to detach himself from the atmosphere of suffering and dying by turning into himself. He had understood for a long time that without an escape into the past and without dreams of the future the present was unbearable.

The sick inmate who was lying on the same plank-bed as him moaned with the wail of a little monkey that wanted motherly attention. He delicately pushed aside the blanket that covered his neighbour. For a moment, he observed his gray-brownish face. He knew since yesterday that what he was looking at was reminiscent of dying rather than of sleep.

When twelve days previously he stood at the door of the *revier*, almost all the places on the 22 person plank-beds had been taken. Only one place had remained unoccupied. Before he went over to the plank-bed and occupied the empty place, he guessed – guessed? No! He knew for certain with whom he would have to share the mattress that was filled with wood shavings, who was the patient with whom he would have to spend the following days and nights in a contact as close as the intimacy of lovers. Therefore he was not surprised when, coming nearer, he noticed the bulging eyes of Maks Bejgelman fixed on him through glasses in a thin frame, and heard his melodious voice: 'Good morning, doctor!' This was a greeting in accordance with tradition. So, it was Maks Bejgelman again. People call it by a variety of names: accident, fate, or destiny.

He knew Maks Bejgelman from Łódź. From the Łódź of yesteryear, from before the war. From the Łódź that was coloured with his own youth and that was as unreal as a myth or a legend. Maks's father, Dawid, had been a well-known Jewish musician, the composer of many light and more serious musical works. By the means of little theatres such as the 'Azazel' or the 'Ararat,' or by means of ensembles cobbled together for some occasion, his musical works reached the sad, gray dwellings of tailors, shoemakers, merchants, the storekeepers of Nowomiejska Street and the vegetable merchants of Wschodnia Street. It was Jewish music in an unadulterated wrapping. In the ghetto, Dawid Bejgelman founded a symphony orchestra. Each of its concerts was a cultural and social event and even a pitiful political one since it usually ended with a speech by the Eldest.[2]

He attended the same *gymnasium* as Maks, except that Maks was five years older than he and five grades ahead. Maks was nearing graduation when he was still a twelve-year-old youngster in the second grade. Their first accidental encounter took place on the third floor of the school, in the hall on the right. That was where the school lavatory was located.

Even at school, Maks had an unusually elegant bearing. He behaved with distinction, expressed himself exquisitely, and even buttoned his trousers with grace. Such elegance and exquisiteness had characterized his whole life.

His whole life? Instinctively he looked at the figure nearby, which was wrapped in a blanket. Elegance and exquisiteness had characterized Maks as long as his world had not found itself within the reach of madness and had not been pushed off its tracks into an abyss.

There, in the lavatory on the third floor, they discovered that they liked each other. It stood to reason that Maks had impressed him. But he could never understand why that exquisite young man took to him. In any case, Maks had led him across the threshold of the first indispensable experiences of a twelve-year-old. In the first place, he taught him to smoke cigarettes. It was to him that he owed the first inhalation of cigarette smoke and the nausea connected with it. Thanks to Maks he also acquired the theoretical foundations of extra-curricular sex education, and primarily the knowledge that the most effective method of protecting oneself from venereal disease was to avoid urinating against the wind.

At the time smoking was a very severely punishable crime. Smoking cigarettes on the school premises was especially severely punished ... And he, a twelve-year-old, had been smoking cigarettes at school. He smoked them in the lavatory on the third floor, exhaling the smoke into the toilet bowl, in the traditional manner. He could therefore say that Maks, by teaching him to smoke cigarettes, had freed in him the reserves of courage that would have otherwise lain dormant. True, that courage had not been used in the most appropriate way. But one does not choose the ways to demonstrate one's manliness when one is twelve years old. What is most important is the first test ...

He heard a sick inmate drag himself down from the plank-bed and approach the bucket swaying. The bucket, needed emptying. At this time, it was certainly already full. Besides, that was one of his duties, this was how he paid for the right to be freed from work at the coal yard. Returning to his plank-bed, the sick inmate stumbled and fell. The bang of the fall disturbed for a while the monotonous background noise of groans and moans that accompanied the uneven struggle between the angels of life and the angels of death.

It so happened that Maks's family had changed their residence and, for a few months, Maks and he walked to school together. Their route took them along Narutowicza Street, through the Dąbrowski Square, Nowotargowa Street (later called Sterling Street), and Południowa Street. How proudly he looked at his peers who passed him when he was in the company of Maks! ... But shortly after that Maks had graduated and in the years that followed he disappeared from his life.

The time came when he too had graduated. He had no doubts about the direction that his life would take. At the time he was fascinated with the possibilities of medicine and dreamt of successes in prolonging human life. Castles in the air. He already saw himself a laureate of the Nobel Prize. But to study in Poland was out of the question. While Poland had at that time one of the smallest per capita number of doctors, a Jew had to have extraordinary luck, extraordinary pull or an extraordinary amount of money to be accepted into a faculty of medicine in the country. Young Jews were leaving for France, Italy, Yugoslavia or Austria because there was no place for them in the universities at home. They were unwelcome candidates for university places from which they were barred by a *numerus clausus* or a *numerus nullus*. Those who succeeded in being accepted to university were shown the fist of ghetto benches[3] that had the blessing of the clergy and the professors ... At a family council, his father had made an exact calculation of his financial resources and concluded eventually that he could support his only son at a university abroad.

He chose France. On the advice of authorities on this problem, within France he chose Rouen, the capital of Normandy. His father's finances had not allowed him to choose Paris. The only thing he knew about Rouen was that Jeanne D'Arc had been burned on a pyre there. A year previously, the whole press had elaborated on it on the occasion of the 500th anniversary of that 'regrettable error'. When he came to Rouen he started to learn many interesting things about that city. For instance, that it had a splendid cathedral, one of the largest in Europe. That Flaubert had been born there and made Madame Bovary walk its streets. And that it had the largest river port in Europe and that the largest rats in Europe ran around there. That the highest rainfall in France was noted there and the city therefore acquired the nickname of 'the chamber pot of France' – and that Maks Bejgelman was studying medicine there.

In the five years since his graduation, Maks had managed, after three attempts, to pass the entrance year examination to medical school. Many Polish Jews studied in Rouen. In the entrance year, out of the 110 students, 40 were Jews from Poland, 30 from Romania, over ten from South America, and the negligible remaining number were Frenchmen.

How few of those Polish Jews who studied abroad finished their studies! The fate of many of them was a genuine epic of effort and struggle that ended more often in defeat than in victory. They were lucky if they paid for their defeat only with the loss of their illusions and with several years of their lives. Often however they paid the highest price. How numerous were those who, due to lack of character, could not defend themselves against the temptations with which the broad world had been luring them. Suddenly the world had opened to the young people who had not yet shaken off the dust of the provincial little towns. They were the ones who fell to the bottom the soonest, and life, the stormy life of the 1920s and 1930s, covered up their fall just as quicksand buries its victims. The best of the young Jewish intelligentsia were coming to France – from Galicia, the former Congress Poland, from the 'kresy'.[4] While some of them came here simply because of the fat wallets and inflated ambitions of their parents, there were also many young people who were brilliant and talented and of which any country would have been proud.

Maks quickly learned of his arrival in Rouen. In a flash, he surrounded him with his benevolent patronage. It was not of course the kind of patronage a young inexperienced person, who found himself alone far from his homeland, would need. It was patronage of a strictly selective character. Maks assumed that the newcomer from Poland would manage without him in dealing with such insignificant and marginal matters as course registration, the purchase of textbooks, use of the library and even finding a suitable residence. There remained however matters in Maks's field of interests in which his competence was irreplaceable.

First of all, Maks became his guide to the coffee-houses of Rouen. Maks had been a well-known and well-liked figure in all the large and small coffee-houses of that port city. Coffee-house life was connected with another interest of Maks's. In the coffee-houses was concentrated everything that had to do with the green table, with card games. And Maks Bejgelman was an ace in each of those games. He taught him the principles of bellotte, introduced him to the complexities of bridge, of blackjack and baccarat, and above all infected him with the addiction to and admiration for poker. And what a poker player Maks was! In France he later met another ace in poker who was equal to Maks. This was Bimba-Dowbór, the son of the famous general Dowbór-Muśnicki. He was well known to the students of Toulouse. He came to Toulouse sometime in the middle of the 1920s. When his father had stopped the flow of money from Poland, money that the son devoted to purposes that had nothing to do with his studies, Bimba was faced with the necessity of earning money. And he began to earn it by passing year after year examinations in mathematics, physics and chemistry for other students in all the learning institutions of Toulouse where he was not yet known. Of course, he collected a hefty fee for it. He also played poker for others, taking for himself a percentage of the winnings. He never failed an examination. He never lost at poker.

But neither was Maks just anybody. So, he readily submitted to his practical and theoretical teaching and advice. Besides, Maks had guided his protégé in such a charming manner that it was difficult not to benefit from his instruction.

Luckily, luckily he was able to separate his two fields of interest during the entrance year of his studies. To separate the Academy of Maks from the Academy of Paris to which the

Rouen school was subordinated. To separate the cards from his studies.

Maks had already waved goodbye to his studies a long time before. But his goodbye wave had so much charm that any attempt to bring the prodigal son back to the path of righteousness would only arouse distaste ... The path of righteousness? What was for Maks the path of righteousness?

He continued to have his elegant bearing. Besides, he had not changed his tastes in dress. He always wore a double-breasted navy-blue suit and gray spats over black shoes. He must have been receiving enough money from his father to permit him to lead the life of an authentic dandy. Because this son of a Łódź Jewish musician was indeed one of the last real dandies. He spoke excellent French and apparently frequented the most exclusive homes of Rouen.

Maks fully respected the extravagant, according to him, approach of his younger friend to his studies. Since the latter was such an eccentric and decided to study, he had no choice but to accept it. On the other hand, he was generous with his praise for the progress that his younger friend had been making in the different specialities of the green table.

At the end of the academic year, he could devote increasingly less time to Maks and his pastimes. He passed the examinations of the entrance year and returned to Poland for his vacation. And again Maks disappeared from his life because Maks remained in Rouen while he transferred to Toulouse for the first year of medicine.

Indeed, the bucket needed emptying. At this time, it was certainly overflowing. He slid down heavily from the mattress, put on his wooden clogs and by squeezing himself through between the plank-beds came to the corner where the urine bucket stood on a low wooden stool. In spite of Neumann's strict prohibition, it also served the sick inmates for more serious needs. Because only a few of the sick inmates had the strength to use the camp latrine that was in the next barrack. The bucket was indeed full. The floor around it was wet. Carrying out the bucket was no easy task. First, it was heavy; and second, by going outside the *revier* one exposed oneself not only to the freezing wind that came from the mountains but also to the danger of slipping. The steps leading to the *revier* were completely iced over, and walking on them while wearing wooden clogs was no mean feat. The first night, unaware of the danger, he slipped and fell, and spilled the content of the bucket on himself. Now he was experienced. Night after night, he emptied the bucket at least twice, and several times during the day he supplied the *revier* and the dressing-station with fresh water. This time also he successfully overcame the obstacles, emptied the bucket, rinsed it and returned to the *revier*. He wiped off the floor with paper and, completely stiff from the cold, returned quickly under the blanket. His neighbour had not even moved. For many hours he had not changed his position …

About a year before the outbreak of the war, that is five years after parting with Maks at Rouen, he met him again by chance. That meeting was grotesque, as in a cheap comedy film. After passing the fifth year of medical examinations, he was returning for a vacation to Łódź. He was returning via Paris, as usual. Somewhere in Belgium, he happened to hear that in one of the adjacent railway coaches a student from Poland was collecting donations among the passengers. He claimed that he had lost his money for a return ticket. He did not have to look long for that student … He recognized him after all from afar, by the navy-blue suit and the gray spats. When Maks saw him, he was at first somewhat disconcerted, but soon he realized that the heavens had sent him help. He took him as a witness who could testify that he was a man of pristine integrity who deserved assistance. At that time, he was greatly amused by the situation. Indeed, due to his intervention, Maks succeeded in collecting enough money not only for a ticket but also to invite him to the restaurant coach for dinner. There he admitted that he had had a streak of bad luck with cards. As happens in poker, one may lose not only the money sent by a father for a ticket, but the whole family fortune …

They parted at the Łódź train station. The following year was supposed to be the last year of his studies. And it was. Then history intervened. War was in the air. He barely managed to return to his homeland. A few weeks later came the beginning of the end of the world. He found himself in the cogs of war, although this war was not entirely as he had imagined it. The flight on foot from Łódź to Warsaw. Work in the Warsaw hospitals during the siege. The return to Łódź. The flight of his parents to Warsaw when his father felt threatened by arrest. Work in the first-aid service, ghetto... The world went backward by a few centuries.

In the ghetto, he did not have the time or the occasion to take any interest in Maks's destiny. Several times he saw Maks's father on the conductor's podium. At concerts by the doomed for the doomed. At that time, of course, he did not see it that way ... He was not the only one, besides. He became the head of an infirmary on Brzezińska Street. And at that time, Maks appeared. In a navy-blue suit but already without the spats, which must have drowned somewhere in the ghetto mud. Without the spats but with a certificate that he was a qualified nurse, and with a little case that contained everything that a qualified nurse required. He was posted specifically to him, to work at Brzezińska Street. This was probably due to his father's influence. But what did it matter in the end? There were never too many nurses in the ghetto. And thus their paths had met again. And this time again not for long. Maks worked very well. Everyone praised him – the doctors as well as the patients. Shortly afterwards Maks was transferred to work at the hospital. Besides, he himself did not remain the head of that infirmary for long either. He got sick with abdominal typhus. Various complications ensued ...

It seemed to him that his neighbour on the mattress had said something. He bent over him and drew the blanket aside. Maks had his eyes open and actually tried to bring out some words. But from his mouth came only a mumbling whisper – a soundless complaint. Or perhaps a request? He went over quickly to the still clean bucket and placed it near the bunk bed so that the sick man could relieve himself. But Maks said no with a motion of his head. He distinctly wanted to say something. So, he put the bucket back. When he returned, Maks lay with his back to him, his head covered by some miracle with the blanket. He was barely breathing. The blanket with which Maks was covered was barely lifting.

He lay down again.

When the ghetto had been liquidated, he could only guess that Maks also wound up in Auschwitz. They did not meet until the moment he found himself in the small group of 80 inmates that was sent out from Auschwitz somewhere deep into Germany. And it was in this group that he came across Maks. This was all the more surprising because he himself performed risky escapes and even neck-breaking tricks not to be caught by the SS for a larger transport. He recognized that being sent out in such a small transport was like winning the camp lottery. And here in the same group was Maks again who greeted him cordially: 'Greetings, doctor!' as if they had just met in a Łódź coffeehouse ... The navy-blue suit was clearly out of the question. With some imagination one could at the most notice traces of the former navy-blue colour in the striped camp uniform ...

This time their paths had met only for a while. In Jelenia Góra, where the transport had arrived, they found themselves in two different detachments. That meant that when his detachment worked during the day, Maks's worked at night. So, this way he lost contact with Maks again.

As the days grew colder, work at the coal yard was turning into an ever-greater ordeal. For the first time during the war, he felt that he was declining and coming to the end of his rope. And that nothing could stop his eventual downfall. Then he hit on the idea of malingering. He had nothing to lose. He pretended that he was suffering from some undetermined kidney ailment and found himself in the *revier*. And he was not at all surprised when at that time he found Maks beside the only vacant place in the whole hospital. It had to be this way. Did he rejoice? In any event, it was better to have Maks for a neighbour than someone to whom he could not open his mouth, although those were not the times or circumstances conducive to social conversations.

Being able to freely move around the *revier*, he was in a better situation than Maks. And the fact that he was doing something, and that Neumann from time to time had been using him, had also been of some benefit to poor Maks.

Poor Maks ... As soon as he saw him in the *revier*, he knew that Maks's future was rather bleak. He had a spread-out phlegmona of the sole. From experience, he knew how such cases finish in camp conditions. If all the signs in the skies and on the ground indicated that the end of the war was approaching with fast steps, none of those signs predicted that Maks Bejgelman had a chance of being present at Germany's final encounter with defeat. He was becoming weaker each day. He was feverish.

As his sickness progressed, fascinating changes began to take place in Maks's behaviour. It seemed that due to the jumps in his temperature there occurred a breakdown in the connections between his nerve cells, but only in one part of his brain. This had not expressed itself in the loss of contact with the world or in feverish raving. It had been the sudden concentration of all his mental functions on one, and only one, group of matters from the past. When in the evening his fever was rising, a stream of reflections on card games began flowing from Maks's mouth. Maks's entire gambling past, and possibly even the gambling past of his ancestors that was encoded in some unknown manner, could be found in that stream ... Indeed there were well-known cases of sick persons in fever or during a loss of consciousness, suddenly beginning to speak in strange, unknown languages which later appeared to have been the languages of remote ancestors. Only that to Maks the language of cards had not been strange. Oh no! What he was saying involved unusual baccarat sequences, extraordinary bridge arrangements, and even very surprising and dramatic poker game meetings. All this was mixed up and grew to cosmic dimensions. Of course, it was difficult to know how much of it had been morbid imagination and how much had been authentic memory of his or someone else's defeats and successes ...

Also he began to play an ever more important role in Maks's reminiscences – he, his pupil, his card-game pupil whom fate had placed on the same plank-bed, on the same mattress. So that in the last minutes of his life the master could remind him of his various mistakes, errors and oversights. Maks remembered them. He either remembered them or created them in his sick imagination. He had created a card-game reality at the centre of which were only the two of them. After such a series of reproaches or charges, like an experienced actor showing off the range of his abilities, he suddenly transformed himself from an accuser into an accused. He begged for forgiveness. He felt guilty that it had been he,

Maks, who taught him to smoke cigarettes and put him in the danger of expulsion from school. He was remorseful that he had made him a gambler, that he had almost ruined his life ... There was no point in trying to persuade Maks that actually nothing like that had happened, that he had been able somehow to protect himself from the dangers to which Maks's teachings had exposed him ... In the state in which Maks had found himself nothing of course could reach him. Although if they could have had a normal conversation on this topic, perhaps he could have even thanked Maks. Perhaps ...

As Maks had been deteriorating, as he was weakening, he began on the one hand to show him greater respect, and on the other hand to stress his own dignity. It was as if Maks wanted there, in that camp *revier*, to show to everyone what good manners he had, how he had been able even in those conditions to retain his pride ... He never for instance addressed him in the familiar manner ... He could not get off the plank-bed, and it was necessary to bring him the bucket every few hours, and when Maks had been sitting on it, it was necessary to support him. But each time Maks thanked him so elegantly, one could say so charmingly, as if all this had been taking place in an English club among gentlemen with titles.

The *revier* had been rustling with quiet complaints and heavy breathing. Painful, disabled, maltreated, stinking bodies swollen from hunger were clinging convulsively to their shitty lives. They were fighting for their lives, for the last thing they still possessed in the SS world, although nothing indicated that another world would compensate them for their present suffering. Everything indicated that the paws of the SS and the power of Hitler were reaching there also, and that the last roll call would be met by Satan and God together – in uniforms with a skull and cross-bones.

Maks lay motionless. His wide-open eyes did not react to anything. He checked his pulse and breathing ... It had happened. Their roads had met each other for so long until he brought Maks Bejgelman to the end of the last one.

He covered him carefully with the blanket. Over his head. Then he lay down near him and fell asleep.

In the morning, he acted as if nothing had happened.

Before the arrival of the camp doctor, he emptied the bucket once more. He swept and washed the floor. He took the temperature of several sick inmates, as if it had mattered. He thought for a while and also pushed the thermometer, under the blanket, into Maks. When the camp doctor came, he reported to him about the night and did not mention to him the death of the prisoner Bejgelman, number so and so. Ostentatiously he moved the bucket to the bunk bed on which Maks lay, the way he used to do several times a day. And he even managed to make it appear that he was helping the sick man. Then he talked to him, or rather pretended he was answering his questions. And when bread was distributed that day, he took Maks's portion for himself. That day the bread had been supplemented with a slice of sausage. Midday he took soup for Maks and ate it in the dressing-station so that no one would notice.

Apart from that, the day passed quietly. None of the SS men appeared in the *revier*, and Neumann gave up making rounds, as usual. In the evening, he again busied himself around Maks. He wiped his forehead with a wet rag. Then he lay down again near him and talked to him constantly.

Next morning he had to decide. Should he continue this game or stop it? Common sense dictated him to stop it. But hunger, a very bad adviser, urged him to repeat it. When Neumann came, and he reported to him in the morning again, he did not mention Maks. With a light shudder, he took Maks's portion of bread again. That day there was no supplement ... Automatically he repeated his actions of the previous day. Actually, he was doing everything automatically, though he realized that should one of the SS men peek under the blanket that covered Maks ... Besides, it would have been no better if Neumann had discovered the matter. He was risking his life to obtain a portion of bread ... And soup – he added in his mind as if he looked for one more reason for the risk he had taken.

The day dragged on into infinity. The frost outside and the cold inside the barrack were in his favour. Before the evening, the little Unterscharführer appeared in the door. Luckily, he only had some business with Neumann.

At night, he transferred Maks's corpse, with the help of one of the healthier prisoners, to the closet near the *revier*. In the morning, he reported to Neumann that inmate Bejgelman died at such and such an hour. Neumann filled out the little card used instead of a death certificate. That was a formality the Germans had observed scrupulously. Two hours later Maks' remains made their final trip in the camp cart to the furnace room of the factory.

When he put in order the part of the mattress that Maks had occupied, he found three pieces of dried out and mouldy bread there. When he soaked them in the soup, they had quite a decent taste.

He considered that as a posthumous bonus, a treat from Maks for the risk he took. When relatively sated he was falling asleep, his mind meandered over the topics of relativity of moral judgments and the merits of gambling, but he was unable to think those topics through to the end ...

Notes

1. Pronounced Max Beygelman.
2. Rumkowski.
3. See note 8 to Chapter 3.
4. 'Kresy' meant 'borderlands'. Basically, the eastern areas of pre-war Poland that were ceded after World War II to the Soviet Union.

12 The Goalkeeper

Before the world had become a cesspool, before this part of Europe was covered with ghettos and camps, ethics and the calling of a doctor were the values that he respected the most. He saw in them the proof of the uniqueness of humankind. He was convinced of that uniqueness before he decided to dedicate himself to medicine. He believed in those values whole-heartedly during his studies, not having had the occasion to experience values contrary to them. Soon, however, history had supplied him with many such occasions. The storm of the occupation brought to the surface an abundance of filth – filth and dried-out excreta into which the human conscience was transformed when it was exposed to the test of the concentration camps where life had been only a temporary pass issued during the selection. By instinct, the SS men knew who the people were that they could immediately use to execute their sadistic plans. Besides, they never doubted that the same fog and the same night that engulfed those who had not passed the sieve of the selection would engulf those who had temporarily remained alive. Night and fog.

The proposal with which Neumann, that Neumann, had approached him a while ago at first surprised and then scared him. If a German doctor had approached him with such a proposal, he would have accepted it as a matter of fact. Nothing coming from the Germans could surprise him. But Neumann, the doctor from Sosnowiec, had been after all the same rotting Jewish prisoner as the other 1,500 prisoners in that camp. The Germans, whether in uniform or in civilian clothes, caused in him the same reaction as the germs of tuberculosis or of venereal disease. They could kill him, destroy him, make him rot, but they could not offend him. On the other hand, this creature that prided himself in his white doctor's coat, succeeded in offending and degrading him with his unheard of proposal.

Neumann was the camp doctor at Hirschberg, He had no reason, and particularly no desire, to share with anybody the privileges that this position had given him. There were four doctors in the group of Jews sent from Auschwitz to replace the manpower that had been wiped out in Hirschberg. But they were sent immediately to the hard work at the coal yard. Neumann, who had been in the camp for more than a year already, did not have to go to work every day, he did not have to toil 12 hours a day loading and unloading frozen coal powder, he did not have to breathe in the coal dust. On the contrary, he had the advantage of extra food that he obtained from the kitchen head by barter. From time to time the SS men also threw a morsel of food his way, such as a few potatoes and left over bread.

He was pondering whether the basis on which his attitude to the doctor from Sosnowiec was developing had been jealousy. He had to admit, however, that Neumann had until now actually behaved loyally and even decently toward him. Could it have been because in the group of doctors that had come with the transport from Auschwitz he was the only one from Poland? It was difficult to suspect the camp doctor of this kind of sentiment, however.

Everything began when he became after a short time completely exhausted by his work at the coal yard. He quickly began to feel the consequences of the abdominal typhus and its many complications to which he had succumbed in the Łódź ghetto. Also hunger and the unbearable cold let themselves be felt. He understood that he was only one step away from the border beyond which he would become a *muselmann.* Then he would have only two prospects: he would either be sent back to Auschwitz, and after the next selection to the gas chamber, or he would croak here, in the camp hospital. He already saw his naked legs dangling from the camp cart that day after day carried the bountiful harvest of death to the boiler furnaces of the factory that made artificial wool.

He decided to defend himself. The only way open to him

was to stay in the little hospital for a period of time – the *revier* – as manpower still capable of being repaired. He therefore faked an attack of kidney pain. It was hard to tell whether Neumann saw through the ploy or not. Enough that he took him in into the *revier* and had prolonged his stay there for a few weeks. He therefore had the opportunity to remain in the warmth of the barrack for a period of time. Instead of toiling at the coal yard, he busied himself tidying up, cleaning the instruments and even taking care of the little pharmacy that was kept well supplied by the Germans.

Until the matter of the shot prisoner had suddenly surfaced.

The previous day, the SS men who guarded the prisoners at work brought to the *revier* a Hungarian Jew who had been shot by one of the SS. The wounded prisoner was put in a separate room. Only the camp doctor attended to him. In the evening, Neumann suddenly asked him whether he had ever administered anesthetic.

'I did. During the siege of Warsaw, but …'

'That is very good, I'll be able to use you.'

'For anesthesia?'

'Yes, for anesthesia. We are going to operate on the wounded.'

'Where was he shot?'

'One bullet went through a thigh, and the other smashed an elbow.'

'So what is there to operate on?'

'It will be necessary to operate on the elbow joint, set the bones, and in general …'

'Are you serious?'

'Very serious.'

'Do you intend in this barrack, in these conditions, without instruments, without the possibility to maintain cleanliness, to operate on an open joint?'

'The joint is smashed.'

'So don't operate.'

'I shall operate.'

'Have you ever performed an operation on a joint?'

'I must admit, no. Never. But I twice observed such an operation at the hospital.'

'Dear God! And you are going to undertake something like that in these conditions?'

'The SS men asked me whether I could perform such an operation.'

'And what have you told them?

' I said I could … They were very pleased.'

'What were they so pleased about?'

'That they will finally see a real operation. They have never seen anything like that.'

'You intend to operate in their presence?'

'We shall do it in their presence. You and I.'

'You are probably out of your mind! Do not count on me! I do not know whether you realize that for something like that you may be held accountable after the war.'

Neumann laughed out loud.

'After the war? When will that be? For me only today and tomorrow exist. And tomorrow the war will not be over yet. I suggest that you be guided by a similar philosophy.'

'You can do whatever you like. But I will not administer the anaesthetic.'

'As you wish. Do you prefer to return to work at the coal yard? If you do not help me, I'll discharge you. That is one thing. And the other – I shall operate without anaesthetic.'

'What?'

'You heard me. And now listen to me. The joint is smashed. If I do not try to operate on him immediately, that man will be sent to Auschwitz. Or to Gross-Rosen. And there they will certainly finish him off. In other words, he is doomed in any case. And I shall try to operate on him. I shall prolong his stay at the *revier,* and, in addition to this, I shall please our SS men who in this place are still not the worst. Perhaps they will reciprocate.'

He could not listen to that any longer. In his mind, he was digesting Neumann's proposal. The more he thought of it, the more the reasoning of the camp doctor seemed unreal to him, the product of a sick imagination. However, the experience of the war years had already taught him that ethics were after all the luxury of normal times – like oysters, Coty perfumes or an apartment at the Ritz. Let alone medical ethics … In the camps, where life was joined with death like a pair of lovers in an amorous embrace, medical ethics were becoming often an account containing insufficient funds. He recalled the little hospital at the so-called Gypsy camp at Brzezinka. It had been managed by two doctors from France. They introduced the practice of not giving food to a patient on the first day of his hospital stay. Those patients were simply starving. This was supposed to facilitate diagnosis ... As a matter of course, the doctors took those patients' portions of bread or soup for themselves. Such a diagnostic method only hastened the patients' death. But that was after all the point: the rotation of patients was thus speeded up, and a dead person's place on the hospital plank-bed was taken by the doctors' next supplier of bread and soup which were after all not only nourishment but also a currency more valuable than gold in Auschwitz ... And now this doctor here ...

At least he knew what his position was. One could not deny that Neumann's standpoint had a certain logic, but it was a cynical logic. And vulgar blackmail. To return to work at the coal yard? With his sick spine and in his state of health, that meant a certain death in a few weeks. Shift work to work 12 hours from six in the morning to six in the evening seven days a week, and then for 12 hours for seven nights. Five prisoners to a coal car loaded with 15 tons of wet, frozen coal powder. Three coal rail cars a shift. That meant – it was easy to figure out – nine tons of coal powder per prisoner ... He could not count on any other work. Besides, other work would not have been easier. Those who had not been working at the coal yard went to work in the luxurious conditions of the closed and heated halls of the Schlesische Zellwolle.[1] But there too not all kinds of work were equal. True, at the factory there were also workers of other nationalities. But only the Jews worked in the department where the lumber was treated chemically. It was enough to work in that department for two or three months in order to incur, as a result of the constant contact with some poisonous acids, different kinds of illness – most often polyneuritis. That inflammation of many nerves led to lasting strokes that turned the prisoners into cripples. Most often, it ended for them by being sent back to Auschwitz.

He had one day to make his final decision. And this

decision could determine his fate. To croak miserably now, when everything indicated that the war was coming to its end? Still, this kind of reasoning could lead to conclusions and decisions of which he would be ashamed ... And perhaps a shameful decision would not be so worthy of condemnation? After all, it was not his fault that the laws of camp life have had put before him such an alternative. This was life in the camp and not a novel in which the protagonist could make a decision in accordance with the author's imagination. He was not particularly brave, but neither did he want to be a swine in his own eyes. The worst of it was that he had to make a decision by himself. There was no one there who could help him.

Although there was still Emil. Emil Vogel – a doctor from Prague, a man of exemplary honesty whose opinion he valued greatly. Vogel knew life and he knew the Germans. He was over 50 years old and would certainly not have survived the work at the coal yard if it were not for his position as a sort of helper to the foreman – so his work was easier. The coal Kommando,[2] as far as he remembered correctly, worked at night this week. At this hour, Emil must have been sleeping. Indeed, he found him in the barrack, in the barrack to which he would have to return if he decided not to accept Neumann's proposal. On plank-beds the prisoners of the night shift, slept snoring heavily. He felt sorry for Emil but he had no choice – he had to wake him up. He sat down near him and in a few words told him everything.

'That son of a bitch,' Emil commented on his story in Polish. He was not given to quick decisions. He thought for a long while.

'It is not easy to give any wise advice here. This must be thought through. I'll drop in on you in the evening before I go to work or immediately after I return from the yard.'

He returned to the *revier*. Neumann was dressing a prisoner's leg.

'So? Have you decided to administer the anaesthetic?' he asked.

'I don't know. I don't know. I'll tell you in the evening or tomorrow morning.'

'In the morning we'll be operating, you must hurry up.'

180

'Yes, yes ... I would still like, however, with your permission to see the wound.'

Apparently, Neumann saw this request as a favourable prognosis for his participation in the operation.

'Of course. He remains unconscious. Little Henio is sitting near him.'

He entered a little room that had probably at one time been used for storage. Neumann had succeeded in making it look like a hospital room. In the centre stood a plank-bed and on it lay the wounded that was indeed still unconscious. He looked closer at the gray face that was hardly distinguishable from the felt cushion stuffed with artificial wool. He immediately realized that actually he knew that man well. Still, he could not identify the face before him among the thousands of similarly emaciated faces. Near the patient sat little Henio, a sixteen-year-old boy from Dąbrowa. The palms of both Henio's hands were paralyzed – the result of his work at the factory. The boy was waiting to be deported to Auschwitz and had no illusions about the fate that awaited him. The camp authorities probably wanted to collect a larger quantity of such waste product in order not to incur the cost of transporting a single Jew.

'Who is he?' he asked Henio.

'Don't you know? He is Moros of course. Ferenc Moros.'

'Moros?'

'Moros, the goalkeeper.'

Moros – the goalkeeper ...

The transport of prisoners from Auschwitz came to this camp at the end of October. That year the autumn was warm so he never felt the harsh mountain air, and the newly-issued striped prison uniforms made of artificial wool still protected them from the morning and evening chill. The first week they worked at night. As it happened, the day shift started to work on Monday, so they had the first Sunday free, which was unusual. He decided to use the occasion to look around the new camp. The Germans had assembled about 1,500 Jews there, mostly from Hungary. Some prisoners also came from Silesia, and now, of course, from the Łódź ghetto. The more than ten barracks were put up without any specific plan. Those were typical camp barracks, the same as in Brzezinka.

The warm sun was shining joyously as if it had wanted to leave behind it pleasant memories for the winter. He breathed deeply. At least he did not have before his eyes the nightmare of constantly smoking crematoria chimneys, and the sharp, heavy smell of their smoke did not eat into his lungs. He had not yet felt in his bones the hard toil of unloading the coal cars. All this gave him the illusory feeling of lasting security. He had the vision of quietly waiting for the end of the war in this mountainous area. Here there was no threat of selection and the immediate sending away to the gas ... Although he could already believe that here also everything was geared to reminding the prisoners that they belonged to a subhuman species that was completely at the mercy of the master nation. The previous day, they had been taken after work to the bath-house. They had all been delighted at the opportunity to bathe and to get rid of the streaks of coal dust in all the wrinkles of the skin, in the corners of the mouth and under the nails. But they had forgotten that the bath attendants were Germans. From the faucets came water that was either ice cold or boiling hot. The SS men and the bath-house attendants were bursting with laughter when they looked at the funny dances of the emaciated naked figures that attempted to avoid the painful streams of water. While they were in the bath-house, their striped prisoner uniforms went through delousing. By itself this operation was very necessary but, after the painful bath, they were forced to put on their wet bodies their still-wet striped uniforms. They returned to the camp shivering from cold ... But all this was yesterday.

Now he could stroll over the *Lagerplatz*[3] in the temporarily clean uniform, which was already dry. He had hoped to find some acquaintances from the Łódź transport. For the time being, he had not met anyone. But he had the occasion to see how badly the Hungarian Jews adapted to life in the camp. Not having had the experience of ghetto life, they suddenly found themselves in conditions of hunger and murderous hard work.

As he looked around, he saw a group of prisoners busy with a strange activity. They were fencing off the centre of the square with a heavy rope. The fenced-off part was of considerable size. Four poles driven into the ground marked the four corners of a big rectangle – some 70–80 metres by 30–40 metres. (The camp occupied a large area. In setting it up no land had been skimped.) The ropes created something like a triple barrier around the rectangle. Inside, however, some prisoners were marking lines with crushed chalk. One line divided the rectangle into two even sections. In the middle of the short sides of the rectangle were erected – he could not believe his eyes – two most authentic goalposts. Yes, there was no doubt that they were goalposts, built like hockey goalposts but larger and without a net.

For a while he observed those preparations in silence and finally asked a prisoner who stood nearby what was the purpose of it all. The prisoner – he was a Jew from Sosnowiec, which made for easier communication – answered briefly:

'Those are preparations for a match.'

'For a match? A soccer match?'

'Yes, it starts shortly.'

'Is it an order from the Germans?'

'An order? Not at all. You will see for yourself,' the prisoner's gaze lingered on him. 'The Jews play against the Germans.'

He was dumbfounded by such an amazing reply. His conversation partner disappeared somewhere and he moved closer to the ropes and observed with increasing curiosity the preparations that converted the centre of the square into an authentic soccer field. The goalposts were erected with the help of hooks driven into the ground. Inside the field the prisoners were finishing drawing the remaining lines of the penalty area and the outside lines.

In the meantime, spectators from all the barracks began to arrive – an animated little crowd that flickered with faded white and blue stripes. Finally the preparations ended, and running – yes, running – two teams entered the field. The prisoners – in their striped uniforms but not wearing the wooden clogs that they wore every day – now they had on their feet leather boots that apparently had been issued to them for the duration of the match. They had tied up the legs of their uniforms with string and pushed them inside the boots. The SS men wore white undershirts and the green breeches of their uniforms. He counted fast: each team had eight players. After a while the referee appeared. This one had not thrown off his uniform. It was Oberscharführer Handtke or Hanke himself – the highest-ranking officer of the camp personnel. After a short training session, the captains of the two teams shook hands ... They really shook hands! The referee's whistle began the match.

What began to happen inside the rectangular field surrounded by ropes, and outside among the spectators, was a spectacle as surrealistic and it was tragicomic. The prisoner team was made up of Hungarian Jews. It also had, as he was later told, one Jew from Poland, from Będzin. Those starved, exhausted, beaten and deprived-of-sleep prisoners, to whom the greatest optimist would not have given more than a few months to live, were moving briskly on the field. It was obvious that many of them were experienced players. Their play was not only self-sacrificing, but also showed quite a good technique. Thanks to that technique, they moved economically and effectively. While the SS men were chasing the ball running from one end of the field to the other, the prisoners spent their strength judiciously and gained ground with a few short passes.

The history of those weekly matches, he was told, went back to the summer of that year. The camp attached to Schlesische Zellwolle had already been in existence for several months when Jews from Hungary began to arrive there during the summer. The SS men apparently had some knowledge of European soccer and must have heard of eminent Hungarian teams, such as Ferencvaros, Ujpesti or MTK, which had many Jewish players. They therefore decided to take advantage of the inflow of slave manpower to have some sport entertainment that would break up the monotony of their boring work routine of escorting and guarding the prisoners. The idea was apparently a lucky one, although from a racial point of view inadmissible.

In forming a team of Hungarian Jews, the SS men must have assumed that since only the prisoners who looked the strongest and the healthiest were sent to the camp, they would certainly find among them skilful soccer players. And so it was. Unusual? Yes, unusual. This was already the fifth year of the war. The spectacle of extermination of human life continued before the eyes of Europe. Thousands of executioners and millions of victims participated in it. The spectacle apparently called for the occasional intermission during which both the executioners and the victims went out to smoke a cigarette. They lighted the cigarettes from the sparks of the crematoria ovens. The director of the spectacle could afford such a change of pace ...

A fierce struggle was taking place on the field. The striped jackets flew in the air like the wings of some grotesque exotic birds. From time to time, the players of the prisoner team raced along the field as if those wings could lift them behind the barbed-wire fence, away from the Germans, to the freedom they longed for. They often showed off for the public, their public, soccer tricks that were all the more rash because they were performed in the boots that they were given for the duration of the match only. Besides, those boots must have been very uncomfortable for some – two Hungarians had changed them for their own primitive wooden clogs, which were now dully knocking on the hard surface of the Lagerplatz.

The competitors of both teams played with smiles, and it was not the fake smile of a photograph. The SS men smiled indulgently as if to remind them that this temporary interruption of the normal relationship between prisoners and guards would eventually come to an end. The smiles of the Jews were brought about by the joy that humiliated people feel when aware of their transient superiority. The SS men were joking the whole time, and when they lost the ball they laughed loudly and hid that way their momentary defeat. When one of the Jews lost the ball or played poorly, it was obvious that he exposed himself to the bitter reproaches of his colleagues and, of course, the spectators. For them, something much more important was behind the sport contest: something that allowed them through the intermediary of their representatives to taste illusory revenge, to win an imaginary victory.

Four or five hundred of those spectators had gathered. In concert, they cheered on their own, in concert they protested against what they considered unfavourable rulings by the referee against the prisoners. They whistled, got excited, wrung their hands and were happy as if this was not just a short break in their everyday tragic existence but an immediate radical change in their miserable condition. As if the removal of the barbed-wire fence behind their backs had depended on a well-received ball or on gaining a point.

The encouragement that the prisoner team received was that much more evident since, as is easy to understand, no one cheered on the SS men. Most of the SS personnel was on the field, others took advantage of the Sunday, and still others performed their normal duties at the camp gate and the fence.

Right before him on the field, two SS men struggled fiercely with a prisoner for the possession of the ball. Finally, they got it. During the struggle, the player in the striped prison uniform fell to the ground. The referee had not called foul play, which actually it had not been. But the spectators hissed to protest against what they considered the dirty play of the opponent. The protest had been so vehement as if it were not just the case of foul play on the field but the grievance of the whole Jewish people that for centuries had been subjected to foul play with the silent approval of history and its referees ...

The hissing was a short moment of retaliation, all the more precious because it could be done openly and would not result in punishment. And that was what was the most surprising. The SS men fully accepted the rules of the soccer spectacle as if the match had been not at the camp but somewhere in a nearby town. When he looked at the spectacle, it seemed to him at times impossible that those players would again become what they really were as soon as they left the field and put on their green jackets with the insignia. He also understood why the SS men did not wear normal sport shorts, which would have certainly made it easier for them to run over the field. They must have recognized that the part of the uniform that they still wore would remind the prisoner team that even during the match not all the camp rules were suspended. Also, that was probably the reason why the Jews had to play in their striped garb. Who knows how the soccer match would have been played if the teams had not been wearing their respective uniforms that reflected the durability of the camp system. And who knows how the spectators would have behaved if the sight of the green breeches of the SS on the field had not restrained their excitement.

In spite of everything, the superiority of the well-fed over the starving was evident on the field. The SS men were pressing – the prisoners were defending themselves desperately. The outcome of the match would actually have been decided beforehand if it were not for the goalkeeper of the prisoner team, who was also its captain and who shook the hand of the captain of the German team before the match. He had really been an inspired player, a player graced by God, whose name the spectators had been constantly chanting. Sonorous shouts: 'Moros! Moros!' resounded through the whole camp and probably beyond the fence surrounding it.

This player had intrigued him at that time. During the intermission, one of the Hungarian Jews satisfied his curiosity. Moros's first name was Ferenc. He came from some small town near Budapest and since childhood had the promise of a great soccer player. He was indeed endowed with excellent attributes to be a good goalkeeper. He was tall, unusually flexible and had long arms. His performance would have been admired by the most refined expert in the soccer art. He was able to defend the goal in the most unimaginable situations. When it was necessary, he ran out into the field. He always placed himself where the ball was. If until half-time the score was only one to zero in favour of the SS, it was primarily because of him. On several occasions he even got the recognition of the Germans: they slapped him patronizingly on the back when by some miracle he kicked out the ball to the corner or caught it from the goal line at the last moment.

The intermission in the game lasted about ten minutes, and during that time both teams stretched out on the field. The prisoners fortified themselves with some warm swill that was generously delivered by the kitchen Kapo. The SS men of course with beer. Everything indicated that the second half of the match would be similar to the first, and that meant the prisoners being superior in technique, and the Germans in strength, energy and physical condition. It appeared, however, that strength was not everything. The prisoner team played the game very cleverly from a tactical point of view.

What the spectators who had observed the first part of the match, and he among them, considered the weak point of the prisoner team, proved an ingenious tactical trick. From experience, the prisoners probably knew that the SS men did not know how to distribute their forces judiciously. And perhaps the beer they drank during the intermission began to have its effect? Enough said, by the end of the match the Jewish team almost completely dominated the field. If the loss of power by the Germans could still be explained, it was absolutely impossible to find a rational explanation for the endurance and ambition of the prisoners. It got to the point that in some instances the play of the Germans was so inept that it made the spectators burst out in a merry laughter.

At the end of the match, the spectators were inflamed by two events. The first was the goal that equalized the score. It was scored by the lanky fellow from Będzin. The second was the unjustified penalty against the prisoner team called by the referee. The prisoners outside the rope reacted vehemently against the referee's decision. It looked as if the striped uniforms would invade the field and beat up the culprit. Luckily for him, the culprit wore not just the breeches but the complete SS uniform. In any event, there was no lack of epithets at his address in Polish and Hungarian. Here and there, someone even called out something fitting also in German. Silence fell when a German positioned the ball for the penalty shot, and everyone went wild when Moros stopped the shot. This was already in the last minute of the match. Before the referee could whistle the end of the match, the spectators jumped over the ropes or went under them and ran toward Moros and hugged and kissed him for joy.

The SS men looked at that outburst of enthusiasm without anger, and even smiled indulgently, somewhat as an owner smiles at his bullock gamboling in the meadow before being sent to the slaughterhouse.

This was the only match that he saw. In fact, it was the last match because after the first autumn rains the Lagerplatz became one big puddle. Besides, all the prisoners began working also on Sundays. One of the players on the prisoner team, the Jew from Będzin, died – he was poisoned by the factory acids. The match itself was commented on for a long time afterwards, particularly by the Hungarians who knighted Moros a hero of two nations – the Hungarians and the Jews.

And now Moros lay here in the *revier*. Shot. In short – he was already doomed.

The very event was rather banal, though such events in general had been rare. Because until now the guards had been aiming accurately and the doctor had no trouble on their account. With Moros apparently the following had happened: he worked at loading lumber onto small trolleys to move it into the factory from the lumber yard. The work here was lighter than at the coal yard where the prisoner crew had to be almost completely replaced three times during the year

Apparently, Moros developed a stomach-ache at work, which was understandable given the quality of the soup the prisoners received. So, he asked the foreman for permission to go to the nailed-together-from-boards outhouse that stood between the coal yard and the lumber yard. The foreman refused. Moros asked for such permission several times, and each time the foreman refused. Having no other choice, Moros squatted somewhere behind a pile of logs and pulled down his trousers. The foreman considered this to be a lack of respect for a German order, pointed out Moros to one of the guards and shouted that the prisoner intended to escape. The German guard, without hesitation, fired several shots, although a moment's reflection would have allowed him to realize that in order to escape one need not pull down one's trousers.

He thought that for Moros it would have been better if the German guard had had a better aim. Not even one of the shots had proved fatal.

Only then there would have been no new spectacle. Instead of a soccer match – an operation. With Moros in the role of the patient. He wanted to exchange at least a few words with Moros. But the Hungarian was still unconscious.

He did not sleep a wink the whole night. He was tormented by the dark conviction that he was acting, or would act, not as he should have acted, that he was looking in advance for a justification to himself in case he accepted Neumann's proposal. When he finally fell asleep, nightmares

189

began to torture him. He saw the rifle of an SS man aimed at him – he was shooting at him and counted soundlessly: one-zero. two-zero… He woke up terrified, shivering from cold. Near him stood Emil, who shook him by the shoulder …

'What happened? Have you returned from work already?' he asked absent-mindedly.

'The coal cars had not arrived. It appears that there is no transport service to Silesia … Listen, take me to that wounded.'

'Neumann does not permit it.'

'What does it matter what he permits. Besides, at this time he is still sleeping. Let's go there.'

He hesitated because he did not want unnecessarily to aggravate the camp doctor. But after all Emil was a doctor too. No one was in the room where Moros lay. Even little Henio had disappeared somewhere. The wounded was still unconscious. He was certainly running a high fever. Emil bent down over the dressing on his arm and with a few movements pulled down the bandage and the gauze. Both of them now looked in silence at the hopeless-looking wound.

'The best surgeon could not help here.'

'Only that Neumann is doing it for the Germans.'

Emil thought for a while and said:

'If Neumann wants to operate, let him amputate. Tell him so.'

This was a way out! Emil Vogel had at one time worked as a surgeon and knew what he was talking about. While it was true that an amputation in those conditions did not augur any hope for the patient, it was still an operation that made more sense than the one Neumann intended to perform. Only Neumann would not listen to him. He was too young to give such advice.

Emil was as if reading his thoughts.

'I'll try to tell it to him myself. Don't be afraid, I won't betray that I was here. And besides … In your place, I would give him the anesthetic.'

'But …'

'Don't interrupt. I hope that after the war Neumann will be held to account for all this … He will operate regardless of your decision. And if depending on your decision the miserable Moros can be made to suffer as little as possible, you understand yourself ...'

Neumann appeared in the *revier* shortly after Emil had left.

'So what? Have you decided?'

'Yes. I'll give the anesthetic.'

'I am very glad. I knew you would agree,' Neumann rejoiced.

'You know, I despise myself for agreeing to do it.'

'No matter. Everyone should despise himself occasionally. There would be fewer people in the world who admire their own nobility. Besides, you are a good actor.'

'Why?'

'You perform excellently in the role of a seduced virgin. You know there is no way out. Only you don't like, let us say, my sincerity. You probably think that I am a cynic, that I am taking advantage of someone else's misfortune... You have not been in the camp very long ...'

'I am truly convinced that both of us will one day have to account for it.'

'You are an incorrigible optimist. In order to account for something after the war, one has to survive it. Besides, I assure you that greater violence inflicted on medical ethics will be forgotten.'

This was tiresome and fruitless verbal fencing. He waved his hand and went again into the room where Moros lay. Nothing had changed there. The wounded man was drenched in sweat and was breathing heavily. He looked at Moros and suddenly felt choking pity in his chest. He felt like crying. And he already did not know whom he pitied more – Moros or himself.

In the meantime, Neumann turned the dressing station into an operating theatre. He gathered all the instruments of the *revier*. He also gathered an impressive quantity of dressing material. It could be that the Germans gave him some of it because never before had there been in the *revier* such an abundance of gauze and cotton. In spite of all this, he was reminded of an engraving that depicted an operating theatre during the Thirty Years War, not one of modern times. Neumann however was very pleased with himself.

'Do you find all of this pitiable?'

'Since you see it yourself ...'

'I see, but I assure you that in the olden days operations had been performed in even more primitive conditions, and the patients came out of them ...'

He wanted to tell Neumann about Emil's suggestion but did not have the time. The Oberscharführer himself (the referee during the soccer match) came to Neumann to talk over some business. Later, he did not have the occasion to remind Neumann of the possibility of an amputation. Around noon, Moros, still unconscious, was brought in and put on the long wooden table had that become the operating table. It turned out that they had one more helper – a Hungarian Jew who was a nurse.

There were about ten Germans in the little room when he began to administer the anaesthetic. And as the number of spectators was increasing, Neumann was increasingly getting into the role of the main protagonist of the spectacle that he himself had mounted.

In the beginning, Moros had been very agitated, but a few drops of ether on the mask were sufficient to put him to sleep. Neumann quickly set out to work. At times with the scalpel, at others with tweezers or some other instrument, he showed the Germans the fragments of the smashed elbow.

'This is the arm bone, those are the fore-arm bones, the elbow bone and the radius bone ... And here is the joint sac. Here we have the damaged vessels and the torn nerve.'

He talked slowly using excessively correct German. He wanted to make it obvious to the Germans that he was treating the whole black comedy produced for the benefit of the Nazi spectators seriously. Perhaps he remembered Rembrandt's picture and now he dreamt of imitating Doctor Tulp? Although, this was rather reminiscent of a provincial Grand Guignol ...

The Germans leaned over Neumann and watched his movements attentively. From time to time they exchanged some comments among themselves and nodded in appreciation. They probably thought that after Neumann's lecture the elbow joint would not hold any secrets for them ...

At one moment Neumann interrupted his demonstration. He closed his eyes and for a long while pondered intensively.

After that, clearly drawling every word, he said not in the direction of the spectators but to him:

'You see yourself that there is nothing that can be done here. Unfortunately we have no choice but amputate.'

That man had certainly missed his calling. He should have been an actor, he thought, forgetting that not long ago the camp doctor had said the same to him. Now Neumann talked only to the SS spectators and explained why he had suddenly changed his plan during the operation. The Germans listened to his exposition and nodded with even greater appreciation. This sounded convincing ...

After a while, he realized that in praising Neumann's thespian talent in his mind he had not done him justice. Because Neumann decided to give the spectators two performances instead of one. Two shows for one ticket ... He must have at one time already done an amputation because while explaining his every move he performed the operation and brought it to an end quickly and efficiently. Even the stump had not looked too bad. The Germans were really fascinated and had almost applauded after the operation its star actor and director ...

The SS men left. The patient's pulse was barely noticeable.

'Did you see how well it went? Moros will never again be a goalkeeper, but perhaps he will survive.'

'But the Germans will in any case send him back to Auschwitz, and there ...'

'For the time being we'll keep him here, and later we'll see. Perhaps we will succeed in keeping him in the camp.'

Now he could not even hope that Neumann would at any time answer for it all. After all, in this case an amputation had been the only solution. It is interesting whether that solution had been suggested to him by Emil. Probably not. He did not have the time. He began to suspect that Neumann knew from the beginning that an amputation was unavoidable ...

But he did not want to think about this. What Neumann managed to achieve in two days was that he held in contempt not only Neumann but also himself. He went to the front of the barrack. A few SS men still lingered there and shared their impressions. He could not hear much of what they said. Only the last remark of the Oberscharführer reached him:

'Der Bursch war ein wunderbarer Torwart ...'[4]
The next day Moros's body was on the cart making its last journey – in the direction of the factory furnace room. No one escorted it except him. Even Neumann was busy with something. The last spectacle with Moros as its hero had not attracted anyone. He escorted the cart to the gate of the camp. He thought to himself that the Oberscharführer's remark yesterday was perhaps the only eulogy with which that dead Jew was bid farewell in the SS camp system.

Notes

1. Silesian Cellulose Wool.
2. Detachment.
3. Camp square.
4. 'That chap was an extraordinary goalkeeper.'

13 The Barometer

What kept alive in the camp the prisoner of the lowest category, the Jew? What kept him alive was incorrigible optimism and hope. What could nurture that hope in a camp that was cut off from the world by a barricade of barbed wire and the barrier of ill will of the population surrounding the camp? Speaking generally, that hope was nurtured by gossip, scraps of information heard sometime during work, and primarily by omens derived from various signs, such as the facial expressions, words and gestures of the SS men.

Well, not only the SS men.

In the second half of January 1945 the rumour spread among the Jelenia Góra camp prisoners who worked at the coal yard of the Schlesische Zellwolle factory that the Soviet offensive had begun. He and Emil Vogel worked at that time together at the coal yard. The working conditions at the coal yard were terrible. Although people from France, Belgium, the Netherlands and Poland had also worked at the factory, none of them was sent to work at the coal yard. Only the slaves worked here. The Jewish prisoners were underfed and dressed only in the striped prison uniforms of artificial cellulose fiber that did not at all protect them from the cold. The effort by itself was unusually strenuous since the delivery of the coal powder – indispensable for the factory's continuous operation – could not be interrupted even for a moment.

The only brighter spot in this servitude was the person of Müller, the German foreman who had charge of the prisoners' work. One could even say about him that he was a 'humane person', with of course the qualification, 'for a German'. Müller was a member of the Nazi party, as evidenced by the badge he always wore in the lapel of his heavy woollen jacket. Though Foreman Müller used to get angry and yelled when the prisoners, barely moving the shovels, loaded the frozen coal powder with difficulty from the coal cars onto the conveyer, he was not a sadist. Unlike most Germans they dealt with, he had not tormented the group of Jewish slaves entrusted to him.

This Müller took a fancy to the two of them, to Emil and himself. It must be said that he never yelled at them and had on several occasions brought them a few slices of buttered bread. That was an exceptional gesture. They concluded that Müller must have had some snobbish satisfaction of having two physicians in the group of prisoners subordinate to him. That this might have been so was confirmed by the fact that one Sunday he brought to the coal yard his wife and grown-up daughter and pointed at them as a zoo director would show off a specially rare and interesting animal to an excursion.

But, oppressed by hunger and cold, even Müller's benevolence could not raise their spirits. And indeed at that time, news began to spread of the Soviet offensive and of its success. While the information that the offensive had begun was reliable, the details of the situation at the front were not clear. Here all kinds of rumours played pitilessly with their hopes.

According to some rumours, the Soviet army was advancing rapidly. Other rumours claimed that the offensive had stalled. That last version was supported by the camp 'elite'. As if out of spite, even the prisoners who cleaned the SS quarters and usually brought pieces of newspapers, began returning empty-handed, and the Polish railway men who usually brought some news from the fronts lately stopped showing up at all. Even Emil, who knew the Germans best, was unable to draw from their behaviour any conclusions about the war situation.

That day new transports of coal had arrived and all the Kommandos worked at full steam, if such a description could be applied to the work of the tortured Jewish prisoners. The weather was frosty and beautiful ... The sky dazzled the eyes with its sharp, clean blue. The coal yard was actually located at the foot of the Snieżka Mountain, whose slope was covered with a silky white coat ... Tired by the many hours of uninterrupted work (the conveyer had to be filled continuously), he rested for a moment delighting in the shimmer of the sun rays playing in the icy diamonds that decorated the snow covering. Breathing heavily, he leaned on the shovel and waved to Emil who worked some distance away. Suddenly he saw Müller near him. As usual, he said to the foreman 'good morning'. He, however, seemingly participating in his admiration of the snowy mountain slope, suddenly said:

'*Schön ist die Welt …*'[1]

'*O ja, sehr schön!*'[2]

And to this Müller:

'*Aber die Menschen, die Menschen sind schlecht! …*'[3]

And, as if to support his words, he hit him in the face once and again. When he fell to the ground as a result of the unexpected blows, Müller began to kick him furiously, getting increasingly enraged … Lying on the ground, he covered his face with his hands to protect it from the boot of the enraged German. At the same time he turned on his belly remembering – he still had that much presence of mind – that a German's favourite way of kicking a prisoner who fell to the ground was hitting him with his heel in the area of the heart.

This lasted several minutes. Suddenly Müller, as if he had unloaded his rage, stopped kicking him, said something that no one could hear, and left.

Everyone who witnessed the scene was shaken up. It would have been understandable if one of the gendarmes had done so. But the humane Müller?

Half-conscious, he lay on the ground. He could not get up on his own. His whole body ached. His face and lips were swollen and blood was gushing from his nose.

As if through a fog, he saw Emil who leaned over him. With the help of a few prisoners, Emil sat him down on one of the logs that separated the coal yard from the factory courtyard. Someone brought him warm water. Someone washed his face, someone wrapped him in a blanket found who knows where.

Slowly he recovered. He only shivered from the cold and from nervousness. Wrapping him in the blanket, Emil leaned over him and quietly said:

'So, I congratulate you.'

Confused he looked at Emil. He was even unable to ask Emil what was on his mind. And Emil, still leaning over him, completed his thought.

'Thanks to you we now know for certain ... We now know for certain...'

He drew out from himself that one syllable:

'What?'

'Don't you understand? You still don't understand? We wanted to know what was the situation at the front. How the Soviet offensive was going. So now we know ...'

And when in the evening he was lying in pain on his plank-bed, Emil stood near him and summed up the day's events:

'That Müller. Who would have thought that he would be such an excellent barometer?'

Notes

1. 'The world is beautiful!'
2. 'Oh yes, very beautiful!'
3. 'But the people, the people are bad! ...'

14 The Little Flat in the Spa

The memorable year 1981 was rolling over the length and breadth of Poland. Whirlwinds and storms were rocking the country. The issues that faced this middle-sized country between the Tatra Mountains and the Baltic Sea swelled to dimensions large enough to threaten world peace.[1]

Still, that had not prevented matters other than those that filled the front pages of the newspapers to preoccupy people's minds. So that life could go on. This was as comforting as seeing during the whirlwind of war a ploughman who follows the plough thinking of tomorrow's harvest.

In the spring of that year, he was invited to Cieplice to lecture on some scientific topics. Those topics fascinated many people, but were viewed with suspicion by the more cautious journalists or scientists. From Warsaw to Cieplice was a long journey. Still, he decided to take advantage of the invitation. To take advantage of the opportunity that enabled him to return to a place that at one time had played an important role in his life. Until now, he had avoided this place in the course of his wanderings over the country for reasons that he had not even understood. Consciously? Subconsciously? He would have to think a long time to explain his erstwhile behaviour rationally.

The spring was sunny and warm. Through the coach windows, the countryside seemed a tower of calm. The journey allowed him to escape the everyday stress, and this had a calming effect. It was not dragging at all, although the train from Wrocław reminded more of an old-fashioned choo-choo than of a means of transportation of the end of the twentieth century. But after all, this had not been the only evidence of the country's backwardness.

Somewhat excited, he went out on the street in front of the

Jelenia Góra train station. Thirty-seven years passed from the day he had walked along the same, well, almost the same, road. Other journeys he could forget – this one he would never forget.

Experience taught him that waiting for a taxi at a train station prolongs the journey by at least an hour – if the final destination is at all in the range of the taxi driver's goodwill. And so it was – this was more or less the time that passed before he found himself in the taxi that was to bring him to the Cieplice hotel.

The driver's melodious speech betrayed that, if not he, then certainly his ancestors originated from the 'kresy'. He was, however, an unusually friendly man who lived with the rhythm of his times. The driver assumed that on the way he should show the guest from Warsaw (he found out previously from where he had come) the places worthy of attention, places that were in the news lately because of strikes, or signed agreements, or still unresolved conflicts. He had done it very conscientiously. Besides, he had such a lot to show.

The driver did not find in him, however, a receptive listener. The passenger was more interested in the city itself. They travelled over the gray, dilapidated streets that carried Polish names. There were Polish signs over Polish stores. He attempted to find here and there a trace of something that would connect the present day with the day when he came in contact with that city for the first time. His attempts to find the past remained, however, completely fruitless. A new era in the history of the city had arrived. The other images had been covered with dust, and only on the bottom of his memory could he find their foggy outlines.

'Have you lived here long?' he suddenly asked the taxi driver.

'Thirty-five years, sir. I was born here.'

'Your parents probably came from Lwów.'

'No, from Stryj.'

'I wanted to ask you something … Did you hear anything about a camp, a Nazi camp, in Jelenia Góra?'

'People were saying that apparently there was something like that here.'

'Does anything remain of the camp?'

'Probably not, or I would have known.'

'That camp was not far from the artificial fiber factory …'

'I really cannot tell you anything about it.'

'And have you perhaps heard of the camp at Cieplice?'

The driver became animated.

'Oh yes, there certainly was a camp at Cieplice. Everyone knows that. A few years ago, on the occasion of some anniversary, even a commemorative plaque or something like that was put up there.'

He was surprised.

'In Cieplice traces of the camp remained but in Jelenia Góra nothing remained?'

'That's what it looks like.'

'In that case I have a request to you. Before you take me to the hotel, let us drive up to the Cieplice camp.'

As a rule, taxi drivers are not surprised at anything, and neither was this one at the peculiar request of his passenger. After all, it was an opportunity for a longer fare.

They left Jelenia Góra, driving past the factory that in the German times had been called Schlesische Zellwolle. Here he found a greater number of reference points for the remnants of what had been preserved in his memory. Up there, on the left, was the coal yard, and nearby was the railway track on which the rail cars with coal powder would arrive. Behind the coal yard was another yard where the lumber that the factory was converting into artificial fiber was stored.

The taxi passed the factory, and after five minutes it turned right, then immediately left, stopping among some buildings.

'It's here,' said the driver.

'Already?' He was genuinely surprised.

He got out of the taxi-cab and looked around. The surroundings meant nothing to him. He remembered the area covered with snow. He made several dozen steps in the direction of a seemingly chaotically put up group of one-storey buildings and suddenly … Suddenly he found himself on the territory of the former camp. Under his feet, he had the same sandy Lagerstrasse as he remembered it when, in the last year of the war, the first rays of the spring sun had melted the plump layer of snow on it. Along the little narrow street stood at that time, as stood now, concrete-block one-storey houses.

At that time the houses were not plastered, today they are covered with gray mortar. Years ago they reminded one of large storehouses, today they look like military barracks. That was actually the only difference that he could notice at first glance. Only now did he understand why this camp had remained while the other one, at Jelenia Góra, had not. The other one consisted of wooden barracks. And after the war wood was too valuable a raw material to leave those barracks as an exhibit illustrating the Nazi camp system. Here, in Cieplice, the barracks were of concrete blocks ...

For a long while he stood lost in thought among those one-storey buildings. He was seized by a kind of idiotic outrage that they had not disappeared together with the system that had put them up.

He returned to the driver who stood by the taxi.

'What is in those buildings now?'

The driver was surprised.

'What do you mean ... People live there ... Normally, that means they live there ...'

Normal people living normally...

His experience with Cieplice began at the beginning of February 1945, that is 36 years ago, when the Nazi world was coming to an end. That world was dying in convulsive spasms and took along with it into the abyss of non-existence hundreds of thousands of prisoners who perished from hunger and exhaustion, from the cold and from SS men's bullets in the camps and during their evacuation. There were very many camps in that area. Their purpose was to save the perishing Reich by squeezing out from the still living Jews, who had been sent here from all of Europe, the remnants of bloody sweat ... The camp at Hirschberg, today's Jelenia Góra, was far from the front. And although from the East and the West the crackle of fascism's cracking skeleton could be heard, here there were no changes. Indeed! Two or three months previously the camp had expanded as if bloated. In November of the previous year, the prisoners who worked at the coal yard near the railway ramp noticed several transports of prisoners escorted by SS men that went on foot on the road that led from Jelenia Góra to Cieplice. That those were transports of Jews was evident from the yellow stars attached to the prisoners' coats. The prisoners were dressed in civilian clothes because they had not had time to put on the striped camp uniforms. Some of the prisoners carried hand baggage ...

Shortly it became clear that those were Jews from the West. From Belgium, the Netherlands. In general, at that time no more Jews were left in the East, let alone any so elegantly dressed. Compared with the human shreds that the Jews from Poland, Hungary and Greece who worked here had become, those people, if one could forget the SS men that escorted them, looked like tourists who were visiting an interesting country on foot.

At that time, there was no camp at Cieplice. Suitable barracks were built for the new arrivals, and the mother camp at Jelenia Góra took care of the rest of the arrangements. So, from Jelenia Góra some indispensable specialists were sent to Cieplice – a few Kapos, a few barrack heads, a dentist and a cook. The above dentist and two nurses were to provide the inmates with medical help. Sending the dentist there showed the Nazis' specific care about the Jewish prisoners' teeth. The Germans had recognized that the gold from Jewish teeth could be of substantial help in the fight against the Allies. Therefore, in Jelenia Góra as well as in Cieplice, every new prisoner was registered in a special card index where the number of gold crowns that brazenly dared to hide in his mouth was noted. When he died, and before his remains were taken to the factory boiler room, the dentist was obliged to break out – he did it with ordinary pliers – parts of the upper and lower jaws together with the gold attached to them. Thanks to the card index, the SS men knew what each prisoner owed them. It was only surprising that there was no order to remove those crowns from the prisoners while they were still alive. It was clear that the Belgian, Dutch or French Jews were a much richer source of gold than the Jews from Poland or Hungary. Therefore a dentist was really necessary in Cieplice, and that was also why he was promoted to camp doctor.

While it is true that the distance between Jelenia Góra and Cieplice was not great, still only meager news about the new camp was reaching the mother camp. And besides, the interest in this new camp had not been very great. The Jelenia Góra prisoners had enough troubles of their own to care about the troubles of others. Nothing was known about the Cieplice camp throughout the whole of November, December and January. Then suddenly came the news that the dentist, the gold prospector for the SS, had died. Also, that one of the nurses had died, and that people in general had been dying like flies from some epidemic. And that actually no one was there to treat them.

At that time, he worked at the Jelenia Góra coal yard. He worked together with his friend Emil Vogel from Prague, also a doctor. It was clear to both of them that if the war lasted another month or two, they would end up, like many others, in the factory boiler room.

When the news from Cieplice had reached them, they decided to do something that had probably never before been noted in camp chronicles. From the premise that it was better to die treating the sick than to croak at the senseless loading of coal, they decided to approach the camp SS administration to be sent to Cieplice as doctors. There they could after all be more useful than at Jelenia Góra.

Such a suggestion seemed plainly insane. The kapo of the Kommando at the coal yard assured them that they should be happy if the whole story ended with 25 lashes. He promised that he himself would add a few more as a bonus for idlers who did not feel like working.

But here something unusual happened. The SS men probably concluded that while it was true that the idea had come from sub-humans, it made common sense. Somewhere an understanding was reached with someone, somewhere something was decided. And three days after they had approached the Oberscharführer himself, in the first half of February, dressed in new striped prison uniforms and new coats of the same material (which did not protect them from the cold), they started out from Jelenia Góra to Cieplice escorted by an armed gendarme.

They went of course on foot. The temperature was reaching 25 degrees below zero. On their bare feet, they wore wooden clogs. If the distance between Jelenia Góra and Cieplice had been even one kilometre greater, they would not have got there alive. The whole distance they snuggled up to each other, and their only consolation was the appearance of the gendarme who guarded them. In spite of the woollen hood, the woollen boots and the thick cloth coat that he wore, he had endured the cold worse than the prisoners whom he guarded.

After the hour that it took them to cover the distance between the two camps, the delighted SS man handed them over to his colleagues at Cieplice. Indeed ... They had been handed over at exactly the same spot where he stood now, 36 years later. The cement-block barracks that they saw then, as he sees them now, seemed to them a good omen for the future after the wooden barracks at Jelenia Góra. Shortly they would also know who, that is whether Emil or he, was the lucky one. The point of the matter was that, as they could guess from the rumours, the illness decimating the Cieplice camp was either spotted typhus or abdominal typhus. Their ghetto and camp medical experience had taught them that. And if a person had been through one or both of those illnesses, it was almost impossible for him to succumb to them for a second time. He himself had had abdominal typhus in the ghetto. Vogel, on the other hand, worked for ten days at the Gypsy camp attached to the Łódź ghetto and had become infected with spotted typhus there. If the epidemic in Cieplice had been that of abdominal typhus, he would be the winner, if of spotted typhus, the winner would be Emil ...

Their acquaintance with Cieplice began with their being handed over by the local SS men to the chef, the kitchen Kapo Dawidek. Dawidek had previously been the cook at Jelenia Góra. When he opened his mouth, the gold in it shone brightly. It was not clear from where that gold had come and why Dawidek was flaunting his oral wealth. Emil concluded that if that gold had been in Dawidek's mouth before the war, the SS men would have long ago guided the destiny of its owner in a way that all those crowns would have strengthened the treasury of the Third Reich. On the other hand, as the kitchen Kapo, Dawidek had been certainly able to take skilfully care of his interests. He was probably exchanging the food stolen from the prisoners for the very valuable metal. The SS men had certainly also made a large profit on it.

However, he was a pleasant man, and if he could amass a fortune in his mouth at the expense of the prisoners ... To tell the truth, he aroused greater admiration for his commercial abilities than anger for stealing from the prisoners ...

To welcome them, Dawidek treated each of them to two slices of bread with margarine and a bowl of thick soup. Two beautiful veal cutlets sizzled on a frying pan on the stove. They looked at them as archaeologists must have looked at the first clay tablets they discovered in Mesopotamia. Unfortunately, the cutlets were destined for the SS men, and even Dawidek dared not touch them.

Quite soon, their initial optimism cooled. Dawidek, who knew everything, introduced them to the situation in the camp and to their future prospects.

The only positive information, whose truthfulness they later had many opportunities to confirm, was that the SS men dreaded more than anything being sent to the front. Therefore, they would do everything to preserve that camp. Everything – even things that were completely contrary to discipline or the official rules, and even contrary to common sense. Dawidek was of the opinion that at the present stage of the war, the whole camp system existed only to save thousands of SS men from the terrible alternative that was for them the front, the eastern front of course. This was encouraging. Unfortunately, Dawidek's other information was less encouraging.

The Cieplice prisoners worked at the paper machine factory. There were about 700 of them. No more than 300 were still working. The rest were either ill or so weak after the illness that for them work was out of the question. The very fact that several hundred prisoners were going out to work at the factory, in spite of the epidemic in the camp, proved that the SS men were prepared to spread the epidemic to the whole town to save their skin. The epidemic could spread because at the factory itself, contact between the Jews and the Germans was unavoidable. The worst, however, was what Dawidek was telling them of the German plans for the near future. And that was that they intended to set up inside the camp a kind of quarantine. The quarantine was supposed to be separated from the rest of the camp by a barbed-wire fence.

All the prisoners who were ill or suspected of being ill would be placed there. The two doctors who had arrived, that meant he and Emil, as well as the one nurse that had survived the typhus would stay permanently with the sick prisoners. This was a gloomy prospect. It was beyond doubt that the food rations for those enclosed in the quarantine, minimal in any case, would be further reduced.

But for the moment they were full – which had not happened in a long time. After resting for a while, they decided to have a look at the sick prisoners. Dawidek took them to the barrack designated as the camp hospital. All the five barracks were identical. In each of them, on the ground floor and on the first floor, there were two larger halls and several very small cells on both sides of the stairs. In each of the larger halls there were about 20 two-storey plank-beds. In the whole barrack, there were about 160 places for the sick prisoners. There were however more sick prisoners than that, and two lay on some straw mattresses. The first prisoner, the one at the edge, ran a high fever and was unconscious. When they opened his shirt at the chest, they had no difficulty making a diagnosis. Emil was the lucky one. It was without doubt spotted typhus.

One of the cells was allocated to the two of them. There was in it, in addition to a two-storey plank-bed, only one wooden stool. They quickly inspected all the halls – they were monstrously dirty and littered. The lice infestation at Cieplice was much greater than at Jelenia Góra. No wonder that the epidemic had spread over almost the whole camp.

Next day in the morning one of the SS men appeared and announced the creation of the quarantine. For them, the most important information was that the doctors would be responsible for everything that was happening in the quarantined hospital barrack. They would be responsible with their heads – the language of the camp authorities had not allowed for any other formulation. What was interesting was that this SS man had not shown any interest in what the epidemic was. Emil attempted to tell him something about it, but the SS man just waved his hand as if to say either that he knew everything on that topic or that it was all the same to him. In reality, both interpretations were correct. The SS men had known perfectly well that it was spotted typhus that was rampant in the camp. They preferred, however, to pretend that they did not know what the illness was. In the atmosphere of disorganization brought on by the approaching end of the war, such a policy could be advantageous to them. In any event, it justified the camp authorities before the factory management and the town authorities.

The doctors were put in charge of the distribution of the bread and soup. Every day they had to report on the condition of the live patients, and to put those who had died outside the barrack. The Germans were concerned that the numbers of the live and dead prisoners should agree with the total, and also that the number of food rations delivered to the quarantine should correspond exactly to the number of live prisoners and the live medical personnel. They had figured out everything precisely: the doctors were incarcerated behind barbed wires and were taking care of the patients, and they, the Germans, supplied the food and the new patients. Beside that, no contact. Well, no, there still was one. The doctors were obliged to take blood samples from new patients, and this was considered important. The test tubes with the blood samples were to be handed over to the SS men who were supposed to send them off further for diagnosis. To Emil's question where those samples would be tested, the SS man calmly replied that there was one central laboratory for all the camps and that it was located in Auschwitz. Saying that, he looked at them attentively ... But they had not even reacted when they heard that the samples would be sent to Auschwitz, which had been already in Soviet hands for four weeks ...

Besides, the Germans never rescinded the order about taking blood samples for tests to see whether a prisoner had spotted or abdominal typhus. That was an important element in their game to prolong the existence of the camp. In addition, they could always justify themselves that, due to the situation at the front, they could not determine what the illness had been ... If such an epidemic had broken out a year or two earlier, the whole camp would certainly have been sent to the gas chamber. However, in February of 1945 the interests of the prisoners and of the SS men responsible for the camp

were identical. Both were anxious for the camp not to be liquidated ...

By the end of the first few days, they had examined all the
sick prisoners in a fashion. There was no doubt that they were
all sick with spotted typhus. More than ten of them were in a
hopeless condition, and among those there was one whose
presence here in such a condition gave them genuine
pleasure. That was a Kapo sent from Jelenia Góra. His name
had been Chmielnicki and he came from Paris. At the Jelenia
Góra camp he had been a sadistic animal who had been
tormenting the prisoners for no reason. Even the Germans
had not demanded of him that much ...

In the meantime, a barbed-wire barricade was put up
around the hospital barrack. Only a narrow passage was left
for the transfer of patients in one direction and corpses in the
other. So, he and Emil found themselves in a quarantine
surrounded by a barbed-wire barricade, which separated
them from a camp that in turn had been surrounded by a
barbed-wire fence ... That was an unusual situation. Unusual,
but for them catastrophic.

Normally, as camp doctors, they could still count on some
occasional additional food rations, perhaps a bowl of soup or
a portion of bread ... Incarcerated in the quarantine, they
could not count on anything any more ...

On anything?

Ultimately there was a way. The situation had forced it on
them. Since inside the quarantine everything was under their
control and depended on them, all they had to do was to hold
over the remains of the dead prisoners for a day or two before
handing them over to the Germans. That way they, the
doctors, would get additional portions of bread and soup.
Emil hesitated. Not so much for reasons of ethics as for the
normal fear of the risk connected with such a manipulation.
However, he swiftly persuaded Emil that the risk was really
not so great since the Germans would stay away from the
quarantine. And after all, it was better to feed on the dead
than to steal from the living, as Dawidek was doing. There
remained the matter of storing the corpses. Here experience
suggested a solution. The best and safest place was the cell
that they had occupied. Under the lower plank-bed, there was

room for two or three bodies. Very seldom did more than that number of sick prisoners die in one day. They had only to be careful not to hand over the corpses in a too advanced state of decay. Besides, it was winter.

The quarantine had tied them to the sick prisoners. They were with them day and night. The very presence of doctors strengthened the sick prisoners psychologically: they had those doctors at their disposal day and night. It also turned out that the little camp pharmacy contained a fair quantity of heart remedies that ultimately had been the only medication of possible usefulness in cases of spotted typhus …

The rest was happening as they had planned it, or rather as he had planned it. They did not have to hold over the corpses for more than one day. Besides, in the first period there were more of them. The arrival of the doctors could have some minimal results only after a certain time.

He looked at the buildings that at one time had formed the camp. In the rays of the hot spring sun, they were peaceful and as if asleep. That first building on the right had actually been the quarantine barrack. Precisely here – he came closer to the building – ran the barbed-wire fence that separated the quarantine from the rest of the camp. In front of that house, and actually between the building and the gate that had been fitted into the barbed-wire fence, they had been taking out the corpses day after day. The Germans had scrupulously deducted their number from the number of the live patients incarcerated in the quarantine. There, in the building on the left, had been the SS offices, and straight-ahead in the distance had been the gate that led to the camp. The prisoners passed it day after day on the way to work.

At first, the system that he and Emil had planned performed smoothly. But already after the second week, complications arose. The first complication was the decision of the Germans to treat the whole hospital building with an insecticide. This of course made no sense at all. Treatment with an insecticide was more needed in the other buildings of the camp. Together with delousing each recovered prisoner that left the hospital, such treatment could check the spread of the epidemic. But to treat with an insecticide the halls inside the quarantine, without delousing the prisoners, doomed the project to failure in advance. In any event, a group of SS men, apparently experts in this work, quite possibly from the company that had at one time serviced the camps at Treblinka, Chełmno or Auschwitz, began the fight against the lice using the same Zyklon. Out of necessity, they must have changed the range of their activities. This of course required that the patients be moved for the duration of the procedure from one room to the other.

That was the first complication. The second one was considerably more serious. A treacherous louse had found access to his body and he in turn became ill. There was no doubt that this was spotted typhus. The whole burden of managing the quarantine fell on Emil's shoulders.

The third complication could have been the most dangerous in its consequences. After the barrack had been treated with an insecticide, in the most acute phase of his illness, a high-ranking commission of the SS leadership visited the Cieplice camp. He had learned of this event later from Emil, who described it most dramatically. The fact that at the head of that commission stood Doctor Mengele himself added a dark spiciness to this event.

It was the beginning of March 1945. We know now that this was two months before the end of the war, but even then no one doubted what the outcome of the war would be. And so an SS commission visits a tiny camp somewhere in Lower Silesia where some kind of epidemic had broken out. It visits that camp in all seriousness, as if the Third Reich had no other troubles.

In any event, as Emil related it to him, Mengele in the company of several SS officers had arrived at the camp with great pomp. He entered it through the very gate that was located directly across from the place where he now stood. Of course, Emil showed the commission around the hospital. Everything was proceeding in a civilized and elegant manner, as between gentlemen. And here, on entering the hall that underwent delousing a few days before and was now being aired – a catastrophe! And what a catastrophe! From behind the door fell out a corpse in a state of considerable decay. They forgot about it when they had liquidated all the hiding places of that kind at the beginning of his illness. And the corpse literally fell on the SS man who had opened the door to the hall ...

As Emil had dramatically reported to him later, the SS man immediately reached for his gun to shoot it. It was difficult to say whether the Germans realized for what purpose the corpse had been kept hidden behind the door. In any case, the culprit should not remain alive. Someone had restrained the SS man, Emil managed to blame everything on the other doctor, that is on him ... He was in the right. First, that was what they had agreed on. Second, his chances of surviving the typhus were slim. Mengele apparently had asked where the *Scheisskerl*, the person responsible for hiding the corpse, was. Emil showed him the cell that they occupied as doctors. Whether on the way Mengele's rage had cooled off, or he was affected by the sight of the dying doctor, in any case, the former chief doctor of Auschwitz only waved his hand and left their cell ...

The commission inspected the rest of the quarantine, talked with the local SS men, issued some instructions that no one intended to follow, and left. And he survived. He came out whole from a perilous situation that could have cost him his life, and from an illness whose price could have been no less.

After the illness, he felt terribly exhausted. The worst of it was that he could not soothe his hunger, since it was for the time being unthinkable to continue the previous method of acquiring additional food. The need to soothe the oppressive and disabling feeling of emptiness in the stomach, a feeling particularly strong after spotted typhus, became the mother of the invention of a method equal to that of holding over the corpses ...

To make the treatment with insecticide more effective, and also to prevent the escape of the dangerous gas from the treated area, it was necessary to seal the cracks in the windows and doors. The Germans sealed those cracks with strips of paper and for glue they used dextrin powder dissolved in water. They had completed the treatment with the insecticide but luckily left behind full bags of dextrin. From his studies of chemistry, he remembered that dextrin is obtained from starch or glycogen. The final product involved additional chemical processing but, as far as he remembered, no substances poisonous or dangerous to the human organism were added.

He began at first with small portions – just once daily and then twice. After those first experiments, he had not noticed in himself any signs that would indicate poisoning. Greater portions proved harmless as well. What was most important was that they effectively soothed the feeling of hunger. He also deluded himself into thinking that they provided the organism with some calories. Later he never attempted to verify how all this appeared from a theoretical point of view. Emil, who endured hunger much more easily than he, told him that he was a madman, that it was madness to attempt suicide on the eve of the war's end.

There was no doubt that the war was swiftly coming to an end. Dawidek, when delivering food for the sick prisoners, always brought them the latest news from the fronts. The SS men were increasingly afraid that the camp would be liquidated.

The epidemic began to subside. True, the number of prisoners at the camp declined from 800 to no more than 400, but still they went out to work and, as it turned out, helped in the removal of the factory machinery deep into Germany. However, it was difficult to say where to since probably only the area of Lower Silesia had not been affected by war operations.

The number of patients was constantly declining. In the whole of the quarantine – barely eighty. Among them the *kapo* Chmielnicki who overcame the disease. He emerged victorious from his encounter with typhus but not from the encounter with his destiny. When the war ended, he returned to Paris. There he was tried and sentenced to death. The guillotine specialist took care of what typhus had not …

It was becoming warmer. Here and there, verdure began to appear. At the beginning of April – he remembered that indeed now was also the beginning of April – they were hit by the dismal news that the authorities decided that the Cieplice camp would after all have to be evacuated. The bearer of the news was of course Dawidek. That was bad news. Each new camp could become the place where the few prisoners who survived – Jewish and non-Jewish – could be exterminated. Because after all they were extremely inconvenient and dangerous witnesses. At that time, Emil was hoping for the best. He thought that the Germans would pamper them. For them, the vision of the front was scarier than the vision of any responsibility.

The evacuation of the Cieplice camp was a story altogether different. When he started out at that time on an unknown road, he left behind a stage of suffering that, while occupying little space in his biography, had carved in him deep traces. He was not always aware of the existence of those traces, or rather scars. He thought that the current of life would erase those traces as the sea erases footprints in the sand on the coast. But this was an illusion. He was returning to the Cieplice of his memories, and what was worse, he was returning to it in nightmares. He had never returned to a place to confront his memories and dreams with reality. At least, with what remained of the reality of that other time. Perhaps it was laziness. Perhaps it was a superstition that he could not understand. In a certain period, it was fear. The fear of delving too much in his own past, because that meant that he was getting old. For the same reason, he did not like to look at photographs that recalled the old days …

Standing here now, in front of the five buildings that at one time made up the Cieplice camp, he felt a kind of regret that he had treated his past that way. And not only his past at the camps. He treated it as if it had belonged to someone else. And this was, after all, a deception. One cannot create an artificial separation between the different periods of one's own life as he had done – between the period of his life that ended with the liberation and the period that began with the liberation. You are what you are: the tears of your mother, the laughter of your friend, the stone that was thrown at you because of your ethnic origin, the song with which you bid farewell to the train with volunteers that went to the Spanish front, the yellow star that you wore attached to your chest, the dead person's bread that saved you from death. Is it too late to correct that deception?

When he had stood in that very place 36 years ago, clinging to Emil, all the world's problems were condensed into one: to survive. Actually to survive and to soothe his hunger.

214

He survived and avowed that all his accounts with the past had been settled. They had not been ...

He survived in that barrack on the right. At that time there were no curtains there, only veils carved on the windows by the frost. Now one could see neat curtains everywhere. He raised his head and stared at the first floor. A face appeared in the window. That was not a ghost but a face of flesh and blood ... And the very building is not a remnant from the times that are now unreal. People live there ... This is their home... In the buildings that once formed the German camp, where people that were branded by their ethnic origin were suffering, perishing from hunger and epidemics, now live normal people who love, quarrel, have children, watch television, read newspapers, are bored – live, normal people. And when they leave this world, no one sullies their dignity ...

He asked the taxi driver to wait a while longer. The taxi driver was not very pleased, but the promise to reward his waiting put him in a better mood.

He entered the building on the right. At first glance, the corridor had not been rebuilt. The same stairs on both sides of the entrance ... He climbed to the first floor. Here, on the right, should have been the door to the cell that he had occupied with Emil at the time. The door was not there. Instead of it – a white wall. However, the door leading to the large hospital hall had remained.

On the door – a calling card with a name. At the side of the door – a bell. He pressed. An elderly woman opened the door and blocked the entrance. The same woman whose face he had noticed from below. A somewhat frightened little girl was hiding behind her.

'What's it about?' asked the woman. She had a sincere, smiling face.

'You know ... its about me... a strictly private matter ... I wanted ... I would like to ask you to allow me to look around the apartment. What is it like to live here?'

'Are you from the housing department?'

'No, no, not at all. This is a strictly private matter. You should not be afraid.'

Luckily, he inspired trust, and the woman allowed him into the apartment.

Inside he did not recognize anything. He could only guess how the hall had been rebuilt. It had been divided with a number of partitions. This allowed for two rooms in sequence to be created and for a narrow little corridor. Near the little corridor but connected to it by a door, was a space that was neither a room nor a kitchen.

'Forgive my intrusion. But I am interested in this building, which means these buildings, that ...' he was looking for the right words, 'were a camp in the German time.'

'We know that, sir. There at the entrance there is, you know, a plaque.'

'I have not seen it yet, but ... Here on the right of the corridor there was a little room ...'

'There was, there was. The door to the room from the side of the corridor was walled up and the entrance to it is now from the kitchen. I'll show you.'

She took him politely to the room near the corridor. On the way, he tried to glimpse through the open door into the room across the entrance. A television set, probably a colour one, a piano, and in general furniture showing prosperity. Very clean everywhere ... Walking slowly not to scare off the visions of the past, he entered his – his and Emil's – cell. He entered from the side where at that time stood the plank-beds. The little room was completely empty. Almost empty. Only in the middle stood a small gas stove. To tell the truth, there was no room for much more. On the stove a kettle. So banal.

'Have all the apartments in the building been rebuilt the same way?'

The woman was not certain about that.

'Probably, yes. Perhaps differently on the ground floor.'

For a while they were silent. He looked around eagerly as if he wanted to pluck off and take away with him a fragment of the period that would shortly disappear from his sight. He asked again:

'What's it like to live here?'

'Fine. My son obtained this apartment. He lives here with his wife and child. Well, and me. Granny, you know ... Pardon me, sir, were you in this camp?'

'Yes, I was.'

'Why had the Germans sent you there?'

He thought for a while how to say it as briefly as possible.

'Only Jews were in that camp.'

'Are you a Jew?'

'Yes.'

The silence was longer.

'You know, where I lived before the war, in Wohńy?[2], there were many Jews. They were poor, poor. Later the Germans deported them.'

'The Germans killed them.'

'Indeed. But later some appeared again.'

'They appeared?'

'Yes, the newspapers wrote about it.'

He did not want to inquire what the woman had in mind. Besides, it made no sense to prolong the conversation. The woman was obviously preparing dinner.

'Tell me though, isn't it sometimes unpleasant to live in a house where at one time there was a Nazi camp?'

'Eh, you know sir, when one does not have a roof over one's head one is not choosy. But it is good to live here. There is no noise from the street. The children have a place to play. And one does not worry because cars do not come here.'

'I thank you very much. And I apologize again for the intrusion.'

'Do not mention it. I am by myself the whole day. And this way I chatted a bit … Goodbye.'

He descended the stone stairs on which at one time he had slipped and fallen downstairs. He descended slowly. Again, he found himself on the previous camp street – the Lagerstrasse – on which the children of this building could now safely play. And of the second building. And of the third one. He had no desire to go into the other buildings. Neither to the one where the SS had had their headquarters. Nor to the one where Dawidek reigned.

When he left the little square between the buildings, he noticed on the right, on a low pedestal, a commemorative plaque, and in front of it a jar with a little flower … The plaque proclaimed that here had been a Nazi camp that was a branch of the camp in Rogożnica-Gross-Rosen.

Before he entered the taxi, he looked back once more. How

many buildings were there after all? Five or six? It seemed if one building was missing ... But perhaps after all there were only five. There was no one he could ask. No one ...

'Are we going to the hotel?' asked the taxi driver.

'Of course, of course.'

'Are you pleased, sir?'

'Am I pleased? I don't know ...'

'No matter. Soon we shall pass the militia sanatorium. A big scandal about that sanatorium ...'

Over Poland rolled the memorable year of 1981.

Notes

1. A reference to the Solidarity movement.
2. Volhynia.

15 Joachim

The Germans decided to evacuate the camp in the evening. No one had any idea how the evacuation would proceed. The SS men did not hide their irritation. They had thought, of course, that the camp would protect them until the end of the war from going to the front. They had not taken into account that, for the authorities above them, the evacuation of the camps and the transportation of the prisoners were also pretexts for actions to protect them from the same danger.

A few hours before they had left the camp, they were told that the evacuation would proceed by train. Moreover, the authorities decided that the sick prisoners from the quarantine would continue to remain separated from the rest of the prisoners, and would be placed in special rail cars. Both the physicians, that is he and Emil, were to travel with them.

They had heard enough about the evacuation of other camps to be afraid of what the coming hours could bring. From various signs, they attempted to divine the intentions of the SS men. They were certain of at least one thing. Since it was the beginning of April, they were not threatened by the frost that a few months previously had effectively assisted the SS men who escorted the evacuees, by decimating the transports of prisoners that were evacuated from the east to the west of Germany.

At four o'clock, they were led out to the railway ramp where the rail cars already stood. Luckily, the tracks were quite close to the camp, and they did not have to carry the most seriously ill prisoners very far. As it turned out, the rail cars waiting for them were coal cars. The height of such a car was no more than one metre. He was to stay with the sick prisoners in one rail car, and Emil in the other. Even squeezed together as tightly as possible, the sick prisoners could not all be fitted into two coal cars. It was necessary to bring another one from Jelenia Góra where there were very many of them: they had stood there idle since the time when almost all of Silesia fell into Soviet hands.

The floors of the rail cars were covered with a thick layer of straw. This gave them the hope that they were not being taken to their death. One could have expected that even the Germans would not be so perfidious as to make the train journey somewhat tolerable for those whom they were sending to the gas chambers or to be shot. Besides, they could have shot the prisoners here on the spot – this would relieve the difficulties of the overburdened transport system of the Third Reich. He hoped that the SS men still kept to the basic idea that as long as the live prisoners were around, they too would be needed – to guard them. The victims and the executioners were continually tied by a common interest. The question was only for how long ...

There were 30, perhaps 35, sick prisoners together with him in the rail car. Several of them were unconscious, the rest very weak. The epidemic had subsided, but it left in its wake completely wasted human bodies.

When everyone from the quarantine was in the rail cars, some workers appeared and began covering the cars with boards. This way each rail car received something of a roof that turned the car into a flat box reminding one of a casket. Only by crawling or walking on all fours could one move inside it. It was impossible to stand straight.

He lay close to the door, which was open for the time being. Behind the Karkonosze Mountains, the sun was slowly setting and it wrapped with a gray-red glare the parts of the railroad track and of the nearby forest that were visible from the door. He wondered what the SS men had in mind by installing those roofs over each coal car. It was doubtful they were afraid that a prisoner would attempt to escape, and it was even more doubtful that they wanted to protect the sick prisoners from possible rain. In the unlikely event that this was their intention, however, it would indicate that they were preparing for a long journey. This was not comforting because it would take them farther away from Poland. What he feared most, however, was that the door of the rail car would be shut. Thinking about it, he began to feel suffocated.

The over 30 sick prisoners could not comfortably lie on the floor of the coal car. Some lay partially on top of the others. The inside of the rail car was drowning in half-darkness, and the thirty rolled up bodies in striped camp uniforms formed a pulsating, shapeless mass.

Three or four hours later, nothing had changed: they still stood at the station. Suddenly, in one rail car after the other, the doors were shut. Still, the train did not move. When the doors were shut, the inside of the coal cars became cut off from the noise of the railroad track. The rail car began to live with a rhythm of its own. The initial quiet moaning of the sick prisoners turned into increasingly mournful and loud complaints, and even screams. The straw mattresses on the plank-beds at the camp were the height of comfort compared to the floor, even if it was covered with straw.

The calls and the whistles of the SS men and railway men outside stopped, and finally the train began to move. They had been standing at the station for at least five hours, and all that time the sick prisoners had received nothing to eat and, what was worse, nothing to drink. Luckily, he realized, it was less stuffy inside the rail car than he had expected. At least for the time being.

The rhythmic din of the wheels had gradually calmed the sick prisoners. For several hours, the train moved in a stop-and-go fashion, occasionally backing up as if changing direction. And finally it stopped again … Someone opened the door. They found themselves at a blacked-out station. After a while, someone's hands – owing to the darkness he could not see whose they were – began to throw pieces of bread into the coal car. No one saw where the pieces of bread had landed. In the darkness, a desperate struggle began. It proceeded invisibly and quietly, and only the wheezing respiration, the hushed swearing, and the rustle of the straw indicated what was going on. Of course, the stronger and more agile prisoners grabbed several pieces of bread for themselves; the weakest and most crushed of them probably obtained nothing. True, he felt responsible for order in the car, but how could he maintain order if he was unable to stand straight? He looked on passively, or rather tried to listen to the confusion caused by the fight for the bread … The train did not stop for

221

long. After a certain time, the doors were shut again by someone's hand, and the train began to move again. Due to the constant changes in direction, he did not even know whether they were heading south or west ... It was difficult to imagine the train would be heading in any other direction.

Several hours had passed. The rail car was becoming increasingly stuffy. The Germans had not provided a bucket before they shut the car. Besides, even if they had, reaching it would have required a balancing act of which none of the sick prisoners were capable. He touched the straw with his hand. As he had anticipated – it was wet. At the same time, he found a piece of bread. He had no intention of giving it up ...

The rhythm of the train and the heavy air put him to sleep. When he woke up, it was still dark. He had completely lost his sense of time. The train stopped again. The sick prisoners were snoring heavily in the darkness ...

Suddenly he heard something entirely different. He did not believe his ears. Someone in the rail car was whistling. However, what was the most surprising was that the unknown person was whistling Beethoven's violin concerto. He listened for a while to satisfy himself that in the whistling there had not been a single wrong note. The person who was whistling it must have been tremendously musical. He attempted to detect from where the sound was coming. It definitely came from the opposite wall of the rail car. He did not have to think long to know who among the sick prisoners could in those conditions and in this situation have had the need to whistle, and precisely Beethoven's violin concerto. Yes, it could not have been anyone else. Quietly and clearly, not to wake the others, he threw into the darkness of the rail car a question:

'Doctor Joachim?'

The whistling stopped:

'Yes?'

'Was it you who whistled?'

'Yes.'

The questions and the answers came in German. Doctor Joachim was a lawyer who came from Prague. He came along the same route as Emil. From Prague, he was resettled to the Łódź ghetto. After the liquidation of the ghetto, he found himself in Auschwitz. From Auschwitz, he was sent to Jelenia Góra in the same group as he and Emil. When the camp at Cieplice was created, he became a clerk there ... He must have been fifty-two or fifty-three years old. The epidemic had not spared him, and he suffered from the illness much worse than the others. It had been a miracle he was still alive, and even more so because, in addition to his illness, a leg of his became suppurated.

He screwed up his courage. Crawling on all fours, pushing himself through across the sick prisoners on the floor, he made his way to Joachim. Joachim continued whistling:

'What makes you so happy?'

'I am not happy at all.'

'So why are you whistling?'

For a while there was no reply. Later:

'I am whistling because this night I shall die.'

He did not know how to react. Joachim could have been right. His condition was hopeless.

'Have you studied music?' he asked stupidly to break the silence.

'Oh, yes. I studied at the conservatory. I come from a very musical family.'

'Joachim, Joachim ... Josef Joachim. There was in Germany a great violinist by that name.'

'Yes, yes. He was my close family.'

The train was now moving faster. Beating time on the rail joints, it forced its way through the Germany that was wrapped in darkness. Somewhere multi-million armies were fighting, somewhere deliberations were taking place on what conditions to put to the dying Nazism, and Doctor Joachim from Prague was preparing to die by whistling Beethoven's violin concerto.

'Tell me something about yourself.'

Joachim had been waiting just for that. He began to talk, or rather to whisper, faster and faster as though he feared that he would not have the time to finish. From time to time he stopped the monologue to catch his breath, and immediately continued as if he feared he would be interrupted.

'My family comes from Prague. Father was a brother of the great Joachim. When I was a little boy, my uncle often visited us. He used to meet in our house with Dvořák and Fibich who were regular guests. Also Janáček used to come … Have you heard of him?'

'I have.'

'They played music. Joachim played the violin. He used to be accompanied by my mother or by Fibich. How they played! From childhood, I was taught to play the violin. Joachim predicted a great future for me. Worthy of his name and fame. In the beginning, I was taught by my mother. Later I was sent to the conservatory. Already as a ten-year-old, I had performed at a concert. Janáček sat in the first row. He applauded. Then the world war came. The first one. I had to interrupt my studies at the conservator, But I continued with music. I played in a quintet. We went to play concerts in France.'

He spoke with increasing difficulty. He interrupted him:

'Now rest. You will finish tomorrow.'

'Tomorrow? … Janáček, my uncle … No, no, Joachim … Always encouraged me…'

Suddenly the train stopped. Again the door of the coal car was opened, and cool April night air penetrated inside. Someone pushed a big pot with a steaming hot liquid into the rail car. A voice announced: 'Coffee!'

Swiftly he crawled back to his place at the door. In those conditions, only he could distribute that coffee among the sick prisoners. He lifted the lid. It was neither tea nor coffee but a liquid with a disgusting smell and taste.

Luckily, the train was still standing. He could therefore pour the liquid into the cups that were either stretched out to him or handed over from inside the rail car without fear of scalding the people nearby.

He finished at the very moment that the train began to move again. He also poured that swill for himself. He sipped it and thought about Joachim. He hoped he would still hear the whistling from inside the rail car. But nothing disturbed the snoring of the sick prisoners and the din of the wheels …

He fell asleep …

He woke up when the merry rays of sunshine began to penetrate into the car through the cracks between the boards of the roof and the walls of the rail car. The rays brought out

from the darkness a narrow strip of the floor that was covered with filthy straw and left the rest of the rail car in darkness. Some of the sick prisoners moved groaning, others lay motionless. It was difficult to say who among them had not survived the hardship of the journey, and who survived it despite the hardship. Who made it easier to continue the evacuation of the transport by ceasing to be a burden to it, and who had not taken advantage of that opportunity ...
The train was still standing.

Some minutes had passed. Finally, the SS men forcefully opened the door the whole width of the coal car. As usual, they shouted something loudly and with a barking voice gave some orders. As it turned out, they had arrived at their destination. He clambered out from the car. Not far, near the other rail car, stood Emil. He was helping his patients get out of the rail car.

He had not had the time to shake off the straw from himself when the SS men ordered a roll call. Of course, they could not do without a roll call. This time it lasted a long time because, in addition to those who stood in rows of five and those who sat and lay on the ground, it was also necessary to count the corpses that were taken out from the coal cars.

The SS men were adding, subtracting and verifying. Luckily, the total checked out. In his rail car, seven people did not make it. Among them was Joachim. In Emil's rail car – nine. Those alive as well as those who died were covered with wet, stinking straw mixed with faeces. The SS men, holding their noses and laughing, ordered the weakest among the sick prisoners to climb onto carts. The corpses remained near the train. The rest of the prisoners went on foot to the camp nearby.

He walked with Emil, barely dragging his feet. On the way he told him about Joachim and reported his conversation with him in the rail car. For a while Emil was silent. Then he said:
'Y-e-e-s ... Only that his family name had not been Joachim at all. That was his given name. His name was Joachim Hirsch. When he was registered in the ghetto, someone mistakenly turned Joachim Hirsch into Hirsch Joachim. I had known his family in Prague. The parents owned a very good tavern not far from the Old City. They kept a Jewish kitchen. They were

very successful. He did not attend any conservatory and never played in a quintet. He was only a lawyer, perhaps a musical one. Aha, something else. The great Josef Joachim came not from Czechoslovakia but from Hungary, and I do not even know if he was a Jew ...'

After a while, they stood in front of a barbed-wire fence that surrounded a factory building where the camp was located.

16 Job and the Others

The soil smelled of spring. No. The spring smelled of the soil that was moist, rotten, and in which the dead leaves gathered during the winter, the superfluous shoots, and generally all kinds of field refuse were decomposing. It smelled of the soil that was dug out from a long ditch by prisoners who were sinking in mud. That soil was later put up along the edges of that ditch and beaten down with spades heavy with clay. This created a sort of rampart reminiscent of trenches as shown in films about the First World War.

He stood leaning with his back against the rough, friendly trunk of a tree. He was breathing in deeply the April air that foretold a time that was late in coming. He observed the uneven, slow movements of hands and spades. True, he was a prisoner like the others, but he was exempt from that work. In a bag that hung at his side, he carried some handy medications. He was a nurse. From time to time, one or another of the SS men also gave him his haversack with a thermos and sandwiches to carry. It was a sign of a patronizing trust on the part of the Germans and indicated a peculiar relationship that the other prisoners envied.

As a nurse, he was exempt from digging the ditch. But he was not exempt from walking. He had to walk back and forth along the ditch for ten hours. Perhaps the obligatory presence of a nurse raised, at the end of the war, the morale of the Germans, although the help he could to provide to his co-prisoners was as illusory as the concern of the SS men for the health of the Jews. Luckily, there was a third possibility between walking and sitting on the ground, and he used it extensively. As indeed now, when he stood with his back against the solitary oak tree that grew nearby. It was his good fortune that the SS men paid no attention to this avoidance of their orders.

He did not have much to do. However, he had a lot of time for reflection. Of course, he had some vague visions of a future that in April 1945 had not looked as impossible as it had a few months earlier. He was also immersed in banal reminiscences of the distant and not-so-distant past. That was a hygienic procedure that protected him with a shield of intimacy from succumbing to camp stagnation. Like many other prisoners, he was threatened with being swallowed up by matters that did not go beyond the everyday camp struggle for survival. And this, like quicksand, gave the victim no chance. He had many opportunities to come in to contact with such instances of decline. Particularly among those prisoners who had survived longer than the average time that the SS had anticipated in the Nazi camp.

The camp at Erlenbusch was the same absurd fiction as almost everything else that had happened after the evacuation from Warmbrunn. The most absurd thing of course was the ditch that the Jewish slaves had been digging for the last three weeks. The little town or village of Erlenbusch was not far from Świdnica. The camp itself was located in the open field. Every day, about 300 prisoners were leaving the camp to dig a ditch of two metres deep for ten hours. The ditch extended on both sides of the paved road, and after a few hundred metres ended somewhere in the field. Two concrete bunkers stood in the places where it touched on the road. The purpose of fortifications like these was probably to stop the Soviet army, if it would occur to it to move deep into Germany through that particular spot. One did not have to be a specialist to conclude that this was a ridiculous obstacle; neither the ditch nor the bunkers would present any particular difficulty to tanks.

Whenever he observed the digging of those ditches, he remembered the year 1939 in Warsaw. At that time, people were also digging ditches. It was not clear whether this was done to hinder the German armies' invasion of Warsaw, or to protect the civilian population from the bombs of the Nazi aeroplanes. In any case, the ditches had not met any of those hopes, except for a third one, which at the beginning had been only marginal. The digging of the ditches gave the tens of thousands of civilians the illusion of participating in the defence of the capital, and created a feeling of solidarity and unity that overcame the bitterness created by the bombastic display of patriotism by the authorities who were about to run away.

In Erlenbusch, the digging of the ditches did not even have this meaning, at the very least because it was the Jewish prisoners who were digging them, compelled to work by Nazi guards. And the German civilians? They were almost nowhere to be seen. After the evacuation from Warmbrunn, the prisoners were crossing a country that appeared as if outside of life and time and war concerns. In untouched little towns and villages neat little houses with flowers and curtains in the windows could be seen. It was like a child's toy town: empty, depopulated. On the clean streets some elderly women appeared from time to time who did not pay the least attention to the prisoners in their striped uniforms. A country under the spell of a sorceress! The only element that disturbed this idyllic view had been the camps and the SS men who guarded them. Of course, that was how it appeared from the outside to the eyes of the Jews who thirsted finally to see here the horrors of war – destruction and death. From the inside, it was certainly different than the seeming calm and the flapping Nazi flags would suggest. The approaching end of the war must have somehow disturbed the way of life of a society that tumbled from the heights of triumph and pride to the bottom of defeat …

Also, the very evacuation of the Warmbrunn camp was absurd – from the Nazi point of view, of course. The evacuation involved 500 or 600 prisoners, three-quarters of whom were exhausted, having just recovered from spotted typhus, and one-quarter who were still sick. Until that time, less expensive methods were being used to finish off Jewish and non-Jewish prisoners who were in a considerably better physical condition than the human tatters from Warmbrunn that were so carefully transported to the camp at Dörnau. Given the labour shortage, those who had been exterminated would have been much more useful as manpower to the Thousand-year Reich.

And at Dörnau, actually nothing made sense. First, they were quartered as if they were to remain there, and then they were assembled for a further ordeal. They were taken to the bath-house, received new striped uniforms, and started out on foot on the way to Świdnica. In the evening, they arrived at the camp for Jews at Schottenwerk. Here the whole ceremony was repeated. They were again taken to the bath-house and again received clean striped uniforms. This was incomprehensible but certainly comforting. People condemned to death are not taken twice to the bath-house and given new striped uniforms each time. Of course, also this time there were SS men who took advantage of the bath-house routine to torment the tired and sickly prisoners. But this was a ritual.

In the morning, they started out on the road again, and after a few hours found themselves at Erlenbusch. One must say in favour of the SS men that on the road they had not performed that other ritual: they had not beaten to death or shot any of the prisoners, though most of them barely dragged their feet. At the most they looked at the breaking ranks of the condemned with disgust which, luckily, was not a feeling arousing in them the desire to murder ...

The situation was clear. Both the Jews and the SS men who escorted them knew that the war was coming to an end. Only that both were anxious with uncertainty. The prisoners were not sure how indispensable they were to the SS men. The SS men were not sure how strong the fear was of being sent to the front at the higher levels of the SS hierarchy, and how long the fiction of utilizing the Jews for unnecessary work and the need to escort them would last. Both sides knew that they needed each other. But if the whole strategy was sinking in a sea of nonsense, and if bringing that strategy to reality was accompanied by a surrealistic pantomime of absurd moves on the chessboard of the SS camp empire – that was a different matter. Nevertheless, any work, however unnecessary, found for the Jews was like a lifeline thrown equally to the prisoners and to the guards. They were chained together, drowning together, and trying to remain as long as possible on the surface of the river that threatened to suck them into a deadly abyss.

The Dörnau camp, to which they were evacuated from Warmbrunn, had been filled to the rafters with beings that by some miracle remained alive and were even being taken to work in the nearby quarries. There were rumours that not far, somewhere in the mountains, quarters were being constructed for Hitler in case Berlin fell. One could presume that the construction of such quarters was also dreamt up by people in the highest ranks of the SS hierarchy who wanted in this way to protect themselves from being sent to the front.

As it turned out, at the Dörnau camp there were many Jews from the Łódź ghetto. They had been sent there directly from Auschwitz not long ago. Those who remembered him and knew him as a ghetto doctor peppered him with questions about the situation at the front, as if the fact that he had been evacuated from Lower Silesia had given him a better insight into matters of war strategy.

After arriving to Dörnau, all the prisoners from Warmbrunn were stripped naked and put on the first and second floors of a former factory. A barrack Kapo assigned to him a place on an upper plank-bed. He created that place by hitting two other prisoners with a truncheon to make them move over. When he clambered to the assigned place and tried to lie down, the prisoner lying on the left to him began to hit him with his fists as if he wanted to get even for the Kapo's truncheon. He of course responded in kind. Sitting on the plank-bed they hit, choked, scratched, and bit each other without saying a word, at the accompaniment of the monotonous gasping and snoring of the other prisoners. The furious fight went on for several minutes. They had hardly harmed each other – after all, they were two weak human tatters not in the least dangerous to each other. Finally, they collapsed exhausted on the mattress. There was just enough room for him to lie on his side with his hand lifted above his head. He immediately fell asleep and almost immediately woke up. Or rather jumped up as if scalded. He had indeed been scalded. The whole side on which he lay was itching and like on fire. It was covered with soft blisters and hot like a cake just taken from the oven. He jumped down on the floor. As in all the camps, the mattress on the plank-bed was filled with wood-shavings. In the dim shine of the light bulb, he saw above the mattress an unusual phenomenon: something reminiscent of mist rising above a swamp, or morning fog. The phenomenon was caused by tens of thousands, and perhaps millions, of

jumping fleas… This was a terrifying and fascinating spectacle. The fleas shimmered in the half-darkness, which made
the whole spectacle even more eerie. He had been thoroughly
bitten – from the underarm to the thigh. He did not return to
the plank-bed. Since childhood he had been allergic to
fleabites. Each such bite caused in him a painful reaction over
his whole body … It seemed to him that the jumping and
wriggling beasts were created to finish the work started by the
Germans.

He sat on a wooden stool for two nights. Luckily, the
barrack Kapo had not noticed it. On the third day, the
evacuees from Warmbrunn that were not sick were gathered
on the Lagerplatz and during the roll call it was announced
that they would be moving on. For him it was deliverance …

The camp at Erlenbusch consisted of five brand new
barracks painted bright green. They were actually the first
larger group of prisoners there. When they arrived at the
camp, they found there only the few dozen Jewish prisoners
who had erected those barracks. That camp, set up at the end
of the war, was an amazing phenomenon. The prisoners
already understood that new camps did not at all mean that
the war would continue for a long time. The purpose of this
additional fiction was to protect the SS men from the Soviet
katyushas. That was a game transparent to everyone.
However, it gave the Jews who were still alive the feeling of at
least temporary safety and allowed them to spin optimistic
dreams about the nearest future.

It was the first time he had found himself in such new
barracks – they still smelled of the pine forest. It was also
pleasant to lie down on mattresses that, while filled with
wood shavings like those at Dörnau, were free from fleas or
lice.

Among the prisoners who erected the barracks he met S. –
his neighbour from the Łódź ghetto. Both used to be co-
tenants of the apartment on Jakuba Street. In the ghetto, S. had
been quite an important person – something like a minister of
finance. As a co-tenant, he behaved decently. As a dignitary
probably also – he belonged to the few who apparently had
clean hands. Both rejoiced at the meeting. It gave them the
opportunity to talk about life, about the ruefully remembered

times. For those who found themselves in Brzezinka, and later in other camps, the stagnation in the ghetto that was dying from hunger, sickness and filth had plainly been a nostalgic memory. And so had been life in Łódź before the war, for the Jews incarcerated behind the barbed wires of the Bałuty.

However, he remembered that short, red-haired man particularly well for reasons other than sharing a ghetto apartment. Not from the time when S. handled the ghetto finances, but from the time when he became, like everyone else, a Jew marked for extermination ...

'Hey, you, nurse!' He started. The SS man who stood near him pointed to a prisoner who lay on the bottom of the ditch. The prisoner lay on his back. His partially pulled down striped trousers revealed a belly and thighs thin like the handle of the spade that lay nearby. He jumped into the ditch and poured, between the lips of the prisoner who lay in it, some of the solution concocted from various common heart remedies – straight from the bottle. It was naïve to expect that this help would bring any results. Besides, the prisoner most certainly did not need that kind of medication. He likely had a terrible diarrhea – the result of bad food and an atrophied mucous membrane. He did not have the time to pull down his trousers and now lay in mud and excrement, which made the SS guard laugh out loud.

He helped the prisoner get out from the ditch. He was a Hungarian Jew. His name was Kohn. His twin brother had perished in Hirschberg. Perished? He was murdered in unusual circumstances. In the Jelenia Góra coal yard where the prisoners were working, there were huge piles of powdered coal that were constantly glowing at the bottom due to pressure. Since the frost was great – at times, it was nearly 25 degrees below zero – the poorly dressed prisoners, who actually had no protection from the cold, used to warm themselves by lying down on the powdered coal. When they later returned to the normal temperature, they felt the cold even more strongly. One of the prisoners the brother of the one that now lay in the ditch, dug out for himself a little pit in the powdered coal, lay down and immediately fell asleep. If he had not fallen asleep, he would have perhaps noticed that a mountain of coal powder was sliding down on him. In a few seconds he was buried, and the

SS men had not given permission to save him, because they felt that he received the punishment he deserved for lazing around. His brother worked on a different shift and had not witnessed it … The twins were already *muselmanns* in Hirschberg, although the one who found himself in Erlenbusch endured the camp better than his brother. This could seem strange since they were identical twins. The one who perished under the pile of coal was greatly swollen from hunger. Someone convinced them that cumin was the best remedy for such situations. Unanimously each of them spent a portion of bread daily to buy this remedy … He remembered how the healthier brother had asked him with hope in his eyes whether that remedy would help his brother. What could he tell him at that time? That it was nonsense? That some camp crook had simply fooled them? He only said they were doing the right thing… They did not have the opportunity to find out that they were duped. The pile of coal powder made it impossible …

Such exploitation of the *muselmanns* took place in all the camps. No one was particularly shocked by it. A *muselmann* was condemned. It was therefore natural that he became the fertilizer on which some other prisoner, who had a better chance to endure to the end, could survive …

Now that brother was also dying here. There was of course no possibility at all of healing him … He helped him take off his trousers and wash up in the puddle nearby. Having fulfilled this way his obligation as a nurse, he went back under the tree.

This S. believed every word of Chairman Rumkowski more than most people did. His belief and trust in the Eldest had no limits. Besides, he had reasons for it. He knew that the Łódź ghetto was the last one that the Germans had still maintained. All the other ghettos had been liquidated a long time before, and their inhabitants were deported and exterminated.

When the Germans decided to liquidate this last ghetto too, Rumkowski went from *ressort* to *ressort* and assured everyone that nothing bad would happen to anyone and that those who voluntarily reported for deportation would be in a privileged position. S. believed him also this time …

He would never forget this scene. At dusk, on the first day of the deportation from the ghetto, a multitude of people poured out onto the street, either in a state of panic in view of the situation, or in order to move to the houses that were already empty of inhabitants. Preparing to be deported some carried pieces of luggage. In the noisy bustle, in the half-darkness swollen with fear, he saw his neighbour. S. carried an enormous knapsack and dragged his weeping children behind him. His wife ran behind him equally burdened, with a knapsack and an enormous suitcase. S. adored his offspring. The ten-year-old boy was exceptionally capable, and the teenaged daughter attracted attention with her beauty. The sight of the man who dragged the resisting children behind him and pushed himself though the crowd to the tram that was to take the deportees to the Marysin station made a weird impression. Even at this moment, when everything was coming to an end, S. obediently obeyed the Chairman's commands ...

After three weeks, almost the entire population of the ghetto was deported and taken to Auschwitz. So was the tailoring workshop where he was the factory doctor. The last of the deportees already knew the destination of the train. They knew about the Auschwitz hell although they had no idea about the selection and the gas chambers ... When, thanks to the favourable evaluation of Doctor Mengele, he avoided the threshold of death by Zyklon B and found himself on the territory of the former Gypsy camp he noticed, on the first day of camp life, in one group of Jews from Łódź, his neighbour from the ghetto, S., sat on the ground. His odd attire consisted of fancy shoes and a very short jacket. He sat staring at a point in the sand, indifferent to everything that was happening around him. He was in a state of complete despondency. One could imagine what he felt when suddenly, at the railway ramp, surrounded by yelling SS men, he was pushed in the direction of Mengele who conducted the selection. And, when separated from those closest to him, he looked at the receding column of Jews that carried off his children and wife with it. One could imagine his reaction when he heard, as did the other prisoners, that the black smoke coming out from the chimney was the mournful shroud surrounding the burning remains of those closest to him. One could imagine that he accused himself for what had happened, for his belief in Rumkowski's assurances. For

235

having urged those who were the most dear to him to be among the first ones to go from the ghetto to the gas …

And what if they had been the last ones? Would anything be different? The sentence on those closest to him was passed when Hitler created his ideology and conquered power.

At the time when they met in Brzezinka, S. had not dared to lift his head. He pretended not to see him. Was he ashamed? Perhaps he did not want to see that cursed black smoke. He was defeat personified. Job sitting on the ground among the Brzezinka barracks. All he did was move his lips, as if he was talking to himself. What words were coming into his head? *Ish haya be-erets hus?* … There was once a man in the land of Uz? … Job …

And now this meeting in Erlenbusch. Only that now it was with an entirely different person. To tell the truth, in Brzezinka at that time he had not believed that, in the state S. had been, he could survive the camp régime. As it turned out, he did survive. He survived and it was as if he had found his second wind. Smiling, even joyous, he joked at every opportunity. He was not emaciated, and perhaps had even gained some weight … At least at the first glance, the feeling of despair and defeat was out of the question. Just the opposite. It seemed that he had armed himself internally against the adversity and misery of camp life. He worked in the kitchen. He was interested in everything. He knew about everything. Nothing that happened at the Erlenbusch camp was a secret to him … He was the one who informed the new arrivals where they would be working, how the local SS men were behaving, and what they thought about the approaching end of the war … It seemed, but this could have been an illusion, that in the new environment S. had shaken off the burden of his experiences of the previous few months. He forgot them or he did everything to make others think that he did …

From the corner of his eye he noticed that Kohn had crept back into the ditch. He was half-naked – he left his trousers at the edge of the ditch – and had this way became even more exposed to the malice of the SS men and to the chill of the April afternoon.

He will probably be the first who dies in the new camp, he thought without special emotion. Emotion belonged to feelings that in the camps were a luxury few could afford. Though, on the other hand, it would be a pity to die when the war was coming to an end. If he had to commiserate with someone, it would be first of all with himself. He had been steadily getting weaker. He constantly had a fever. He knew what it meant. And besides, he was troubled by a painful abscess in the anus.

It was actually S. who had three days previously foretold that the Erlenbusch prisoners would be sent back to Dörnau. It looked as if on the fourth or the fifth of May they would start out on the road again. What influenced that decision? Even the SS men did not know. In face of the approaching apocalypse, the strictness of the German organization disappeared. For the prisoners it was important that the play was coming to an end. For the remnants of the army of Jewish prisoners that were being shuffled from one end of the stage to the other, it was important only to succeed in holding out on the stage until the end. Yes, the play was coming to an end. Unfortunately, the accompaniment to the play's final act – the roar of the guns of the approaching front line – was not reaching the camps.

Usually S. was right. He really knew everything that concerned camp matters. Sometime during the second half of April he foretold the arrival of an important commission of the SS authorities. Indeed, two days later they had not gone out to work. They were ordered to clean the barracks, to wash the floors so that they would shine. The Berlin hotel 'Adlon' would not have been ashamed of the camp kitchen. At the designated hour, they all stood in fives on the square among the barracks. The important commission arrived in three automobiles. It consisted of six SS officers. The silhouette of the one in front seemed familiar to him.

As if reading his thoughts, S., who stood near him, whispered: 'That is Doctor Thilo.'

Yes, that was Doctor Thilo himself, the one from Brzezinka and Auschwitz. The one who accompanied Mengele during the selection at the railway ramp. An ominous figure probably remembered best by the prisoners of the women's camp where he had been the chief physician. Why on earth did Obersturmführer Thilo appear in Erlenbusch?

After a while the matter became clear. As he passed slowly

in front of the human remnants that stood rigidly in fives, the Obersturmführer indicated the prisoners that looked the most weak with a finger, or the palm of his hand, so that they would be separated from the rest. The gestures were the same as on the railway ramp in Auschwitz, and so were obviously the intentions. Doctor Thilo had continued in Erlenbusch the Auschwitz ritual two weeks? days? hours? before the end of the war.

Having done the selection, that is having selected the few dozen prisoners who looked to him for some reason the worst, Thilo stayed on to explain something to the camp SS men then got into the automobile, and the whole cavalcade disappeared on the road to Świdnica.

S. swiftly got some information from an SS man. It turned out that Thilo had indeed considered the prisoners indicated by him as already of no use to the Third Reich. At the nearest opportunity, they had to be disposed of. Apparently, the SS man had struck his forehead when he shared this information with S., with the implication that those at the top were crazy: '*In solch einem Moment*,'[1] he apparently said.

Nothing changed in the camp after the inspection. The prisoners selected by Thilo to be shot continued to go out to work every morning.

Another sensation was that one of the SS men had deserted the camp. Of course, S. was the one who had the most to say about it. That SS man was a Hungarian. When he learned that the Soviet army occupied the locality where he came from, he concluded that this freed him of any obligations to Germany. The fugitive was not found the following week, and S. convincingly contended that the remaining SS men wished the fugitive luck.

All this had happened two weeks or perhaps one week before. Tomorrow, he thought they would probably go out for the last time to dig the useless ditch that was intended to save Germany from the Soviet army ... He glanced at the sky. Luckily, the day was coming to an end. Although he did not work, he was exhausted. The tree against which he leaned sheltered him in a friendly manner and absorbed his fatigue. After returning to the camp, he tumbled down exhausted on the plank-bed. He had a high fever again. He had barely lain down when an excited S. stormed into the barrack. He was obviously bursting with some news he had to convey to him immediately. He sat down on the plank-bed and attempted to tell him something in a confidential whisper which joy transformed into a hoarse falsetto.

'Read this. Carefully! Aloud! I must hear it again!'

He took out a charred piece of newspaper from the blouse of his striped uniform.

'Here. In black and white! With what letters!'

It was a piece of the front page of some newspaper whose name ended with '*Zeitung*'. The content of that most important news was in the headline in large type: 'The Führer fell in the battle for Berlin'. After the headline followed some text, whose legible fragment told the same. The newspaper gave the date of that event as the 13 April ... He read it again. And again ... The end? It probably was ...

S. was raving. He even made no attempt to control himself. He was jumping on the plank-bed and shook with giggling laughter. All the time he was striking his thighs with his hands. He could not contain his joy.

'I knew it! I knew I would overcome him! That I would survive him! He is already gone, and I am here! I am! At last something good from God's hand!'

'I don't understand. What are you talking about?'

'I know well what I am talking about. You obviously do not know the Book of Job. It says there: "Shall we receive the good from the hand of God, and not receive the bad?" I think the idea in this full of submission verse should be reversed: "Shall we receive the bad from the hand of God, and not receive the good?" This would have been a hundred times more fair.'

'Are you a believer, Józef?' He addressed him this way for the first time.

On hearing this question, S. immediately became serious. His previous mood changed as if he recognized that the reply called for a different atmosphere. After all, before going to the synagogue on Saturday one changes one's everyday garments for festive ones.

'Am I a believer? Of course, I am a believer. I believe in God. Could a Jew in general not believe in God? How do you imagine that? After our experiences of so many years? If the good and the bad, happiness and defeat, joy and sorrow, fat days and lean days had been equally divided among all the nations, one could have said that chance determined everything. Do you understand? Perhaps I am not expressing myself clearly ... What I want to say is that if the Jews had received the same share of all the disasters and defeats that befell mankind over 3,000 years – perhaps somewhat more or less than the other nations – this would have been normal. Simply statistics, and not a superior power – probability, and not providence. Simply, once on the wagon, and once under it. But do we Jews have the right to speak about chance? Do we have the right to complain only about bad luck, of a disastrous lottery ticket that we are constantly pulling out from that ... from that ...' He was searching for the right word.

'From the revolving drum, you wanted to say?'

'Indeed. You got it right. From the revolving drum of events. Thousands of years of our history were thousands of years of tears, degradation and plagues. The Egyptians held us in slavery. The Assyrians and Babylonians chased us out from our homeland. The Romans slaughtered us. The Crusaders murdered us and raped our wives and daughters. The spiritual rulers cursed us. The secular ones robbed our property. The Inquisition burned our forefathers on the stake. The Cossacks killed us and taught us to fear pogroms during which entire Jewish villages and little towns perished. The ground of Eastern as well as Western Europe is soaked with Jewish blood. Finally came the Nazis and perfected all those means of violence. They almost brought about our nation's destruction. And I am to believe that this is only a caprice of history and not God's hand? No, it is not possible that God had not intervened in the history of our nation. This was His work! It was He who decided that other nations would experience various fates, and that the lot of one, only one, would be a string of disasters. Therefore I believe in the existence of God and accept now joyfully this crumb of goodness from His hand – because what is the death of Hitler in the sea of His, God's, possibilities, when I as well as my forefathers had to accept evil constantly from His hand? Hitler is dead! Thank You, God! Thank You for allowing me to live to see that moment, after having punished so harshly my impatience and false hope that I would succeed in avoiding the fate predestined for me ...'

He fell silent. For a moment it looked as if his red hair parted in the middle of this head – ingeniously shaved by the Germans – was on fire. After a while, as if ashamed, he controlled himself and smiled again.

'Tell me, Józef, how did it happen that you know the Book of Job so well?'

'I learned it by heart. In Auschwitz I bought the whole Bible from a "Canadian" for two portions of bread. Cheap. Later, in Dörnau, they took it away from me ...'

He pondered.

'Well, I have to return to the kitchen.' And on leaving, he added: 'I'll bring you some soup later.'

Of course, he was happy that Hitler went to hell, but the feeling was as if incomplete. He did not feel capable of the joy commensurate with that event. He was increasingly bothered by the abscess. Tormented by the fever... He saw the immediate future and primarily the expected road to Dörnau, in shades of black ...

He returned in his thought to the conversation with S. Job. How many of them still remained in the German camps? They paid for their experience as did their archetype; no one was entitled to a discount ...

Notes

1. 'At such a moment.'

17 Finale Giocoso

A few minutes before noon, a small Soviet military vehicle passed the gate and entered the grounds of the concentration camp. A very young and very handsome officer sat in the vehicle beside the driver. This was on the ninth day of May 1945, when the whole world had already known for 24 hours that the war was over. For the prisoners of that camp, this was confirmed only by the arrival of the Soviet vehicle.

True, the SS men had disappeared in the morning of the previous day. They disappeared, but were they not scheming something? No one dared leave the camp. There were even some who claimed that they saw with their own eyes the SS men lurking in the vicinity. There was of course no radio in the camp. Neither was there any news coming to the camp from the little town nearby. That day, a few daring prisoners were preparing to slip into the area, primarily to obtain some food – the camp food supplies had been finished a long time ago. The prisoners who remained were wandering around the camp yard like Leah haunted by the *dybbuk* in the chalk circle marked out by the *tsaddik*[1]... Those who remained? Of course, there were those who managed to die when the Germans ruled the camp, and those who took advantage of the first 24 hours of freedom to do so – as if death free of the Germans were different from death under the SS men's boot.

The arrival of a vehicle with the first Soviet soldiers in the grounds of the camp was greeted by the prisoners with screams of joy and happiness. They had been waiting for the Soviet army, they followed its progress as much as they could, and blessed its victory. Only when that vehicle arrived were they certain that the war had really come to an end. The young officer, with a face rosy like an apple, with blue eyes like the sky in May, wearing a cap that sat playfully on his head, was not allowed to get out of the vehicle. Everyone wanted to shake his hand. Everyone wanted at least to touch him, to verify that this was not a dream. They examined his uniform, they counted the medals on his chest with admiration. The medals showed that their owner had been chasing the enemy from far away. It took the emotional officer a long time to quiet down the rejoicing prisoners. In the meantime, a Soviet truck with an open platform arrived in the grounds of the camp. The young officer jumped up gracefully onto the platform, and in a clear, loud voice greeted the liberated prisoners in the name of the Soviet army. He spoke in Russian, and even if not everyone understood his words, everyone understood the content of his speech.

Next the officer told about the suffering and determination of the Soviet people, about the casualties it incurred for the final victory. He talked about the successive stages of the victorious march of the Soviet army, about how the neck of the Nazi beast had been wrung forever, and precisely in Berlin. He spoke about the genius of Stalin, the father of those victories. Finally he spoke about the unconquerable ideas of communism that were triumphant everywhere in Europe and written on all the workers' banners …

The prisoners listened to the young officer and swallowed his every word. When he finished by appealing to them that now everyone should return to his liberated homeland and build a new life there, the prisoners raised shouts in honour of the Soviet Union, Stalin and the Soviet army.

The young officer had tears in his eyes. He jumped down from the platform and fell again into the arms of the prisoners who did not want to let him go. Finally, after he waited a while, the young officer asked where the Nazi camp actually was.

Where? Oh, here …

It was a two-storey building of red brick which had previously been a textile factory. The Germans removed all the machines from it and, some time in the fourth year of the war, turned the previous factory into a concentration camp. The prisoners that were brought here were mainly from Poland, but there were also some from Hungary and Greece. They worked in the nearby factories, quarries, but primarily in all kinds of farm work. In the two-storey building, the prisoners occupied the two top floors. The main floor housed the SS administration, the clerks and the camp kitchen. On the first and second floor along the whole building there were halls. In each hall there were six rows of two-storey plank-beds. They stood so close to each other that the upper beds formed one large sleeping surface with countless straw mattresses full of lice and fleas. On that surface any number of prisoners could be placed. It was difficult, however, to say how many there were. Perhaps close to a thousand, but that number was constantly changing, particularly in the last months of the war. Because that camp had become a sort of transit point for the transports of prisoners heading west.

The living conditions here were immeasurably worse than in other camps. There was no water. The latrines were far from the main building. The food rations were constantly reduced. Besides, the SS men hit on the idea of differentiating the rations. The prisoners who were strong enough to go out to work received increased rations. The rations of those who could not move from their plank-beds were reduced. The rations of those who worked were increased at the expense of the rations of those who were unable to work. This way the selection once begun could end only in one way. To make their task easier and to prevent the sick and exhausted prisoners from seizing the rations of those so-so healthy, the Germans decided that those who went out to work should occupy the first floor, and those who stayed in the camp – the second. This division was still reinforced: the prisoners on the second floor were deprived of even the smallest piece of clothing. They had nothing left except the wooden clogs. They were completely naked and could in no way pretend to be working in order to obtain for themselves a somewhat larger bread ration …

The prisoners had not managed to tell the young officer all that when they began to show him around the camp building. Neither had they managed to explain that for the last thirty-six hours those on the second floor had been completely deprived of food.

The first floor was almost completely empty. Not stopping there, they immediately led the officer to the second floor, and explained to him that it had been designated for the sick prisoners.

This was not the best introduction. In any case, it was not a definition that could have prepared the young officer for the view that spread before his eyes when he opened the door that led to the hall on the second floor with an energetic gesture.

The floor was covered with a layer of urine of perhaps a few centimetres. Wooden clogs and pieces of dissolved feces were swimming in it. Near the plank-beds, and also between them and the door, lay the naked remains of dead prisoners in the most unusual positions – mostly on their bellies, spread-eagled, with their faces immersed in the urine. The remains of dead prisoners lay also on the plank-beds among bodies that still showed signs of life. Those still alive looked at the group that stood at the door with dull, expressionless eyes. Those alive as well as those that were dead were emaciated and black ... All of them had swollen legs and cracked skin.

They opened the windows of the hall. But the spring did not cross the opening from the outside. It seemed that it did not have the courage to penetrate into the building. Frightened by what it saw inside, having resigned from visiting the hall of the condemned, it swiftly shuffled someplace else to announce through the windows of other houses that it was taking over the command of the tired world.

For a few moments, the young officer looked dumbfounded at the view before him. He had not had the time to extinguish the smile on his lips when he turned pale, staggered and was at the last moment supported by the prisoners who stood near him and, when he was literally pulled out from the hall, he vomited. Luckily, he did not soil his uniform or the medals that bore witness to his courage. Only in the yard did he recover.

From the nearby church the bells were ringing for Angelus. The sound was spreading joyfully far and wide and announced the arrival of the era of peace. In Europe the guns fell silent. Bells were ringing everywhere in praise of the victory. There was rejoicing in London, Moscow, Paris and Warsaw! Hosanna! Never ag ...

Notes

1.   A reference to the play 'The Dybbuk' by the Yiddish writer An-ski.